GROWING SOLES

A ninety-six year journey
around the world

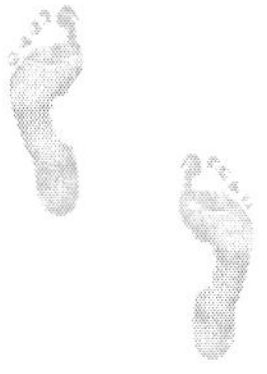

Micae Martinet

Growing Soles Inc.

Growing Soles: A ninety-six year journey around the world
Published by Growing Soles Inc.

ISBN 978-0-578-71776-0

This book is dedicated to

Douglas Andrew Parker,

wǒ de nán péngyou. Wǒ ài nǐ.

CONTENTS

ACKNOWLEDGMENTS

I owe thanks to so many people. First and most of all, thank you Doug Parker. I can't think of anyone else in the world who would hear the question "Do you want to finish Hippolyte's walk with me?" and without even thinking about it or knowing how far it would be, answer, "Okay." We have so many more adventures ahead of us and I look forward to them. I am so grateful to have you in my life. I love you more than I can express.

I'd also like to thank my cousin Clare Martinet who, ten seconds before Doug answered "okay" mused, "I wish someone from our family would finish the walk for Hippolyte." Thank you for sending Doug and me on such an amazing journey. I wish you could have been there with us, for even just one day, to experience the beauty, kindness and generosity that is China. The experience has changed me.

This book would not have been possible if not for Christophe Landry and my cousins Brian Eloy Martinet, Thomas Edward Martinet and Thomas Arthur Martinet. Their extensive research into the Martinet family and Hippolyte were the catalyst for the most amazing journey I've ever been on.

Nouria Demini Harvey and Fatima Demini Mooney, thank you for your help translating the French newspaper article and Hippolyte's letter. Je Vous aime tous les deux.

Thank you Luxi, for translating directions to the western cemetery behind the Muslim village, for mailing our packages to us, for your advice, for translating phone calls and for a lovely dinner our last night in Dali.

Peter Michael Nyman, I can't thank you enough for helping us locate Hippolyte's grave. Standing before it was one of the most amazingly beautiful and moving moments of my life.

Qimei Long, thank you for being our Mandarin teacher. I'm sorry we weren't better students. Xièxie lǎoshī!

Thank you Steve and Marie Long for your invaluable feedback and editing help. It never felt like work when we sat down in your backyard and went over the first half of this book, line by line. I love you both.

Tom and Jeff Forrester, thank you for your advice and counsel on publishing. You both helped alleviate my fears.

John Weiss, thank you for sending me copies of your Hippolyte postcards. Your words about what set my uncle apart from other globetrotters moved me. "There were hundreds and perhaps thousands roaming the world, but Hippolyte was unique. I don't recall there was another traveler who went barefoot, but more importantly, he was genuine." I got chills when I first read them.

Dr. Vincent, Steve and Ruby, thank you for the hospitality and for a lovely dinner at your home.

Thanks to everyone we met in China. Thank you for your kindness, generosity and enthusiasm. It sustained us and carried us up some steep, long hills on hot days.

Thanks are also in order to Dawn Lewis Brown who painstakingly edited this book over the course of nearly five years—sometimes line by line and over the phone. You have my deepest gratitude.

All newspaper articles, letters and other documents in this book appear in their original form. None have been edited and as such contain spelling, grammatical and typographical errors.

November 1, 1922

Mr. Honorat Martinet,
218 Richard Street
Los Angeles, California

Sir:

The Department regrets very much to have to inform you of the receipt of a telegram dated October 4, 1922, from the American Consul at Yunnan, China, reporting that your brother Hippolyte Martinet died at Siakwa, Yunnan, on September 30, 1922.

Upon receipt of further information in regard to the death of Mr. Martinet, you will be promptly advised.

I am, Sir,
Your obedient servant,
For the Secretary of State:
Director of the Consular Service.

REVEAL DEATH IN CHINA OF L.A. MAN WALKING ROUND GLOBE BAREFOOT

The last official record of Hippolyte Martinet's heroic attempt to walk around the world barefoot was written in Judge Paul McCormick's court Friday, when administrators of Martinet's estate were appointed.

Martinet succumbed to exposure and privations in the province of Yunnanfu, China, where consular reports said his death was due to fever.

He had walked from Los Angeles to New York, and with the exception of sea voyages across the Atlantic, the English Channel and the Hellespont, he'd walked every foot of the way to China. His route led him across France, Switzerland, the Balkans, Greece, Turkey, Persia, Afghanistan and through the Khyber Pass into India. Skirting the southern foothills of the Himalayas, he had swung through Indo-China up into the Chinese republic where he met his death September 30, 1922.

Martinet according to his brother, Honorat Martinet 218 Richard Street, who was appointed his administrator had money forwarded to him in care of American consuls on his route. Most of his estate consisted of money in banks where he had stopped. It aggregated $4000, it was said.

Martinet left Los Angeles in 1920, expecting to make the circuit in three years and then settle down in his business.

He resolved to wear neither hat nor shoe during his trip and to distribute money as charity wherever he went. He refused to accept money, however, although his letters told of many efforts to "endow" him by wealthy men who heard his story on four continents.

(The wording in this article is somewhat ambiguous.
To be clear, Hippolyte would wire money home
to his brother Honorat)

CHAPTER ONE

Searching For His Grave

September 29, 1922—Xiaguan, Yunnan China

The man staggered through the outdoor market. With one hand, he tugged at the waist of his pants, pulling them up over his bony hips. Just days ago he had used a borrowed knife to bore another hole through his leather belt so it could be cinched tighter, but already his khaki trousers were slipping off his gaunt frame. He tried to count how many days it had been since he had eaten but couldn't keep his thoughts straight. He was used to walking long distances as well as circumstances that resulted in involuntary fasting. However, in recent weeks he had missed more meals than usual while still walking thirty to thirty-five miles each day. He swayed as his vision darkened and faded into a pinpoint and then his sight slowly returned. Looking down, he scanned his surroundings for the dog that had been his companion for the last nine months. He caught site of the skinny mongrel snatching the entrails of a freshly slaughtered chicken and stealing away with his prize, tail tucked between his legs.

Although accustomed to the sound and cadence of strange languages, just now his environment seemed especially confusing. It lacked order; it didn't make sense and seemed somehow surreal. Market places were often boisterous and active, but today it seemed different. It was overwhelming and confusing. Everything about it assaulted his senses. He tugged again at the waist of his pants as his empty stomach cramped into painful knots.

Had he not been woken that morning by hunger pangs, he might have been able to sleep through the headache. Now, there was no ignoring the vice-like pain that gripped his temples. Confused, he watched women fanning themselves while he was overcome with shivers and a chill he couldn't shake. Turning in a slow circle, he looked again for his dog, but it was nowhere to be seen.

Of the many odors that wafted and mingled throughout the market place, one scent above all others attracted his attention... meat. He needed calories and protein; meat was dense in both. His stomach rumbled again in anticipation of food. He approached a butcher, extended his arm and exposed his cupped and empty palm. It was a universal gesture. With pleading eyes, he thrust his hand out further until the butcher cut off a scrap of raw meat and tossed it to the man. He caught it gracelessly and pulled it towards his chest for fear that he would drop it. He gobbled it down and extended his hand for more. *"Filthy foreign beggar,"* the butcher barked, shaking his head as he turned away in disgust. Dejected, the dark-skinned man with the bushy hair left the butcher's stall. He stumbled and paused briefly as the horizon tilted and then righted itself.

Rebuffed, he shuffled through the market, the soles of his bare feet dragging through fish scales and sticky, congealed animal blood. He found his way back to the dusty street, took a moment to orient himself and returned to the place he had left his rucksack hidden in the weeds. It only weighed twenty pounds, but that morning when he tried to put it on his back he nearly crumpled to the ground under its weight. He found it, sunk to his knees and lay with his arm draped protectively over the dusty bag. The rucksack contained all his worldly possessions: his one extra set of clothes, maps, a canteen, towel, comb and an American passport bearing his name: Hippolyte (pronounced Ee-poe-leet) Cervais Martinet. Issued in Seattle, Washington, it was only two and a half years old but already bore stamps of sixteen different countries. His destination, Shenzhen, from where he would take a ferry to Hong Kong and then a ship home to the U.S., was 1,200 miles away.

The crushing pain in his head crept into his joints. His entire body ached. Blindly, his fingers reached for the strap that held his bedroll to his backpack and clumsily unfastened the buckle. He pulled his knees towards his body for added warmth, unrolled the wool blanket, and pulled it over himself before falling into unconsciousness. The itchy bites left by mosquitos had nearly healed, leaving almost no indication that he had been infected with malaria. Later, the dog returned and sat beside his master for a few minutes before getting up to move to the nearest spot of shade where he lie panting. The dog seemed perplexed. They rarely spent more than a single day in one place.

By afternoon, his presence had been reported to the police. Two officers with a handcart picked him up, placed him and his rucksack in the bed of the cart and wheeled him back to their offices. Following orders, they deposited him in the small, empty building next door. When they went to check on him the next morning, he was dead.

The officers contacted local missionaries. They would leave the burial of this Westerner to one of his own. Because it was not permitted to bury Westerners in the same area as the Chinese, the foreigner was laid to rest three days later in a small, missionary cemetery eight miles to the north in Dali.

May 17th, 2015 Dali, Yunnan China

It was midday and we had been searching for hours, parting and meeting up again as we traversed a path up the hillside, eventually making our way to a newly constructed wall that stood approximately eight feet high. The top was strung with what appeared to be electrified wire. At our feet, the ground was littered with broken glass and tiles, pieces of wood with nails sticking out and other construction debris. It was yet another dead end. Behind the wall stood very modern-looking houses. Each one was at least 3,000 square feet and identical. They were all part of China's massive construction boom. Many homes being built and bought in China were only for investment and would never be lived in. However, upon completion, these particular hilltop, lake view homes no doubt would be occupied by city dwellers who appreciated Dali for its 6,500-foot elevation, lake breezes, cooler weather and cleaner air. The Dali that I was looking down upon now was not the Dali my great-great-uncle would have seen nearly a century ago. A busy two-lane highway carved the landscape; a steady stream of cars ran in both directions. From where we stood, we could survey in its entirety the cemetery we had just searched. Somewhere below us was my great-great uncle's grave… if only we could find it.

We picked our way back down the hillside and split up again to search in different directions. We continued hunting for that low, stone wall that I had seen in the photographs my cousin had given me. In my mind, at first and then out loud I pleaded, "Come on Hippolyte, help me find you. Which way do I go?" Minutes later in front of me at eye level I saw it… a tree branch just a little thicker than my thumb that had been purposefully broken and twisted into an upright position. "This is a sign meant for me. It has to be," I thought to myself. Usually I'm more rational and not given to superstition, but the idea of finding his grave after all these years was intoxicating. To come all this way and not find it was a disappointment I wasn't willing to accept. I quickened my pace and continued searching for another ten minutes, but my great-great-uncle's final resting place eluded me. There were no more suspiciously broken branches, no arrows drawn by a ghostly finger in the dirt, no eerily arranged rocks. I had to accept the fact that maybe it was nothing more than just a broken branch after all.

I walked a few more feet until I found myself in a tiny clearing between some trees. In front of me was a quiet view of Erhai Lake. To my left was a nectarine tree bearing small, green fruit. I thought to myself that in a few weeks they would be plump, sweet and ready to eat. It really was a pretty little spot, secluded and private. I heard Doug's voice and I called him over to me. Our limbs were scratched and whatever poisonous plant we had walked through earlier was still burning our legs but strangely only when we stopped moving. My leg and arm still ached fiercely from when I had fallen earlier that morning. "I think it's time to give up," I said. Then I put a bouquet of peach-colored roses into a bag from the St. Martinville, Louisiana gift shop and set them on the ground. We had come to Dali to find Hippolyte's grave and, despite four hours of searching, we had failed. Miserably.

Doug walked off to give me a moment alone. He stood with his back to me and I watched as he pulled off his hat and used a bandana to wipe the sweat off his recently-shaved head and face. I was used to the faint stubble on his head; he had been shaving it for fifteen years, but it had been three years since I had seen him without a beard. He had grown it not long after we started dating. He thought it made him look old. I thought it made him look handsome. I imagine that after retiring from a twenty-five-year career in the Navy, the freedom to do whatever he wanted with his face was liberating.

I turned my attention back to the view in front of me and pulled out my phone so I could film and narrate a short video. I had to start over twice and take several deep, calming breaths to get through it. When I was done, I put my phone into my pocket and walked out of the clearing to meet Doug. "Are you disappointed?" he asked. "A little," I answered tersely in an effort to disguise my disappointment. I lowered my sunglasses when I felt that familiar sting, the precursor to tears. I wanted to tell him exactly how disappointed I was, but I was afraid that doing so would unleash those tears. I was certain we had looked at every headstone in the cemetery yet none of them was Hippolyte's. I felt cruelly taunted and defeated.

When I had imagined this day, I never entertained a scenario in which we didn't locate it. It wasn't in my narrative. Before I descended into a pit of self-loathing, I reminded myself that Peter Nyman, the person who gave me the directions to the Muslim village and this cemetery doubted we would find the grave at all and that likely what remained of it would have been completely destroyed. That knowledge did little to relieve the heaviness in my chest. It felt as if a cold rock sat somewhere behind my ribs. When I inhaled, it stopped my lungs from filling completely. The weight of it drained my energy. I wanted to go back to our hotel room and take a nap, maybe even cry. I felt like a sucker. I had been duped by own romanticism.

I had been so hopeful just a few hours earlier when after breakfast we got into a cab and headed to the Muslim village that sat between Ancient Dali and the more modern Dali City. I handed the directions to the driver, who studied them for a moment and then pulled into the stream of traffic that was headed southbound along the 324, a two-lane highway. Cars, motor scooters and motorcycles honked at us as we joined the flow. We would soon learn that Chinese drivers use their horns very liberally.

As we sat in the back of the cab, I planned out our day. First, find Hippolyte's grave and then take a cab a few miles further south to New Dali and find the location of the old police office—easy peasy. It was a short ride to the Muslim village and within a few minutes we were standing on a sidewalk. The driver pointed out the window to the right and then merged back into the stream of honking traffic. Doug and I headed towards the minaret of a small mosque.

Our presence immediately attracted the attention of a group of teenaged boys gathered on a basketball court. We used the translation app on my phone to ask them, "*Westerner and Muslim cemetery where*?" I had already learned that messages written in simple, direct language garnered the best results, but even then our queries were sometimes met with looks of confusion. One of the boys pointed down an alleyway and indicated that at some point we should turn right.

For some reason, I was expecting the village to be abandoned. I had been entertaining a romantic vision of Doug and me walking hand in hand through cracked and cobbled, empty streets as we explored the silent Muslim hamlet. I envisioned shutters hanging askew over broken windows, doors blowing open and closed by a sudden breeze. Instead, we walked through an occupied yet eerily quiet village. As we walked down the muted streets, women wearing headscarves peered out at us from behind shuttered windows and doorways. I instantly regretted my choice of clothing... Bermuda-length khaki shorts that showed my bare legs. As instructed, we made the first right turn and within moments saw hundreds of headstones fan out and climb the broad hillside that stood before us. My great-great-uncle Hippolyte's grave was somewhere among them.

The sprawling hillside we were about to ascend looked familiar, like the landscape in the two photos I had—three identical headstones in a row with a low, stone wall running behind them. However, in 1925 and 1940 the hillside was bare. There were no other gravestones. Now it was speckled with them and it was impossible to tell in which direction Hippolyte's grave might be. All sense of distance, proximity and depth were altered. Everything had been thrown out of proportion. I sighed as I realized the enormity of the task before us. Doug relieved me of the peach-colored roses and the gift bag, a connection to Hippolyte's hometown, and headed up the hill. I fell in line behind him. At that exact moment it began to rain ever so lightly. "How cliché," I thought to myself, as I tried to recall a single movie with a cemetery scene where it had not been raining.

The flowers and the bag were from my cousin Clare. Months earlier, she asked if she could give me a token to leave in China for Hippolyte. She didn't know yet what the token would be, but she assured me it would be small and light. For months she had been looking for something to give to me. In the end, the item found her.

A week before our departure date, Clare dropped by a library on a whim. She walked through the doors and headed towards the book stacks when something caught her attention. An ordinary cardboard box sat on the checkout counter. Regardless, Clare was inexplicably drawn towards it. She looked inside and found a tangled jumble of eyeglasses. The library was hosting a donation drive for the local Lion's Club. Inside the box was a plain brown paper gift bag, she picked it up, turned it over and saw that the front was stamped with the seal of the St. Martinville Tourist Center. St. Martinville is a town in St. Martin parish of Louisiana. It lies one hundred and forty miles west of New Orleans and seventeen miles south of Lafayette. Even today, it only has a population of 7,000 people. In 1878, Hippolyte's birth pushed the population to just over 1,600. This gift bag had made its way 1,800 miles across the country to Long Beach, a city of a half a million people, and then found its way to my cousin. We were speechless and had goosebumps. That was the exact moment I began to believe in signs.

Our search was systematic and thorough. Doug and I approached each grouping of graves from the opposite sides, examining every headstone until we met in the middle, but our efforts did not produce any results. I hadn't expected to find his grave immediately. There'd be no satisfaction in that, but I did hope to find it. I began doubting myself and feared we'd never locate it. Under different circumstances, this cemetery was a place I could have spent several enjoyable hours casually exploring.

We hunted and pecked our way up the hillside of this odd graveyard. In places it was overgrown with weeds, and the only indications that it hadn't been completely abandoned were the occasional sticks of burned incense we would see stuck in the dirt in front of headstones. It was so unlike any cemetery I had ever seen. There was no signage, no fencing, no groundskeeper's building, and corn had been planted in multiple places. The higher up we went, the more the hillside below us began to resemble some sort of crazy patchwork quilt. In some plots, the corn was knee-high, while in others it had only recently sprouted and was nothing more than hardy, little green shoots that stood three inches above the recently-tilled topsoil. Drops of rain left little dark spots as they landed in the dry dirt.

We walked the perimeter of the beds, looking at headstones that had flat faces and were etched with either Chinese or Arabic writing. The three arched headstones and the low, stone wall we were looking for were nowhere to be found. Occasionally, we would see a low wall and anxiously scramble up the hillside thinking we had located it only to find, on closer inspection, that it was not "the" wall. It wasn't oriented in the right direction in relation to the hillside behind it, it was far too long, or it never veered to the left.

The cornfields gave way to brush and vegetation that had become increasingly thick as we headed further up the hillside. Sometimes grabbing at weeds and bushes to help pull ourselves up, we found our hands reeked of acrid-smelling wormwood plants. I regretted my clothing choice for the second time that day. My legs were scratched all over and bleeding in some places. At one point, Doug turned around and said to me, "I just walked through something poisonous," and an instant later I felt it too, an intense chemical-like burning feeling all over my bare legs from the top of my socks up to the hem of my shorts. We had no idea which plant the culprit was and thus no way of knowing which plant to avoid. Our legs burned for two days straight.

Continuing up the hillside and sometimes veering off in different directions, we agreed to meet again at a central point further ahead. The weeds became dense and more resistant. Walking through them felt like wading in a river against a current that pushed us backwards. Doug was off to my left and had disappeared from sight when my ankles were snared in a tangle of weeds. Before I knew it, I was falling forward. The weeds that were so resistant as I struggled to push through them almost vindictively offered little opposition as I went crashing face-first into the dirt. I was able to raise my left arm to break my fall a bit, but my right arm remained trapped at my side, unable to tear through the weeds. Soft dirt cushioned the left side of my body, but two baseball-sized rocks lay under my right side. My thigh landed on one; the second rock was lodged under my right upper arm. The force of the fall knocked the wind out of me and the muscles of my right arm and leg cramped and were immobilized by pain.

I'm a huge klutz and accustomed to stumbling and tripping, but I don't often take falls like this one. I lay there in the dirt and weeds for nearly a minute before getting up. All morning I had been hearing the call of a single bird, and at that moment I heard him again from a nearby tree. Only now he seemed to be mocking me. "Cuckoo, cuckoo, cuckoo," it called. It had just gotten personal. I did my best to brush the dirt from my legs which were wet from the rain, but I only succeeded in making my hands dirtier. I headed back up the hill cursing that annoying little bird rather than my own clumsiness. The top of the hill and the tract houses lay hundreds of yards ahead of us. It marked the farthest end of the cemetery. I figured that Hippolyte was somewhere between where I stood and the houses at the top of the hill. "Cuckoo, cuckoo, cuckoo," the bird continued to call. Maybe he was onto something. Maybe I was crazy.

Our search continued and I berated myself. "If Hippolyte could walk from Seattle to southwestern China, the very least you could do is find his grave with the directions that you've been given!" My frustration was beginning to wear on me. This search and this journey were deeply important to me. My life for the last eight months had been leading up to this point and my dream was blurring and receding further away from me.

I had no idea that it was going to come back into focus and materialize before my own eyes. I submitted to defeat and chastised myself for believing in signs. Maybe they were for other people but not for me. I felt foolish, even more foolish than I had two weeks before I left when I went to see a psychic, hoping to make a connection with my uncle.

If at that moment I had seen Doug and myself having just placed the flowers beside the nectarine tree, I might have called out. "Wait! It's not over yet" ... because that broken branch was a sign, and it was meant for me. It was put there to delay me. Had I not been led on a ten-minute wild goose chase, our paths never would have intersected with that of a Chinese farmer and his grandson, as was meant to be.

Doug and I started our trek back down the hillside while I mentally berated myself for the folly of believing in something as random and meaningless as a broken tree branch. Off to our left, a metallic creaking noise broke the silence. I turned my head towards the sound and watched as an older man carrying a boy of about three stepped through a rusted, metal and wooden gate. It creaked again as he dutifully pulled it closed behind him. A stone and wood house stood behind the gate. The man waved to us. We waved back and walked towards him. The four of us met on a narrow, dirt trail.

Doug used the translation app on his phone and asked if he knew where the cemetery for Westerners was located. The man pointed past us. Too surprised to believe that it could possibly be true, I pulled out my phone and wrote, "*Three graves together, white woman, missionary*" and I gestured to indicate that her grave was in the middle. Nonchalantly, with a tilt of his head he indicated an area behind us. He took the lead and waved for us to follow. The boy peered suspiciously at us over the man's shoulder. Not twenty-five yards to the left of where we had met him, he stopped at the edge of a cornfield. Sprouts no more than four inches high stood perfectly spaced in orderly little rows. "Yī, èr, sān—*One, two, three,*" the man said matter-of-factly as he pointed out each of the graves. And there they were, the three head stones. All were broken into multiple pieces, weeds and plants growing around them. The stone wall behind them was almost unrecognizable. The mortar had long ago eroded and what was once a wall, was now a linear pile of rocks with something alive and green growing out of the spaces in between. My uncle's headstone, on the far left, had collapsed and the top of the arch sat upon the two broken sides. The headstone to his right, belonging to a missionary named Fanny, was toppled over and almost upside-down. The headstone to the right of hers was broken into several bits. Yet, they were all still there.

We had found it. "Wǒ de yéyede shūshu—*My grandfather's uncle,"* I said to the man as I tried to explain my relationship to the grave on the far left. I looked to Doug; he read my mind. "I'll go back and get the flowers," he said, and headed back up the narrow pathway. Without a sting of warning, I began to cry. My feelings of defeat had been replaced by triumph but humbled by the fact that it was achieved only through the help of benevolent strangers. I took out my phone, shot a new video and took several photos. A few minutes later, Doug returned carrying the bag and the flowers. I carefully put them in front of the remains of his headstone that had a little green fern growing in what was now a very low archway. Even though time and the elements had broken those stone arches, they were still obviously there, and we were standing before them. Hippolyte died September 30th, 1922 and was buried three days later on October 3rd. I felt so honored to be the first family member to visit his grave in the ninety-three years, eight months and two weeks since he had been laid to rest far from home and among strangers. From the moment I learned about my great-great-uncle, I was mesmerized by his story and felt a connection to him that I couldn't yet articulate. For nearly a decade, I had been estranged from members of my family. I didn't feel like I belonged with or to them, and after so many years of that disconnect, it felt like I had lost my place in the Martinet lineage. But when I learned about my uncle, I immediately felt like I fit in again. This man made me feel like I had kin and I proudly reinserted myself back into the family genealogy. I assumed my new place, right next to Hippolyte.

For a few more minutes I stood beaming at my uncle's graveside. The cold rock behind my ribs had vanished and was replaced by something as weightless and exuberant as a hummingbird. The sensation was almost too overwhelming, like the little bird beating its wings inside my chest needed to be set free. I knelt and picked up five small stones that lay in the dirt in front of his headstone. They were like jewels to me. I put them deep and safe inside my pocket. I didn't want to leave but we still had more searching to do. Doug and I headed back to the street to look for a cab. I'm not sure when it had stopped raining, but at some point the clouds must have cleared because by the time we got to the sidewalk, the sun was shining.

Hippolyte's grave with cousin Clare's bag from St. Martinville and the flowers she asked me to place there.

The Straits Times—12 January 1923—Singapore

PASSING OF ANOTHER GLOBETROTTER.

We regret to learn, says the Englishman of December 21, of the death recently in a Chinese village of Mr. H. Martinet, the globe-trotter. Mr. Martinet caused quite a sensation when he passed through Calcutta last July, his bronzed complexion and flowing locks giving him the appearance of a Sadhu. Mr. Martinet was a man of great simplicity of mind and there is plenty of evidence on record, apart from his own assertion, that he actually accomplished the tremendous feat of walking across three continents. Mr. Martinet was a native of Seattle, on the west coast of the United States whence he started some two years ago to walk around the globe. His walking powers were undeniably great and he was quite capable, on occasion, of covering thirty miles in a day for a large number of days. Although apparently a man of robust health he seems to have fallen a victim to the climate of the Chinese frontier. There are many globe-trotters about nowadays, but few of them so picturesque or of so striking a personality as the late Mr. Martinet.

CHAPTER TWO

Dali City

Although buried in Ancient Dali, Hippolyte had succumbed to malaria in Xiaguan, now known as Dali City. This was our next stop. I had documents which indicated he had died next door to the "police office" and it was my hope that we could get our hands on maps of the old city that could help us locate it. The whole purpose of our trip to China was to find Hippolyte's grave, locate the site of his death, and from there begin the 1,065 mile walk southeast to Shenzhen where we would take a ferry to Hong Kong. We were going to finish the walk my great-great-uncle began ninety-five years ago.

I wanted to find the exact site of Hippolyte's death. Aside from finding his grave, it was another way I could connect with my uncle. I can't explain it; I just wanted to be there. I suppose it was a way of honoring and acknowledging him. It made my heart hurt knowing that Hippolyte had died so far from home and all alone. Initially, I had no idea how he wound up next door to the police office. It was just one in a series of unanswered questions, a mystery. Then, just two mornings before, I got a possible although unlikely answer. When Doug and I flew out of Hong Kong and into mainland China, we each filled out an arrival card. On the back of the card, printed instructions explained that if we weren't registering at hotels, we were required to report ourselves to local police stations every three days. Although I didn't know how old this policy was, it might explain why Hippolyte died next to the police office.

Xiaguan, as it was formerly known, had been a major cross point between Tibet, Myanmar and Kunming. When Hippolyte was there in 1922 it was but a village. Today it is the third largest city in Yunnan province with a population of 620,000. The 1990s ushered in a building boom across China that some would describe as devastating. Pre 1990, one might have found traditional style wooden buildings in Xiaguan, although not the same buildings Hippolyte would have seen. A massive earthquake destroyed much of the city on March 16th, 1925. On May 17th of 2015, we found Xiaguan, or Dali City as it is called today, to be a bustling municipality with tall buildings and multi-lane intersections choked with traffic.

The cab dropped us off at the Dali Bai Museum, or at least that's how I'm referring to it here. The sign in front of the museum actually read *Dali Bai Nationality Autonomous Prefecture Museum.* High school students who had just finished a field trip stood in groups out front. Several of them greeted us in English with a "hullo" and then lapsed into fits of shy giggles. Some pulled out their cell phones, aimed them at us and took our photos. The shyer students casually removed cell phones from pockets and purses and snapped pictures of us discretely and surreptitiously. In the last two days, Doug and I had been greeted with beaming smiles and hellos and had photos taken dozens of times. We were beginning to feel like D-List celebrities. We posed for group photos with the students, said goodbye, entered the museum and inquired as to where we might find maps of the city as it stood at the time of my uncle's death. The museum proved to be a dead end, but the consensus was that we should try the local library, which was just a few blocks away.

Once at the library, it was the translation app to the rescue again and we were quickly referred to the third floor. The room we walked into was about five hundred square feet. Several floor-to-ceiling bookshelves were spread out along all four walls. An older woman and a college-aged young man stood up when we entered and we repeated our query. I handed her one of our postcards. We had printed a thousand of them so we could give them out on our trip. "Wǒmen gěi—*we give to you,*" I told her, as I presented her with the card. One side of the card was a reproduction of a postcard that Hippolyte had printed. It bore a photograph of him and his dog with the caption—"I am an American, walking around the globe with my dog as companion. I started on April 19, 1920 at Seattle, Washington without a penny in my pocket. We both earn our livelihood by the sale of our picture post cards." Our Mandarin teacher, Vivian, had translated the caption into Chinese characters for us. The other side of the postcard had a picture of Doug and me standing beneath a tree in our yard. A few short sentences explained that the man on the opposite side of the card was my great-great uncle, that he had died of malaria in Dali before completing an around the world walking journey, and that ninety-five years later we were finishing the walk for him. Our Mandarin teacher had translated this as well.

While the librarian pored over a stack of books she had pulled from the shelves, Doug and I did our best to make simple conversation with her assistant. It was our good luck that he spoke a little English because our Mandarin was awful despite months of weekly lessons. Unfortunately, none of the books or maps dated as far back as the 1920s, so she suggested we inquire at the actual police station. Her assistant was kind enough to walk us there.

We followed our guide out of the tranquil library and out onto the sidewalk. The streets were a hive of activity, swarming with cars and motorcycles that buzzed past us. I have always found trying to negotiate the streets in a foreign country nerve-wracking. In Bangkok, I once spent a good ten minutes on a corner tentatively stepping into the street and then jumping back onto the curb before a man eating at a food stall on the other side of the four-lane road left his lunch to come help me cross the street. Thirty minutes later, the same man took pity on me again and led me back across the street. I learned then and there that the trick to crossing is to commit. Once you start moving, you don't stop.

Traffic signals seemed to be regarded less as laws and more as gentle suggestions. The typical motorist *could* stop for a pedestrian who has the right-of-way in the middle of the crosswalk, but is just as likely to accelerate while honking. Either option is equally plausible and apparently acceptable. A few harrowing minutes later, we were at the police station. My fear sweat mingled with my *it's 85 degrees and 90% humidity* sweat, and I immediately headed towards the glass double doors at our left, anticipating air conditioning and a place to sit down until my knees stopped shaking. However, before my fingers even had the chance to touch the cool glass, we were summoned to a window where a uniformed man sat at a low counter. I approached, bent over and did my best to speak to him through the small, round hole in the glass as though I were asking for two tickets to a matinee. Unfortunately, he did not speak English. Our escort from the library tried to help, and after a brief discourse, the officer got out of his chair, left his office and came through the same double doors that had moments ago teased me with the promise of AC. I thought he was going to invite us in, but instead he walked up to us, barked a few short phrases, and promptly went back through the doors and sat down in his chair. The young librarian translated for us. There were no such records kept by the police station and we had been told to leave. The young man had done his best, but in the end we walked away not being any closer to finding the old police office.

I comforted myself with this... Dali City had changed and grown so much, especially in the past ten years, that it was likely the site of the old police office now lay under the multi-lane road we just crossed. Stopping for a minute, I looked around at the tall buildings and the cars that whizzed past us as we stood on the sidewalk. I closed my eyes and tried to eclipse my other senses, the sounds, the smells and the feeling of people moving past me. I searched for the little bit of Hippolyte that might have remained in this place. I tried to imagine what it must have been like back then... earthen streets, wooden buildings, the creaking wheels of ox-drawn carts, street vendors doing business with customers, and dogs barking at the strange foreigner as he made his way through the marketplace looking for something to take the edge off his hunger. I opened my eyes and the sounds of the city came rushing back into my ears. I watched as a stray dog ambled down the street and I wondered what became of Hippolyte's dog. Oblivious to us, the mutt trotted past, keen on a scent. Doug and I hailed another cab and headed back to our hotel room in Ancient Dali. We were dirty and sweaty and expected for dinner in a couple of hours.

That night we were guests at Luxi's house. Luxi's boyfriend was from Finland and was a friend of Peter Nyman, the Finnish man who had given us the directions to the cemetery. Luxi had been kind enough to translate them into Chinese characters for us. She owned her own cooking school where she taught Western tourists how to prepare traditional Chinese dishes. You would be hard pressed to find General Tsao's chicken or Kung Pao anything anywhere in China. After a day of teaching, she had generously offered to cook dinner for us. We stood in the doorway of her small kitchen, drinking glasses of hot water and talking as our host chopped vegetables for our dinner. We helped her carry everything to the rooftop where she taught her classes. Several large canopies were erected and long, rectangular tables stood underneath them. Each table was outfitted with a few cutting boards and propane burners. Luxi retrieved several pans from a cupboard, lit a couple stoves and began cooking. Nearby, a rice cooker exhaled a plume of fragrant steam. Like most cooking, the preparation is the most time-consuming aspect of the endeavor and, within minutes, dinner was ready. We served ourselves a bowl of sticky rice and took a seat at a circular table, eating our dinner in the Chinese style. All the dishes were placed in the center of the table and we each held a bowl of rice and used our chopsticks to serve ourselves a little food from every dish. In China, it's impolite to load your bowl with food. Rather, a few morsels are taken and placed on top of the rice. Once eaten, you may serve yourself more. I've been a self-taught expert with chopsticks since I was a kid, but I unknowingly grew up using them incorrectly. It's considered poor table manners to put your chopsticks in your mouth, as they are used to serve oneself food from communal plates. I was careful not to commit this social faux pas. That night, Doug and I tried what would become one of our favorite Chinese dishes—scrambled eggs fried with tomatoes.

Over dinner, we told Luxi about our day and how we found Hippolyte's grave. She was very surprised. She was certain that all remains of the cemetery would have been destroyed. I marveled again that we had even been able to find it and that it had been left somewhat intact. In the process of farming, it would have been convenient and easy enough to completely destroy the tiny Western cemetery, to remove what remained of the headstones in order to make way for another row or two of corn. Yet, to a degree, it had been preserved. In a way, I felt Hippolyte had been protected.

CHAPTER THREE

Peter, The Clarkes and Dali

After we left dinner at Luxi's, Doug and I strolled through Dali, stopping for a beer on the way back to our hotel room. I felt like I could finally relax and enjoy this charming and historic town. People walking by smiled and waved to us. The day before while exploring Dali, we saw a few Westerners, but we were clearly a novelty here. A Chinese family—a man, his wife and their adult daughter—walked past us. The man noticed Doug's beer and gave him the "thumbs up" gesture. "Hěn hǎo hé!—*It tastes good,*" Doug said to him in his best Mandarin. The man's daughter, with a perplexed look on her face, asked her father in English and with a distinctly American accent, "What did he just say?" Had we known that they would be the last people we would see for weeks who could speak English, I would have chased them down and made conversation with them. Instead, we just laughed.

I was a little disappointed that we would be leaving the next morning. I would have enjoyed spending a few leisurely days exploring this very pleasant and historically rich town. It would have been nice to visit the famous Three Pagodas. Legend says that Dali was once a swamp occupied by breeding dragons that caused natural disasters to keep humans away. However, the dragons revered pagodas, so three were built to appease and deter them. The pagodas are over 1,000 years old and have survived both man-made and natural disasters. One of the pagodas was said to have split in an earthquake in 1515 but miraculously recovered ten days later during an aftershock.

Ancient Dali was once a major military barracks, the political center of Yunnan province and a gateway to the Silk Road. It is now a picturesque tourist town. It's what Westerners envision when they think of China, a draw that is irresistible to even Chinese tourists who arrive by the busload. Traditional Bai style brick and wood buildings with tiled hip and gable roofs with their classic upturned eaves line streets that are laid out in a grid. Homes hug the side streets; whitewashed outer walls painted with scenes from nature and Mandarin characters hide peaceful inner courtyards. Little canals running with clear water cascade through the streets. Although the canals were once used to distribute water to the residents, their purpose today is purely aesthetic. Clearly, considerable effort has been made to give the visitor the impression that Dali has been "untouched by time" without coming off as kitsch.

Ancient Dali had an allure so irresistible that even ardent wanderers would lay down their backpacks as well as roots and lose weeks, if not months, in this charming town. It still has that vibe, even though consumer culture is alive and thriving with a clear love of all things Western. People of all ages wear clothing printed with absolutely anything written in English—sometimes to comical effect. A random selection of mismatched English words can be a selling point, while other times it's clear that the buyer has purchased knock-off designer wear when sporting a t-shirt bearing the logo "Golvin Klein" printed in an all too familiar font. Women pushing small carts sell delicate flower wreaths woven with vibrant fuchsia bougainvillea, pale purple statice and bits of greenery. Almost every young lady is wearing one in her hair. Music stores showcase school-aged girls performing in drum circles. Other shops sell marble goods, batik-decorated fabrics, flowing dresses and jewelry. The restaurants and food stalls offer everything from traditional Chinese dishes to enormous skewered and grilled chicken feet basted with a spicy red pepper sauce. The truly adventurous can nibble on fried scorpions or something I was never able to acquire a taste for... fermented tofu. Come mid-afternoon, busloads of tourists begin pouring through Dali's four gates. It is a city that comes to life after the sun sets. By nightfall, people of all ages pack its streets. I could see why Peter was so fond of it.

Peter Nyman, a native of Finland, succumbed to Dali's charms and had been living there for several years. He was currently in Indonesia and I was a little disappointed that I wasn't going to have the opportunity to meet him. I wanted to share the high I was experiencing and to celebrate it with him. I owed him so many thanks. In fact, the whole day was possible only because of him. He was the person who gave me the directions to the cemetery behind the Muslim village and an email introduction to Luxi, whose help had proven invaluable.

Peter had a Master's degree in Comparative Religion that fed an interest in Missionary History. From there he became interested in the history of the Yunnan Province, where Dali is located. He stumbled upon the story of Hippolyte Cervais Martinet, a man from the United States who had walked around the globe barefooted and without any money. In a little over two years, this man walked from Seattle, Washington to Dali in the Yunnan province of China, where he died of malaria.

Peter's research eventually led him to a Protestant church where he interviewed a priest who knew of some very old people who had a vague recollection of a cemetery where foreigners were buried, as it was not permitted to bury Westerners alongside the Chinese. A Protestant missionary woman named Fanny Clarke had been buried in this cemetery in the 1880s. Peter also learned that in the 1920s, an America man had been buried next to her. Later, Chinese Muslims were buried in the same vicinity. The priest at the church introduced Peter to an Imam who knew where the cemetery was and took him there. At the time, the area was being farmed. It was early spring, and he was able to locate the headstones in a plot of young corn. He visited again in the fall, but the corn was so high and dense that he was unable to locate the graves. With his curiosity about the intriguing American still unsated, he conducted an internet search and found several newspaper articles about an American man who walked around the world barefoot and died in China. More searching led him to my cousin Artie's email address and a brief correspondence occurred. They exchanged photos and it became abundantly clear that the pictures were of the exact same cemetery and headstones. Oddly enough, Peter and I were discovering Hippolyte at roughly the same time, he from China and I from my home in southern California. Years later, my cousin gave me Peter's name. I conducted my own internet search, which produced several different email addresses for a Peter Nyman. I sent email introductions to all of them and was thrilled to get an immediate response. He even emailed me a copy of a photo he had of the cemetery. Its history was fascinating.

The cemetery came into being because of a woman named Fanny Rossier, a Swiss missionary. She and another young woman named Mary Ann Howland arrived in China in 1878 as members of the Inland Chinese Mission. In a double ceremony on September 15th, 1879, Fanny married George Clarke and Mary Ann married a fellow named Georg Nicol. Two months later, both couples left Shanghai and traveled up the Yangtze River to do missionary work deeper into the interior of China. It was an arduous, ten-week journey that was marked by two shipwrecks in the icy Yangtze River. Although George and Fanny were headed for Guizhou province, they disembarked and spent some time in the town where the Nicols were to make their home.

The Clarkes stayed a short while with the Nicols in late January, a time when local women were busy preparing for the festivities of Chinese New Year. Nonetheless, approximately two hundred Chinese women found time daily and en masse to walk down the street, into the courtyard, and eventually into the home of the Nicols—all for the chance to catch a glimpse of the two white women. When Chinese New Year was over, the crowds increased to five hundred.

Eventually, George and Fanny continued westward over mountain passes flooded by winter rains until they reached Guizhou province. Fanny was the first western woman to travel that deep into China. While in Guizhou, George attempted to open a school, but only one boy attended. It was in Guizhou that their son was born. Tragically, he died when he was only five weeks old. In May of 1881, George and Fanny left Guizhou and moved further west, becoming the first Protestant missionaries in Yunnan. They settled in Dali where they founded a literacy program for the local Bai people, ministered to opium addicts and tried to convert locals to Christianity.

In 1883 a second son, Samuel, was born. Fanny never recovered from his birth and passed away six weeks later. Before she died, Fanny requested that she be buried in Dali. Her husband, acting on her request, bought a piece of land on the outskirts of town and laid her to rest there. George conducted the services at her graveside and walked home alone, their infant son cradled in his arms. Until that time, their attempts at converting the locals were largely unsuccessful. But locals were so touched by her request to be buried in their town that countless Chinese poured into the church and asked to be baptized. It is said that children who died orphans in Dali were buried near Fanny, the woman who had lost one son and left the other without a mother.

During China's Cultural Revolution, many artifacts of western influence were destroyed or re-purposed, including the graveyard created by George Clarke for his wife Fanny. Years later, stories were still told about the beloved Clarkes. They were remembered as the red-haired people with big noses who had endeared themselves to the locals by wearing traditional Bai costumes and dancing in the streets in an effort to attract audiences and, hopefully, converts. Because of the Clarkes, this cemetery, its occupants and history were never completely forgotten.

CHAPTER FOUR

Family History

Back in our hotel room in Ancient Dali, I lie wide awake next to Doug, the five stones from Hippolyte's grave on the nightstand beside me. For once I didn't envy his ability to turn out the light, roll over and almost instantly drift off into uninterrupted sleep. I often struggle to sleep, but this night was different. I was too excited and a bit nervous as well. The next morning, we were going to begin our walk. The waiting seemed nearly unbearable. As I shifted in bed, trying to get comfortable on our unbelievably firm mattress, I remembered the night I first stumbled upon the story of my great-great uncle. I learned some surprising things about my family that night, things that my father likely died not knowing. After reading about Hippolyte, I felt the need to share his story with an urgency I can't describe. That was exactly six years and two weeks ago—to the day.

It was on that night that I got out of bed and turned on my computer. A long-time sufferer of insomnia, I fall into certain familiar routines. I look at real estate listings even though I have no plans to buy or sell a house, or I go on rambling internet searches that can only be characterized as being led by tangential curiosity and my brain's synaptic misfires. But that night something else got me out of bed. It had been a little over nineteen years since my father died and I was missing him, so I went to the internet and typed in his name. I had done this before. He was listed in the California Death Record Index. It sounds morose, but for some reason I found it comforting to see his name there along with his date of birth. I think that seeing my father's name was a reminder that even though he was no longer here, he once had been, and we had been an important part of each other's lives. That's why I conducted those maudlin internet searches.

That night, I saw my father's name mentioned somewhere else. I clicked on a link and found a complete genealogy for the paternal side of his family. Until this time, all I knew about my family was that we had French ancestry to which we owed our "olive complexions." It was in this genealogy that I read about Hippolyte and saw the itinerary of his amazing journey around the world. Chills ran up and down my spine as I thought back to a time in my mid-thirties when something told me I had to walk across the United States from coast to coast. I had no idea what was compelling me. I just felt the need to do it. I considered walking for a charity and finding sponsors but eventually let that fire die. I didn't know it, but an ember still burned and it was stoked back into flame when my cousin Clare suggested that someone from our family finish the walk for Hippolyte. I learned something else that night, something that members of my family decided to hide generations ago. It was a secret so well protected that it would be decades before the truth was discovered.

Sitting in front of my computer at two a.m., I learned that in 1845, the first member of the family who *willingly* came to the U.S. was my great-great-great-grandfather, Pierre. A carpenter from Belgium, he settled in St. Martinville, Louisiana. It was there that he met and fell in love with my great-great-great-grandmother, a mulatto slave named Marie Louise Benoit. It would be a while before the reality of this fact truly hit me, before my mind was ready to make the jump from *slave* to the realization that at least one member of my family had been stolen from ancestral land, torn from family and had come to this country as cargo in the dank and lightless belly of a ship. Some of those humans were strong enough to survive the six to eight-week voyage across the Atlantic; those who perished were tossed unceremoniously overboard, literally dead weight. My ancestor was strong and survived the journey and the devastating heartbreak. I also had to grapple with another fact. Marie Louise Benoit was mulatto, meaning she was part white. I'd be naïve to think that the union that resulted in her conception was consensual. It was likely that both slave and rapist were part of my family lineage.

Learning about my African ancestry was staggering and humbling. Even now, years later, it leaves me somewhat confused. I'm extremely proud that this is part of my DNA. It's in every cell of my body even if it's just a very small part. But I also recognize that it is only in my DNA and that it has never been part of my heritage and in no way distances me from my white privilege.

Marie Louise and her mother, Hortance Armand, were the property of a Doctor Nee. On January 10th, shortly after Marie Louise gave birth to Pierre's first son, Pierre bought Marie, their baby, and Hortance for the sum of $1,840. Adjusting for inflation, in 2020, that would equal $61,267... for three human lives. This raised other questions. Was Doctor Nee my four times great-grandfather? Had he in fact sold his own daughter? Pierre saved Marie from a life of slavery and in return she gave him a family to replace the one that he left behind in Belgium. He would never see his parents or siblings again. Pierre and Marie would have ten children together before it became legal for them to marry. They were finally wed on December 7th, 1869, a twenty-four-year-old relationship finally legitimized. Six years after they wed, Pierre died.

Their fourth born child, Louis Andre, had an illustrious and diverse career. He became the only black notary public in New Orleans and a state representative for St. Martinville Parish, an office to which he was re-elected twice. He was a medical doctor as well as a lawyer and passed the Louisiana bar examination in 1875 before graduating law school at Straight University in 1876. He was appointed to a position on the Orleans Parish school board, a job he would hold until the schools were segregated. He was also a journalist and the founder of *The New South*, a weekly publication that would eventually become a daily newspaper known as *The Daily Crusader*. Both chronicled the struggle for civil rights in the south.

Louis Andre Martinet was also a key figure in the inception and orchestration of the Plessy V. Ferguson Railcar case. I remember hearing about this landmark Supreme Court decision when I was in high school and again when I was in college. I am so proud of this man, my great-great-great uncle, and I am so ashamed of the fact that he was never discussed by relatives because to do so would have been acknowledging our black ancestry. Our family ceased to speak his name and he was forgotten for nearly two generations.

The importance and the relevance of his work and the causes to which he committed his life ceased to be known or celebrated by future generations of my family. His passion, however, did attract the attention of a young woman named Eloise Bibb. Born in 1878, her curriculum vitae are as impressive as my uncle's. Her first book of poems, which might have included this sonnet written for Louis Andre Martinet, was published when she was seventeen years old. She earned multiple degrees in her all too brief fifty years and worked as a journalist, playwright, social worker and public speaker. Bibb began her career as a public school teacher in New Orleans. It's possible that this is how she became aware of or met my uncle, as he was a member of the parish school board.

Sonnet To Dr. L.A. Martinet,
editor of the *New Orleans Crusader*
by Eloise Bibb

O thou who never harbored fear.
Who ever scorned her visage drear,
Who loathes the name of cowardice,
Whose banner bears the brave device,
"For justice, I will give my life,
Though I should perish in the strife!"
To thee, I sing my humble lay.
Posterity will see the day,
When thy exalted name shall stand
Immortalized by every land!
Be though our beacon over-head,
Ay, lead us; blindly we will tread.
Until our dark sky is serene,
May thy unfailing light be seen.

Louis Andre died on June 7th, 1917. In 1957, the Louis Andre Martinet Legal Society was formed in his honor. It dedicates itself to serving African-Americans as well as African-American law students and members of the legal community. I found the following quote on its website.

> "What have I to gain in fighting this battle? Like you, I have asked myself this question a thousand times... Certainly, I gain nothing, but rather spend time, labor and money in it. There is no doubt, that if I turned my attention to, or put my energies in, professional or some private pursuits, I would get along much better in this world. Yes, why do I do this? I want no political influence, no prestige, no office. Why do I do this? Like you, I believe I do it because I am built this way."

CHAPTER FIVE

More History

I knew that my grandfather had moved to Los Angeles as a boy, but I never knew what prompted that move. That question was answered as I continued scrolling through the genealogy document. I stopped when my cursor had made its way to the generation of my great-grandfather, Edouard Droctove Martinet. It was this generation that first left Louisiana in 1913 with a number of family members following over the next few years. The incident that compelled my family to move may be fact, or it may just be family legend. I have never found any documentation to verify that the following is true, understandably, some family members argue that the incident never occurred. My father's cousin Artie interviewed several of his cousins as he was compiling our family's genealogy. One cousin recalled a conversation he'd had with an uncle. Artie quoted him in the genealogy document. "Their house in St. Martinville was burnt down (the reasons for the arson are speculative, but my grandfather made someone mad) and everything went with it. My uncle told me that he hit a black man with a hammer and killed him." I have lost hours thinking about three words from the above quote—"a black man." Why did our uncle make this distinction? In saying that the man was black, was he distancing himself from or denying his own ancestry? Otherwise, why not simply say "he hit a man with a hammer and killed him"?

Another cousin reported that the man he killed had molested one of his daughters. Other family members claim that there was no murder and the reason for the arson was that Edouard, who was a building contractor, was taking away too much business from his competitors. Regardless of motive, the incident made *The Times-Picayune* in New Orleans.

MARTINET HOME BURNS.

> ST. MARTINVILLE, LA., May 25.
>
> The residence of Edward Martinet was destroyed by fire last night at 11 o'clock. The origin of the fire is unknown. Only the piano was saved. The estimated loss is $2,500. The insurance on the building was $1,500.

Several cousins report hearing that my great-grandfather "Pop" stood awestruck in the front yard watching the house burn as my great-grandmother, "Mom" Edwidge, ran in and out of their home rescuing children. I know only a few things about Edwidge. One is that as a child in Louisiana she went to work picking cotton when she was only eight years old. Another is that she and Pop had been in a rollover car accident. She told her husband to refuse the help of a passerby as she was still trapped in the overturned vehicle and was not wearing underwear. Later in life she became an avid fan of televised wrestling. No one, not her husband, children or grandchildren, could convince her that it was all staged and choreographed.

After the fire, my great-grandfather posted two notices in the local newspaper. One read:

> As I am going out of business as contractor and builder I beg any one holding any account against me to have same approved in my absence by Ludovic Martinet.

The second posting read:

> Card Of Thanks—I thank the people of St. Martinville who assisted me in my misfortunes last Friday night and especially those who are assisting my wife in her sewing for the children. Respectfully, EDW MARTINET

As an adult, Mom and Pop's daughter, Val talked about the move and said the arson really frightened Pop. The insurance payment on the house came through in July and they left in the early days of August. Their move was announced in a local newspaper. Although the family was moving to Los Angeles, the article reported they were moving to San Fraucisco [*sic*]. It's possible that Pop intentionally gave misleading information to the newspaper. The article ran as follows on Saturday, August 2nd, 1913 in St. Martinville's local newspaper, *The Weekly Messenger*.

> Mr. Edward Martinez and family,
> the best of our colored people, will
> leave here Monday for San Fraucisco,
> with a view of locating permanently.

They left Louisiana by train and turned up at a sister's door in Los Angeles. There were eleven of them all together requesting accommodations until Pop could build a house for his family. Edwidge would plant cotton in the backyard of their new home. I think it was as much ornamental as it was comforting and familiar to her. Along with a new house, Pop also built a new life for his family in Los Angeles. Shortly after the children were enrolled in school, an administrator paid a visit to the house and advised Mom and Pop only to speak English at home. Pop began giving English lessons to his children every evening after work. No longer in the south, it was time to abandon their native tongue. His was the last generation of my family to be designated as mulatto on any official government document. Free from the south, generations of Jim Crow laws, segregation and lynchings, our black ancestry was buried and forgotten until seventy years later when it was unearthed like hidden treasure.

Cousin Artie told me that when he was a young boy, Pop came to live with his family after Edwidge died. As he tells it, they were the only ones willing to take in the curmudgeon. He, his siblings and cousins remember that Pop had a thick Cajun accent that was sometimes difficult to understand. They also describe him as gruff, grumpy, crotchety, having a short temper, and overall hard to get along with. I've seen pictures of him; he always seemed to have a vaguely disengaged, disinterested look on his face. One family member spoke about him in the context of the autism spectrum, suggesting that perhaps he had Asperger's Syndrome. This insight lends perspective to the fact that he was an inventor who held at least two patents. One was for a brick-making machine and the other was for a type of plasterboard or wallboard that he had formulated for use in Hollywood. It was much easier to make and assemble sets with this material compared to the heavy lath and plaster that was being used at the time. Artie once asked his parents, "What's wrong with Pop? He looks weird." Artie realizes now that he was asking about Pop's faint African-American features. His skin was dark. He had full lips and bushy hair, features that threatened to expose his secret.

There is rumor of a second murder committed by a family member. Again, I have not found any evidence to verify this. It is alleged that Pop's uncle killed a black man with a baseball bat for spitting into a vat of wine. It's unsettling to think about this aspect of my family history. It's dark and scary. Thinking about it now gives added perspective to an event from my childhood.

I was not more than four years old when one evening after dinner I was playing with my Legos. I had built a car and every time I tried to make it roll, the wheels fell off. In a fit of temper, I spiked the car like a football onto the floor and it broke into pieces. My father had been watching me from the doorway and walked over without saying a word. He turned me over his knee and swatted my behind—not hard enough to hurt but hard enough to get my full attention. I was utterly stunned. Nothing like that had ever happened to me before. I remember my father kneeling in front of me, and as he gently put his hands on my shoulders, he asked me calmly, "Do you know why I did that?" "Because I threw my car?" I offered, already feeling embarrassed by my own behavior. "Yes," my father said. "Because you lost your temper. You must always control your temper." I knew from the even tone of his voice and the steadiness of his gaze that he wasn't angry. He was sharing something grave and significant with me. I think I remember this event so clearly because I understood that the message was crucially important to my father and therefore he *had* to share it with me. I felt valued, loved, and in that moment grown up because such an important message had been bestowed upon me. Another reason I have such a vivid memory of that evening is because it was the only spanking I ever received in my life.

In my early 20s my father's girlfriend shared some stories that he had confided to her. With his permission, she revealed that his father had been an alcoholic, didn't control his temper and was very abusive. The stories I heard that day made me profoundly sad. I remember wishing I could have been there to shield the little boy my father had been. I wanted him to feel loved and protected by his father. I wanted him to feel as safe as I felt with mine. These two men were so unalike. It seemed almost impossible that they were related.

Their differences in temperament might have been genetic. Maybe my dad didn't inherit that hair-trigger temper. The only thing I can say is that he always kept his anger in check because that was the behavior he wanted to model for his children. He was so conscientious in his parenting that I never felt any serious conversation he initiated with me was off the cuff. It was always scripted and rehearsed beforehand, his words chosen deliberately and delicately. I have linked those two events together in my memory: the lesson I learned when I was four about controlling my temper and the stories about my alcoholic grandfather and his violent temper. Now the stories about my Pop, his uncle, and even my own speculation as to who Marie Louise's father was have been injected into the family narrative. I carry all their blood in my veins.

I also carry the blood of another family member in my veins. This blood feels more like my own. It's in my marrow. I think it's what makes my feet itch. It's what sparks my own wanderlust. This blood belongs to Pop's younger brother Hippolyte. He looked rather like my Pop but for one exception. Hippolyte, or Polyte as the family called him, had blue eyes.

Oregon Daily Journal November 6, 1922, page two.

WORLD JAUNT PROVES PEOPLE KIND AT HEART

Traveler Dies in India on Strange Quest

"No man will refuse food or shelter if you are worthy of his charity. "So said Hippolyte Martinet in the summer of 1920 to his brother, Honorat Martinet of 218 Richard street. Honorat declared he doubted if that were true. "I'll prove it by walking around the world," said Hipploвласти.

WORKED WAY ACROSS—Then like a Brahmin of India, shoeless and carrying a staff, Hippolyte started his long journey. He hiked across the United States, work his way across the Atlantic and traversed Europe.

He accepted food and shelter only, ate and slept with white, yellow and black men, climbed mountain trails and joined caravans crossing deserts until he arrived in the province of Yunnanfu, China.

There he was stricken with yellow fever and died September 20, 1922 in the hut of believer in Confucius, the great disciple of charity.

Hippolyte Martinet had not completed his circle, but he had shown that all men at heart are kind.

STRANGE STORY REVEALED—The strange story of his wanderings was gathered together by the brother from the letters received from British and American consulates along the path of the pilgrim. They were presented today in the court of Judge Paul J. McCormick where the brother asked to be appointed administrator for the purpose of dividing between three sisters and himself some $4000 which the wanderer left in the bank here. The request was granted.

The sisters who will share with Honorat Martinet, are Mrs. Nicolas Hallsky, Mrs. Blanche Davis and Mrs. Samuel Tachet.

CHAPTER SIX

Why He Walked

The Great War was over and the world was still reeling from the ravages of the 1918-1919 Spanish influenza pandemic. Returning soldiers, crossing oceans and borders, had brought the virus home with them. It infected 500 million people at a time when Earth's population was only 1.8 billion. It killed 20 million people in a period of eight weeks, 675,000 in the United States alone. Worldwide, it is estimated that the Spanish influenza took between 50 million and 100 million lives. Historically, it falls just after smallpox and the bubonic plague in terms of total deaths. Somehow, Hippolyte had managed to survive it.

Like his grandfather, Hippolyte was a carpenter and he found work in a cabinet-making factory in Yakima, a small agricultural town huddled in a valley at the eastern base of the Cascade Mountain Range. One hundred and fifty miles southeast of Seattle, it was considerably drier and warmer, receiving on average only eight inches of rain per year compared to Seattle's thirty-eight inches. Good soil and sunny days with summertime temperatures reaching 100 degrees and mild winters that only occasionally dropped below freezing made Yakima prime real estate for fruit farmers. Orchards irrigated by the Yakima River produced apples, pears and peaches.

In his early 40s Hippolyte had begun to experience respiratory problems. Working indoors and constantly inhaling fine, wood dust had no doubt done damage to Hippolyte's lungs. He might have developed what we now call COPD, chronic obstructive pulmonary disease, which is usually caused by smoking and air pollution but can also be caused by continually inhaling dust. He visited a doctor and was diagnosed with consumption. The doctor prescribed a regimen of plenty of walking and living strictly outdoors.

If it was consumption, also known as tuberculosis, Hippolyte had fallen victim to the same disease that by 1900 had infected fourteen percent of the U.S. population before reaching the age of eighteen. Tuberculosis, or TB, would become the leading cause of death worldwide and an antibiotic cure would not be discovered until the 1940s. For decades, the standard treatment for TB was placement in a sanitarium, a hospital exclusively for people with active TB. Patients were confined to bed in closed rooms and fresh air was forbidden. Although reading quietly was permitted, they were remanded to stay as still as possible. Prohibited activities included writing and speaking to other patients, as they constituted too much activity. It was a very bleak life with a poor prognosis for recovery.

By the turn of the century there was a radical shift in the approach to caring for TB patients. The fresh air cure became the favored method of treatment. Windows were cast open and patients wheeled outdoors. As much fresh air as possible was now the preferred course of medicine. It was believed by some medical professionals that the skin needed to breathe and that being naked and exposed to fresh air was healthy and put the afflicted on the road to recovery. It was thought that the body's immune system was better able to fight TB if it wasn't busy fighting off other airborne contaminates.

TB sufferers across the U.S. and Europe began taking the fresh air cure with not perfect but better results. Those who could afford to take the fresh air cure went to live in private sanitariums. When weather permitted, residents spent their days outdoors. When the seasons changed and temperatures dropped, they were bundled under blankets and furs and placed in chaise lounges where they spent entire days outside, even in the frigid cold. Those who couldn't afford these often lavish sanitariums made do with what was available to them. They lived in as much isolation as possible to avoid infecting others. They slept on verandas, balconies and porches, and in shacks or "sanitary tents" away from the house. Even sleeping on the ground was advocated, and this is where Hippolyte would sleep almost every night during his journey around the world.

Perhaps acting on his doctor's advice, Hippolyte became a lodger at a home in Yakima and slept on an open porch every night, even in the dead of winter when temperatures dropped into the mid-30s. Up until the time he began his walk, he lived at 111 North 1st Street at the home of Frank Kappert, a thirty-six-year-old cook and café owner, his nineteen-year-old wife Maxine, and their one-month-old daughter. The other lodgers included Ella Hall, a twenty-eight-year-old widowed waitress from Missouri, and Ray Riggo, a twenty-eight-year-old married laborer, also from Missouri.

Whereas previous TB treatment demanded complete inactivity from patients, the fresh air cure encouraged plenty of exercise and continual exposure to fresh air, and it was proving successful. Hippolyte took up exercise and began his own hiking regimen. On September 13th, 1919, he wrote a letter to his sister.

> Dear Sister Blanche,
>
> Got to think of you why I make up my mind to stay home and rest today. Practically the first Sunday ever since I'm here.... May I please to say feel much at home for one reason have a bed on an open porch and I never was in a room for the time being, beside on Sunday I go out hike in the hills hike and hike until I get good and tired and then stop, strip myself like Mother nature made me, lie down the mother Earth and let the glorious Sunshine do the rest. But say, before long I'll be a real Indian that is to say all face a well toasted body, but I care not if I did get black as the Ace of Spade for I value my health and this is the way I'm going to regain every bit of it.

He also had some words of advice for Blanche, the baby of the family.

> Now you may question my sanity but whatever you do, if you only value your own health and the wellbeing of the human race ------------—read Barnard Shaw on birth control. Now for my sake, don't take me at heart for advocating same, but read and reread what a great man have to say until you come to understand---------and the chances are that you'll take a layoff until such time as your health will justify the newcomer to be sane and sound. By the way, may be of all this bunk you'll let me have a pleasant letter, that is to say can't have same from the old maid, when she do write takes an expert to read her writing and nothing pleasant at that, you may tell her letter was read also Prosper.
>
> best wishes for sound good health also regard to all
>
> Your affectionate bro,
>
> Hippolyte

Hippolyte's health was indeed improving. His doctor cautioned that if he didn't continue walking and living outdoors, he was likely to relapse and would most certainly die. The seeds for a long walk had been planted. The second reason for the around-the-world walk had its roots in a spirited correspondence between Hippolyte and his brother, Honorat. Hippolyte espoused that "No man will refuse food or shelter if you are worthy of his charity." Honorat disagreed with his brother, prompting Hippolyte to assert that he would prove himself right by walking around the world without any money, surviving solely on what his fellow man gave to him. Furthermore, he added that he'd do it barefoot. His rationale behind this decision was simply this…shoes were too expensive.

I've spent a great deal of time contemplating why Hippolyte was so adamant in his convictions. It's one thing to try to make a point, but he was committing himself to a two-year venture. Was it really that important to prove himself right and save face, or was he saving something else? Was Honorat drowning in disillusionment? Was this Hippolyte's way of throwing his brother a lifeline? If the family legends are true, their brother and uncle had committed violent murders. It's one thing to read about such ugliness in a newspaper; it's another thing all together to feel shared blood coursing through your veins. Perhaps Hippolyte needed to tip Honorat's scale a little bit and show him that there was indeed good in the world. Or, maybe he needed an adventure and his failing health and the debate about man's nature were the excuses needed to indulge his whims.

When my extended family talks about Hippolyte, they are divided into two camps. Many of us are proud of and enamored with this relative whom we never met. The other camp can't get past the fact that Hippolyte left his teenaged boys with his older brother, my great-grandfather. This facet of Hippolyte's story perplexes me. I am told my great-grandfather was very resentful of this, and justifiably so. Perhaps it was because between the ages of fifteen and twenty, their father was absent. In 1890, after an altercation with the police, their father, Pierre Francois, had to leave town for several years.

Pierre and some friends had been having drinks and playing cards in an acquaintance's store. Eventually, the store owner told the intoxicated group that it was time for them to leave so he could close his doors. Two police officers were standing outside and Pierre, who was drunk, mistook one of the police officers for the shopkeeper. He jokingly grabbed at the man's throat for asking him and his friends to leave. The policeman retaliated by pummeling Pierre with his fists. Pierre was knocked to the ground and as the police officer prepared to stomp on his head, one of Pierre's friends offered, "If you don't have a revolver, here's mine." Long story short, six rounds were fired, nobody was shot and Pierre ran off leaving behind his wife, nine children (the youngest just a one-year-old baby) and his boat-building and architecture businesses. This was at the height of vigilantism and it was too dangerous for him to return. It is rumored that he went to New Orleans where his brother Louis Andre was living. Two years later, he tried to return home but was warned by friends that a police officer from the night of the altercation had been tipped off and was in the vicinity of Pierre's house and he was carrying a loaded rifle. Pierre left town again and did not return until 1895. In all, he was absent from his family's life for five years. I don't know how a family of ten survived for so long, but they somehow managed.

Just like his father had been absent in his life, Hippolyte repeated history. He went chasing one thing—his health—only to lose another—his sons. I have to wonder what Hippolyte's sons thought about the man who had left them with their uncle to travel the world. How did they feel about their father? Did they love him, resent him, or miss him? Were they excited their father was having this grand adventure, or did they feel abandoned?

I have always felt that the largeness of the lives my parents led happened before we children were born. When I look at photos of my parents, I marvel at these strange yet familiar young people, smiling with drinks or cigarettes in their hands at a party with people I don't recognize. They were leading lives that didn't include me yet. They did things and went places. I think it was the opposite for Hippolyte. It seems to me that the largeness of his life was lived after walking away from his teenaged boys.

CHAPTER SEVEN

A World of Walkers

There is nothing inherently special about people walking long distances. Before we had modern transportation or domesticated animals to carry us about, humans got around on their own two feet. During the United States' era of westward expansion, scores of pioneers walked as many as twenty-five to thirty miles a day on their migration. I've spent a fair amount of time contemplating this whole business of walking, and I've come to this conclusion: the frequency with which people have embarked upon long distance foot journeys makes it a rather common part of human history. In fact, it's quite... pedestrian.

I had so many questions about my uncle's journey, and each answer spawned more questions. The process was akin to scratching an itch that rather providing relief only made it worse! My questions led me down so many paths of discovery that eventually I had to stop and ask myself why I was so taken with Hippolyte's story. Yes, he walked to China, and although they number only a few, there are other people who have walked just as far or even farther. I eventually realized that it wasn't the fact that he walked that was extraordinary. It is *why* he walked that makes his story special.

I wondered what compels a person to make such a profound commitment of time and energy in a culture that doesn't value such endeavors. It's not even a rite of passage, like the Australian Aboriginal Walkabout. What's the motivation? I did some research and was surprised to learn that quite a few people have attempted to walk cross-country or around the world. They all faced challenges and some, like Hippolyte, lost their lives. Reading about their experiences was exhilarating and inspiring, and I discovered that their inspiration sprung from a variety of wells. Some walked for charity; others walked for peace or to protest war. A few walkers found the lure of a cash prize irresistible. I was especially moved by the story of two remarkable women who walked across the United States in a heroic attempt to save the family farm.

In 1896, a thirty-six-year-old Norwegian immigrant named Helga Etsby heard about an intriguing offer. An anonymous sponsor was giving away $10,000 (valued at $262,000 in 2020) to anyone who would walk across the country. Helga was a mother of eight and her husband had suffered an accident and was incapacitated. Unable to pay the mortgage and taxes on the family home and farm, the Etsbys were at risk of losing both. The $10,000 prize money promised to be the solution to their financial problems. Helga and her eighteen-year-old daughter Clara wrote to the sponsor and agreed to walk from their home in Spokane, Washington to New York City. Of course, the offer was not without stipulations and a legal contract was signed. The contract stated that the women had to walk unescorted and that begging was not permitted; instead, the women were required to work in exchange for their food and lodging. A clause in the contract provided for, upon written request, the extension of their arrival date in the event of accident or illness. The contract also stated that when the journey had been completed, the sponsor would disclose his identity and the women would be awarded their $10,000.

On May 6, 1896, Helga and Clara left their home in Spokane. The women traveled east following the railroad tracks, walking twenty-five to thirty-five miles per day. They earned food and lodging by cooking, cleaning and sewing for their hosts. Helga and Clara also earned money by selling their picture post cards. Over the course of their journey, the mother/daughter team spent only nine nights sleeping outdoors. They endured blistering heat and bitter cold temperatures, rattlesnakes, robbers, and an encounter with a mountain lion. Two postponements were approved and granted due to a bout of food poisoning and a sprained ankle.

On December 23rd, 1896, 230 days after their departure, Helga and

Clara arrived in New York City. With the $10,000 prize they would be able to pay off the mortgage and taxes on the family property. However, on Christmas Eve they received the news that their sponsor was refusing to both disclose his identity and honor their contract, a cowardly and despicable move. It is unclear why the second party was able to break the terms of the contract and why the women were unable to pursue legal recourse. Helga and Clara were stranded in New York City without money, jobs, a place to live or a way to get back to Spokane. Having no intention of walking home, mother and daughter moved to Brooklyn and spent the next several months competing with other immigrant women to earn money for their train passage back to Spokane. By the time Helga and Clara returned home, two of her children had died of diphtheria. Helga was devastated. In the end, their home and farm were lost and Helga was vilified and shunned by her community for, as they perceived it, having abandoned her family.

In 1908, the Touring Club de France upped the ante considerably by announcing an even more daring challenge for an even grander prize. They offered 100,000 francs (valued at 527,000 euros in 2020) to anyone who could complete an around-the-world walking journey. Four teenaged students from Romania, who were at the time studying in Paris, decided to accept the challenge using their own money to fund the expedition. They were Dumitru Dan, Paul Pârvu, Gheorghe Negreanu, and Alexandru Pascu. Clearly, the four came from affluent families, which leads me to believe that the actual incentive was adventure rather than fortune. Two hundred other applicants were turned down. Only the itinerary of the four friends was approved. The boys returned to Romania where they spent the next two years preparing for the expedition by learning additional languages, studying cartography and physically training. In 1910, they were all nineteen years old and finally ready to begin an expedition that would not be completed until 1923. Of the four walkers, only Dumitru Dan would live to complete the challenge, the others dying from opium poisoning, a fall from a precipice, and gangrene. The outbreak of World War I forced Dan to suspend the trip. In 1923, after wearing out 497 pairs of shoes, he was finally able to complete it. By that time, due to a downturn in the economy, the 100,000 francs was only worth the current equivalent of 40,000 euros.

Decades later, the allure of an around-the-globe foot journey still proved to be just as enticing. In 1970, Dave Kunst and his brother John left Waseca, Minnesota and began a walk around the world. Over the course of the next four years, Dave walked 14,452 miles, traveling through thirteen countries and crossing four continents while wearing out twenty-one pairs of shoes. The brothers were accompanied by two dogs and a series of four mules that carted their belongings. In Monaco, the pack mule was novelty enough to garner the brothers an audience with Princess Grace.

While in Afghanistan, the brothers gave an interview to a local newspaper. Dave and John had been encouraging people to donate money to the Children's Fund, but the newspaper mistakenly reported that the two were actively collecting for UNICEF. While traveling through the Hindu Kush Mountains, Dave and John were attacked by bandits who assumed they were flush with donated money. Both brothers were shot and, tragically, John was killed. Dave spent the next four months in a hospital recovering from his injuries.

A third Kunst brother, Pete, stepped in to take the place of his murdered brother. Dave and Pete continued the journey and crossed into Pakistan, where they were escorted by a tribal prince through the Khyber Pass. It was printed in a Pakistani newspaper that the brothers were the first non-Asians to walk through the Khyber Pass since Alexander the Great. However, a newspaper article published after Hippolyte's death reported that he crossed the Khyber Pass on his journey which, if true, means my uncle Hippolyte was the first.

The two brothers made their way to Australia, but halfway across the continent, Pete returned home. Shortly thereafter, the mule that carted Dave's belongings died of a heart attack. An Australian schoolteacher named Jenni came to Dave's rescue and agreed to tow his possessions behind her car as he walked. Jenni followed as Dave journeyed through 1,000 miles of Australian sheep country. The two fell in love and are still married as of writing this book.

On October 18th, 2011, Canadian Jean Beliveau completed an eleven-year, 46,900-mile foot journey that took him around the world. Beliveau passed through sixty-four different countries and wore out fifty-four pairs of shoes. Along the way he was hosted by 1,600 different families, had police escorts in nine countries and a thirty-soldier military escort at one point while in the Philippines. Beliveau said that he walked to promote "peace and non-violence for the profit of the children of the world." He was criticized for his walk because it didn't actually fund a charity. His walk was seen by some as a self-indulgent, over-glorified mid-life crisis.

One of my favorite walkers is Mildred Lisette Norman. On January 1st, 1953, departing from the Los Angeles Rose Bowl Parade, she began a cross-country walk. It was roughly two and a half years since the onset of the Korean War, and the threat of nuclear attack was looming in the minds of many. She continually walked for peace for nearly three decades. She carried with her only a pen, a comb, a toothbrush, a map, and her signature clothing—blue pants and a blue tunic with "Peace Pilgrim" written across the front. This became her adopted name and she vowed to "remain a wanderer until mankind has learned the way of peace." For twenty-eight years she traversed the United States and parts of Canada. It is estimated that she walked coast to coast at least twenty times, covering roughly 56,000 miles. She never carried money; she walked until she found shelter and she fasted until she was offered food. In one interview she said, "I don't even ask. It is given without asking. I tell you, people are good." In a July 1981 interview, her optimism was abundantly clear. "I love people. I see the good in them… and you are apt to reach what you see. The world is like a mirror. If you smile at it, it smiles at you." I think Hippolyte shared this philosophy with her. In 1981, Peace Pilgrim was killed in an automobile accident as she was being taken to a speaking engagement in Knoxx, Indiana. She was seventy-three years old. Peace Pilgrim was born in 1908 in Egg Harbor City, New Jersey and would have been twelve years old when Hippolyte arrived in New York City, one hundred and twenty-one miles away. I wonder if she heard about him. The possibility of it feels magical. It gives me chills.

Hippolyte shared so much in common with these other walkers, be it their motives, philosophies or what they experienced on their journeys. Like Hippolyte, some faced criticism from their family or community until generations later they were revered and written about. For my uncle, the criticism lingers. Maybe it's hard not to feel irked by someone who turned his back on his obligations and chose to live so freely. I remembered the family reunion when my cousin Clare suggested that someone with Hippolyte's last name finish the walk for him. We had all been talking about our amazing Uncle Hippolyte and how remarkable it was that the world took care of him for two years. Then someone interjected with, "Well, he was no angel you know. He left his kids behind." It was true. Hippolyte left his sons in his brother's care while he went traveling around the world. It's something I will never understand. How could he abandon his own children? It's impossible to ignore and it taints my image of him. But, when I share his story with people, I share it all, the good and the bad, because it makes him more human. I wonder how much of his personal life he shared with the people he met.

In the months before Doug and I began our walk, I thought a great deal about the people we would meet. How would we be received? How did I want them to remember me? How would they be changed and how would I be changed? I also thought about my *why.* Why was I walking? Was it just to honor my uncle? Was it really just to finish his walk, to replace the ellipsis that hung at the end of his journey with a period? Or, was there another reason?

CHAPTER EIGHT

Training Days

I would love to know how Hippolyte prepared for his journey. Was he a list maker, or did he wing it? Did he go to the library and pore over almanacs and encyclopedias? Did he know what plants were safe to eat and how to find potable water? Did he study other languages like the Romanian boys? Hippolyte spoke English but French was his first language. Would this be of use to him as he traveled through parts of Europe? Did he know how to read maps and use a compass? Did he lie on his back at night with his hands behind his head, his dog beside him, look up at the stars and use them to plot his course for the next day, or did he just watch them drift across the sky? If I drive an hour and a half away from the pollution of city lights, I can watch those exact same stars.

While Hippolyte was planning to circumnavigate the globe, he had to walk across the entire Northern United States first. It was 1920 and the Eisenhower Interstate Highway System was still thirty-six years away. He would have to make his way through Washington and the panhandle of Idaho before veering south through Montana, South Dakota, Minnesota, Wisconsin, Illinois, Indiana, Ohio, Pennsylvania, New Jersey and New York. Coast to coast, temperatures would range from nighttime lows in the thirties to daytime highs in the eighties. From New York he would cross the Atlantic Ocean and eventually both the Ionian Sea and the Mediterranean. All together he would walk through sixteen different countries and across three different continents.

I believe that Hippolyte's departures and arrivals were planned to coincide with the seasons so he could avoid subjecting himself to scorching heat and freezing cold temperatures. This necessitated a winter layover in France. Regardless of timing, some of his destinations were unavoidably hot or cold, and weather can be unpredictable and even deadly.

The inventory below is as close as I can get to knowing what he might have carried when he left Seattle. The first time I looked at the list, knowing how his journey ended, I experienced an awareness that took me back in time. I remembered going through my father's belongings after he died and what a solemn act it was, how it felt to touch his things knowing that he would never use them again. It's the same sensation seeing the list of Hippolyte's belongings, the things that he carried with him, used and wore...the things that *he* would never use again.

This is a verbatim copy of the list. I have not corrected typing or spelling errors.

1 Gold Watch

1 Passport (from U.S. Government)

1 Passport (Temgy-

ush Civil Magis)

Silver coin (11.50)

1 Compass

1 Dairy

1 Chain (iron for dog)

1 Photo

2 Post Cards

1 Towel

1 Water Tank

1 Canvas Bag (Knapsack)

2 Cloth Bags

2 Maps

1 Sketch

1 Pair Khaki Pantaloons

1 Pair Leather Sandles

2 Leather Belts

1 Suit Underwear

1 Rain Coat

2 Pencils

1 Comb

1 Umbrella

This list indicates that Hippolyte had two passports, one from the U.S. and the second from "Temgyush Civil Magis." I believe that the second "passport" might actually be a visa or some sort of travel document that was issued to him in China. I believe the two postcards were most likely the ones he sold that bore his image. The photo might have been the original picture of him that he would have used for printing more postcards. As for the sketch, I found another postcard of him that bore his image in a pen and ink drawing rather than a photograph. This might be the sketch that was listed.

I had read that Hippolyte used running corks, although they were not listed in his final belongings. In a couple photographs of Hippolyte, he clenches them in his hands. It took a good deal of research to ascertain what exactly they were used for, but I eventually found a reprint of a vintage trivia card that offered an explanation.

DO YOU KNOW
No. 28
Why do runners carry running corks?
Corks are really a focus used to assist mental concentration. Most people under the strain of any violent emotion or pain will instinctively clench their hands as a sort of relief. The muscles of the body and the impulses of the mind act and react upon each other. So the athlete will clench his fists even though he isn't going to use them and the running corks assist him to do this, while at the same time preventing him from digging his nails into his flesh.

I'm not sure when he started using the corks. Perhaps they were self-prescribed and incorporated into his hiking regimen during his initial rehabilitation from consumption. Regardless, his forays into the hillsides of Yakima eventually became training exercises in preparation for his trip.

His lungs might have been healthier and ready for the journey, but Hippolyte knew that if he was going to make it around the globe barefoot, he'd have to toughen up the soles of his feet. Alas, developing calluses proved more challenging than he expected and one of his training hikes was called short by an encounter with the police. The story of his arrest made the local newspaper in a casually-written human interest story.

They butchered his first name and misspelled his last name, but overall Hippolyte came off looking only slightly less silly than the police who took him into custody. The article ran:

EFFORT TO GROW SOLES LANDS FELLOW IN JAIL

Apollos Martinez Strides Barefoot
Over Yakima Hills and Frightens Farmers

Appolos Martinez started out early yesterday morning to grow soles on the bottom of his feet. The pursuit is apparently a harmless one and there is nothing unlawful about it but it landed Martinez in the county jail just the same.

In the interest of the undertaking he started out across the river and into the Terrace Heights district bareheaded and with his shoes tied about his neck walking with a mighty stride. His appearance struck terror into the hearts of some of the natives of the farming district east of the city. Immediately they beseeched the sheriff's office by telephone to send a force of man-hunters out to capture the wild man who had come into their midst.

Answering the call, Sheriff Hutchinson and his deputy J. L. Greenwood set out to track the intruder. He escaped them by turning back toward town, crossing the river at the Cascade mill. Here Deputy Sheriff J. E. Kenney appeared to welcome him into the city. He casually invited Apollos to ride with him. But the man spurned the offer; and Kenney followed him discreetly into town. As they passed the jail, Kenney ran in and invited Thornton out to aid in the capture.

Martinez submitted with only one plaint and that was that he be allowed to take a bath immediately after his violent exercise the officers say. In the jail he confided to them that his walking exploit was so that he might grow soles on his feet thus doing away with the high cost of shoes which prevented him from making a projected journey to New York afoot. Martinez has worked as a painter locally and is known to be an enthusiast on outdoor life.

It's a good thing that Hippolyte was merely caught barefoot because he was also in the habit of nude sunbathing while on his hikes. I don't know how long Hippolyte was held, if he ever got his bath or who bailed him out, but I do know this—it would not be his last arrest.

Doug and I had our own planning to do. Both of us had travel and hiking experience, but neither of us had undertaken this kind of trip. One of the first things we did was examine our map of Southern China. We unfolded it, laid it on the living room floor and opened our travel guidebook. Starting in Dali, the town where Hippolyte had died, we plotted a course south and east to Shenzhen from where we would take a ferry to Hong Kong. Doug measured distance on the map in roughly fifteen-mile increments while I used the book and internet to search for hotels in that area. If we found hotels, I'd put a marker in between the pages and add the town, hotel names and approximate mileage to a list I was compiling. If we didn't find a hotel, we knew we'd have to find other accommodations. Likely, this meant that we'd need to camp. We calculated how many days we would need to complete the walk and moved on to step two—buying our airline tickets.

I had been stockpiling credit card points for nine years and the day after Halloween I traded them in for two round-trip tickets to Hong Kong. We'd be flying out of Los Angeles the morning of May 13th, 2015. Now we were officially committed. With a firm departure date, the trip began to feel more concrete. After weeks of talking about it, it started to feel like it was truly going to happen, which ushered in a whole new level of excitement. We would lose one full day in transit and arrive in Hong Kong at three o'clock the afternoon of the 14th. After spending the night at the airport hotel, we would take a short two-hour and twenty-minute flight northwest to Kunming, spend the entire day there, and then take an overnight train into New Dali, arriving at four o'clock in the morning on the 16th. From there we hoped to catch a local bus into Ancient Dali. We allotted ourselves three days to find Hippolyte's grave, locate the police station next door to where he died and then begin our walk. If everything worked out, we would be on the road by May 18th. At an average of fifteen miles a day, that gave us sixty-nine days to walk 1,065 miles.

We had to get separate visas for Hong Kong and China and downloaded the necessary documents off the internet. When Doug filled out his applications, he ticked the "divorced" box—not that it's anybody's business. But because there was no box labeled, "in a long term, committed, mutually exclusive relationship," I was left with no other option than to check the box next to the word "spinster." The word spinster bothers me the way the word *moist* bothers other people. Spinster, with its hissing *esses* sounds critical and in a way... punitive. When I hear *spinster*, it doesn't bring to mind a happy, independent, unmarried-by-choice woman, or someone who just hasn't found her mate yet. The word conjures images of an unpleasant and unattractive woman who lives alone. Any cats she adopted or perhaps trapped have long since run away. She is perpetually practicing Lent. Her eyebrows are drawn up not by disdain but by a bun ratcheted so tightly as to be tearfully painful. She wears high, upturned, starched collars. On their way to and from school, children cross to the other side of the street rather than pass her home. That is a spinster. I decided to take back and rebrand *spinster* and own it proudly. I can be fulfilled without being a wife or mother. I rock my librarian glasses and they are SEXY! My cats have never run away, I give out the best Halloween candy and for that the neighborhood children love me. Spinster. That's me!

Like Hippolyte, Doug and I also had some physical training to do. In fact, immediately after we agreed to finish the walk for Hippolyte, we committed to doing at least two training walks a month. On either a Saturday or a Sunday we would walk between fifteen and twenty miles. Over the course of the next seven months we completed a total of three walks. Our first walk ended after eight miles when I developed a blister across the top of my right pinky toe and the third walk was cut short at seven miles by the birth of Doug's grandson. Our second walk, bookended by blisters and a baby, was by far our most successful. However, it is best categorized as a hybrid of a pub crawl and a spa day. We stopped three times for alcohol and once to get a massage at a place of dubious integrity, as it was surrounded by strip clubs. At least we didn't get arrested. Unlike Hippolyte, our permanent records remained clean.

My conscience, however, was not clean. The guilt of not following through with our commitment to train weighed on me. I think Doug and

I may have even pinky sworn on it. Late one night in the first week of March, I was sound asleep and brought to complete alertness by a voice that said, "One thousand sixty-five miles." My eyes shot wide open and any trace of grogginess left my body. I thought about what Doug and I were about to do. Our venture wasn't that risky, but I understood that, realistically, anything could happen. We would be walking along a rural highway for over 1,000 miles. All it would take was being in the wrong place at the wrong time. It could be a driver glancing down for a second and... if anything happened, how would Doug's family ever forgive me? As our departure date neared, those miles began to feel even more foreboding. "One thousand sixty-five miles," the voice said to me again. "One thousand sixty-five miles," I whispered back to it. That's really far, I thought. What was I doing? Why did I think I could do this? One thousand sixty-five miles! The voice would wake me up every night until the day we boarded the airplane.

CHAPTER NINE

Hooked On Pinyin

I resist change. My own mother ditched her landline years before I did. In fact, until the spring of 2015, I still had a home phone that plugged into the wall. The cord gave me a walking radius of twelve feet and periodically I'd have to stand on a chair, take the receiver off the hook and let the cord unravel. I'm not what is known as an *early adopter*. My friends all had cell phones years before me, and I finally got one only because pay phones were getting harder and harder to find. I have no interest in self-driving cars and don't ever want to own a personal jet pack.

I used to marvel at my childhood friend David's great-grandmother, Dora. She lived with her daughter and son-in-law, David's grandparents. As a child, he spent every summer with them, and later he lived with them during his college years. Those were some of the best years of my life. I loved dinners with them. There was such a strong sense of family. The fact that the people who sat around the dinner table every night spanned four generations made me feel like I was in a Norman Rockwell painting. His grandmother stood exactly five feet tall, and his great-grandmother peaked out at 4' 10" and couldn't have weighed more than eighty pounds. He called them, respectively, Big Grandma and Little Grandma. Little Grandma was born in 1888, long before the invention of the car. When I was a teenager, Little Grandma told me stories about growing up in Yuma, Arizona. As a young girl, she would take her family's clothes to the river to do the wash alongside local Native American women, both sides silent and suspicious as they beat their clothes against rocks. I mourned her passing keenly and wish I had taken more time to draw those stories out of her, but by the time I was really interested in listening to them, she was in her late nineties and they weren't offered freely. I had to mine for them like precious stones. In her lifetime, she traveled by horse and wagon, automobile and airplane and lived for almost two decades after the first men walked on the moon. The kicker was that she seemed to take it all in stride, like it was no big deal. Had I been her contemporary, I would have been the woman standing on the ground stabilizing myself with my four-prong rubber tipped cane, pointing up at the airplane flying overhead while remarking, "You'll never get me up in one of those!"

Doug and I are in absolute awe of the modern cell phone. While neither of us ever owned it (we were priced out), we both remember the first-generation mobile phone. The only accessory it came with was a carrying case, and the phone itself was so bulky and awkward that you needed two hands just to hold it up to your ear. The device did two things. It made calls and received calls, and while the mobile phone did get smaller, that was about all she wrote for close to two decades. Now they can do a multitude of things. I'm sure I'm only using about three percent of my cell phone's abilities, and I'm okay with that. My car has all sorts of voice commands and I have no interest in them, let alone actually learning how to use them. For me, it's all too overwhelming. Why press a button and tell my car's computer to adjust the air conditioning when I can blindly reach over and do it myself? I honestly tried using the voice commands and I couldn't get the hang of it. In the end, I was the crazy woman shouting profanities at the pleasant-sounding woman with the non-regional British accent who existed non-corporeally somewhere inside her vehicle. Technology is changing and growing at such a rate that it's frustratingly impossible for me to keep up with it. Even so, I'm looking forward to the day I can squish my breasts between two smartphones, press send, and have the results of my mammogram texted back to me in sixty seconds.

Doug is tech-savvy and eager to try out the latest gadgets while I unapologetically identify with the Luddites, the nineteenth century textile workers who destroyed the industrialized looms that threatened to rob them of their jobs. I too destroy machinery. I just don't do it intentionally. There are people who can't wear watches because something about their personal magnetic field breaks them. I have a similar problem with computers and other electronic devices. I can't tell you how many times I have sat down at a computer or picked up a piece of electronics only to have the screen go dark or the device freeze up. Doug thought I was exaggerating until the day I bought a new laptop and, right out of the box, it was broken. I turned it on and it behaved as though possessed. Programs opened and closed on their own, black windows full of text and obscure symbols appeared and disappeared on the monitor, and the screen blinked on and off. It finally made a believer out of Doug.

Despite my bad luck with technology, I was eager to download a translation app into my smartphone. After years of traveling and toting around cumbersome or inadequate dictionaries and phrasebooks, an app for my phone promised to be technology I was ready to get on board with. One night we were having fun testing them out; we set the app to English and Mandarin, pressed the microphone button and said, "Hello." Our phones immediately answered, "Nǐ hǎo," which we verified indeed meant "hello" in Mandarin. We practiced asking for directions, ordering meals, and checking into hotels. Then we decided to test out our ability to speak Mandarin. Doug changed the setting on his app to translate from spoken Mandarin into English and said, "Nǐ hǎo" into the phone. The phone announced, "Hello" and the word appeared printed in English, verifying that he was pronouncing the Mandarin words correctly. We tried out a few more phrases, feeling confident and self-satisfied. *What a lifesaver*, I thought. *This device is a game changer*. The possibilities were endless! Then something happened. Something bad. I can't remember what phrase Doug said in Mandarin, but this is what we saw and heard back in English—"Nice fresh rape." That night we started looking for a Mandarin teacher and found a young woman nearby who would give us private lessons at a reasonable price. We started meeting her for weekly hour and a half lessons.

We weren't going to try to learn traditional written Chinese. It wasn't a good use of our limited time. Besides, I'd heard stories about Westerners who had lived in China for decades and while they could speak passable Mandarin, they were hopelessly lost trying to read anything written in Chinese characters. Most Westerners learn to speak Mandarin the way we were learning it, by reading it written in Pinyin, a phonetic system that uses the Roman alphabet for writing the Mandarin pronunciation of Chinese characters. It was adopted by the Chinese government in 1958 as part of a language reform program. It was thought that Pinyin would help China better connect with other countries, as the Roman alphabet is the most commonly used alphabet in the world. It works like this.

This character 人 means people. It would look like this written in pinyin: *rén.* This is only one example and makes it seem deceptively easy, but let me be clear. It is not.

Part of the problem lies in the fact that in Pinyin the letter "e" is pronounced *er,* "eng" says *un,* and the letters "zh" and "ch" are both bookended by invisible Ts and Rs. "Sh" is pronounced like *szhr* and to my ear sounds exactly like the sound "ch". Then, just when I'm ready to throw up my hands and quit, Mandarin throws me a bone, and "ing" is actually pronounced *ing!* Too little, too late, Mandarin!

But wait, it gets more confusing. Mandarin, like many Asian tongues, is a tonal language. There are five different tones on vowels. The tones have numbers and names and, to make it even more confounding, alternative names.

The first tone is called the high tone, or the soprano tone. Think monotone, how a robot would sound. The symbol for this tone above the vowel looks like this: ā.

The second tone is a rising tone, or the inquiring tone. Your voice starts low and then rises in pitch. The symbol for this tone looks like this: á.

The third tone is a falling rising tone, or the sarcastic tone. Pitch goes down and then rises again. The symbol for this tone looks like this: ǎ.

The fourth tone is a falling tone, or the emphatic tone. Pitch drops quickly and sharply. The symbol for this tone looks like this: à.

The fifth tone is the light tone, or the quiet tone, and has no tone mark over the vowel. It shortens the vowel sound. It looks like this: a.

Thus, the word "mao," depending on how it's accented, can mean a number of different things.

Māo means cat. It can also mean to hide oneself.

Máo means hair or feather. It can also mean mold and spear. When capitalized, it can be a surname.

Mǎo means riveting.

Mào means, among other things, hat and commerce. When capitalized, it can be a surname.

Now, imagine Mr. Máo trying to get a cat fur hat made for himself out of the cat that was trying to hide from him right before he speared it. Riveting, yes? I think tones are Mandarin's way of getting back at English for: tough, bough, cough, though and through. Well played, Mandarin. Well played.

To be fair to Mandarin, I think that tones and I got off to a bad start. Years before, when I was in Vietnam, I went to a fabric store and tailor. I asked in English if there was someone there who could make an áo dài for me. An áo dài is the traditional dress worn by Vietnamese women. It's a tight-fitting calf or ankle length tunic that is slit up the side and worn over pants. It is actually pronounced something like "ow zai." I hadn't quite tuned into the whole tonal thing yet and because I was asking a question, I unintentionally inflected my voice up on the last syllable of the word. The women in the store blushed and giggled. I asked again for an áo dài. I thought that perhaps I wasn't pronouncing the word correctly. I pointed at one woman's clothing and demonstrated emphatically, "áo dài! áo dài!" Nervously, I began to wonder if I was using the wrong word altogether. And I was right, but not for the reason I thought. After more giggles, someone finally told me that áo dài with your voice inflected down on the last syllable is the style of outfit that I wanted to buy. I, however, had inflected my voice up, and inadvertently used the slang word for testicles. My bad. After all was said and done, I finally got my áo dài. It's beautiful and I have worn it only once.

Doug didn't struggle with Mandarin in the way that I did. He has one of those brains that hears something once or twice and it's his forever. For me, Mandarin lessons were a trial. It was very challenging, and unfortunately I did not give it the time it deserved. Our teacher, Vivian, was so patient with us, but I really had to pity her. We often came unprepared and a couple times we even copied each other's homework at the last minute. After our lessons, Doug and I would sometimes go to a Mandarin Chinese restaurant for dinner and practice speaking with the servers, who were very patient with us in the way only a person who works for tips will be.

At first, all we could say was, "Nǐ hǎo—*Hello.* Nǐ hǎo ma—*How are you?* and Zài jiàn—*Good bye.*" Eventually we worked our way up to "Quingwèn, wǒmen yào liǎng píng píjiǔ", which means, *"Please, we want two beers"* and "Hěn hao hé!" which means *"It tastes good,"* if we were talking about drinks. If we were referring to our food, we'd say "Hěn hǎo chī!" I struggled with Mandarin, but Doug took to it like a Peking Duck to water.

CHAPTER TEN

The Walk Begins

The second week of April 1920, Hippolyte traveled northwest to Seattle from his home in Yakima. Only days before on the night of April 7th, a fire broke out at Seattle's most luxurious hotel, The Lincoln. Hundreds of people stood in the dark streets and watched as the building burned and a man and his daughter fatally leapt from the fifth floor of the seven-story building. Four people including one firefighter, died in the blaze. Four blocks north and two blocks to the east, Hippolyte checked into the Hotel Sather at 606 ½ Pike Street, likely very moderately priced accommodations by comparison.

Hippolyte traveled 140 miles from Yakima to Seattle to have postcards made. He planned to sell them on his walk as a way of supporting himself. Hippolyte may have gotten the idea from Helga and Clara Etsby who, in 1896, partially funded their walk across the country by selling postcards bearing their photograph. My uncle would have only been eighteen at the time and living over two thousand miles away. Initially I suspected he also went to Seattle to get his passport but later learned his passport was issued in France. My cousin Brian suggested that beginning his walk in Seattle was done for "wow factor". Hippolyte was planning to wear a sash bearing his start and end points. Yakima, a small town with a population of 18,539 was relatively unknown but most people would have heard of Seattle so, "Seattle To New York", it was. While in Seattle, Hippolyte shipped a package by sea to his sister Blanche and her husband

Prosper. Shipping it by sea might have been cheaper than shipping it over land from Yakima. On Friday, April 16th, 1920, from the Hotel Sather, he composed and sent a letter to his brother-in-law, Prosper.

> Friend Prosper:
>
> I arrived here Monday last. I am shipping you by boat—freight prepaid my box of tools and suit case and enclosed herewith the bill of lading for same.
>
> I hope you will look out for them so you will get them without delay. The suitcase is unlocked and you will find the keys for it and the tool box in my vest pocket. You are welcome to use anything if you can do so. I am making preparations for my trip and expect to get started Monday April 19th. I am having some photographs made and may be able to send you one before I leave—if not, I will later.
>
> If you will write by return mail—addressing it to Yakima General Delivery—I will be able to get it there-but you must answer at once.
>
> I intend to keep in touch with you by mail from time to time so you will know where I am.
>
> You will find in the toolbox cooking utensils which I kindly give to Edevge. They are for her.
>
> I am well and expect to start on my trip Monday.
>
> With kindest wishes,
>
> Sincerely H Martinet

This is the last letter in my possession that was written by or to Hippolyte until the following April in France. It's possible there were other letters; I just don't know what became of them.

While searching online for newspaper articles about my uncle, I found a notice in a newspaper regarding abandoned property. Apparently, Hippolyte left something behind at 617 ½ Pike St. It was categorized as *intangible personal property*. By definition, this means something that cannot be touched or held. Examples of intangible property would be a copyright or trademark. I wonder what he left behind. Did my uncle try to copyright his future? Was he planning to write a book about his walk around the world?

On Monday, April 19th, 1920 with the words "GLOBE TROTTER" stretched across his chest, Hippolyte officially began his journey. He carried a bedroll and the backpack that would contain his sole possessions for the next two years. He set off at 5:30 p.m. I'm not sure why he got started so late in the day. Maybe he was short on cash and didn't have enough money for another night at the hotel. Maybe he was just anxious to begin walking. There would have only been an hour and a half of daylight left; however, there was a full moon that night.

I imagine my uncle walking southeast back to Yakima, the setting sun at his back, and later the moon rising overhead, lighting his way. He is acutely aware of the pack on his back. It feels novel and exciting. He hasn't become used to it; it's not yet part of him. He passes homes with lit windows where families sit down together for dinner and talk about their days. I wonder if he thought about his sons whom he had left in the care of his brother Edward. I've wondered how far he walked that first day, how anxious he must have been in the months and weeks and days before he began his trip.

Because Hippolyte asked Prosper to send a letter to Yakima General Delivery, I believe that he was going to backtrack through Yakima on his way southeast into Montana. Hippolyte was walking on average thirty miles per day and at that rate would be in Yakima by Friday, April 24th. Despite being arrested in Yakima once before for walking barefoot, I believe that Hippolyte made it through without incident this time.

The days before the walk began marked the onset of the annual Lyrid meteor showers, visible only in the early morning hours before sunrise. I picture my uncle lying in the darkness at that hour when the earth is at its coolest. Hippolyte is on his back staring up at the sky as it begins to turn from black to a deep glowing blue that gets lighter with every passing minute. His fingers are laced behind his head as he counts the meteors that streak across the sky, appreciating the miracle of it and thinking to himself, "This is a good omen."

On the same day Hippolyte began his walk, nearly 600 miles away in Butte Montana, copper miners called for a strike in an effort to secure higher wages, an eight-hour work day, and an end to the use of rustling cards—a method of blacklisting employees involved in union organizing.

In fact, miners all over Butte were bravely striking. They did so despite the fact that not quite three years earlier on August 1st, 1917, Frank Little, an American labor leader, was murdered for lending his support to union organizers after 168 miners were killed in a fire at an Anaconda Copper Mine. Six masked men dragged Little from his room at a boarding house. He was beaten and taken to the edge of town where he was hanged from railroad trestles. A note pinned to his pants read, "First and last warning." Thousands attended his funeral.

Three years later, the anti-union vitriol was just as fervent, conditions were just as perilous, and labor relations were just as tense. *The Daily Bulletin,* a local newspaper, quoted the head of the Anaconda Mining Company, who suggested that killings and hangings be used to help end the strike. On April 21st, the local sheriff deputized mine guards. Almost immediately, picketing miners were fired upon. One miner was killed and a total of sixteen others were shot in their backs as they fled gunfire. The following day, federal troops were called in to prevent further violence. Nobody was ever found guilty in what became known as the "Anaconda Road Massacre" or "Bloody Wednesday."

CHAPTER ELEVEN

In Transit

At 9:00 a.m. on May 13th, Doug and I flew to Hong Kong. We arrived at 4:00 p.m. on the 14th and willed ourselves to stay awake until 8:30 p.m. so we could better adjust to the time difference. We stayed one night at the airport hotel and early the next morning flew 751 miles to Kunming. The train that took us to Dali wasn't due to leave until 9:00 p.m., which gave us twelve hours to wander around the city with our backpacks. Doug and I were in the real China now, and it was as different as could be.

In search of Chinese SIM cards for our cell phones, we headed to the main thoroughfare where vendors lined the sidewalks, hawking everything from phone cases to bananas. We passed a girl of about seven who was squatting in the middle of the sidewalk with her pants around her ankles, defecating into a plastic bag. That drew no attention at all; yet, every head turned and followed us. Eventually, we spied a huddle of teenaged boys sitting on a railing. They were all occupied, looking at the cell phone of the boy who sat in the middle. Seeing us approach, their faces broke into excited smiles. We decided to enlist their help. Doug pulled out his cell phone and used the translation app to ask them where we could buy SIM cards. One of the boys took Doug's phone and tried to decipher the message on the screen. His friends gathered close around him, draping their arms over one another—relaxed behavior we'd never see back home. They escorted us to several different stores before eventually giving up. For some reason, the first stores we went to were under the impression that they couldn't sell SIM cards to anybody without a Chinese form of identification. We finally found a place that accepted our passports and after nearly forty-eight hours without connectivity, we were once again linked to the digital world.

Too tired to explore any more of the city, our last few hours in Kunming were spent sitting inside the train station. By the time they began boarding the train for Dali City, we were weary with exhaustion. We shuffled down the aisle to the sleeper compartment we shared with two young women and settled somewhat comfortably into our bunks.

The distance between Kunming and Dali is only 170 miles, but it was an eight-hour train ride. As we trundled along, Doug and I wondered about China's famous 124 mph bullet train. We certainly weren't on it. Our train was agonizingly slow, but at least it afforded us a few hours of much needed sleep. Every so often I would wake up, pull aside the curtain, and peer into the darkness to see us chugging along at no more than 15 mph. Then the steady swaying of the train car would rock me back to sleep.

We arrived in Dali City at 5:00 a.m. It was still dark when we exited our car and followed the throng of people that moved briskly into the train station. A woman dressed in colorful, traditional Bai clothing and headdress homed in on us immediately. We asked about taking a cab into Ancient Dali. She told us that it would be very expensive. She sold us two tickets costing less than three dollars for the tourist bus headed to the outskirts of the city. We later found out that the cab ride would have cost roughly four dollars. Forty minutes later we boarded the bus and took seats in the very back row. As the bus slowly motored its way to Ancient Dali, the woman who had sold us the tickets pulled out a microphone and narrated our journey. When we arrived at 6:00 a.m., the sun had just risen. We hefted our packs onto our backs and headed to the gates of Ancient Dali. The streets were silent and empty except for the men and women in bright orange vests using straw brooms to sweep away the debris from the festivities of the night before.

CHAPTER TWELVE

We Hit the Ground

Our second night in Dali saw us in bed not long after China's 8:30 p.m. sunset. We spent the entire day looking for Hippolyte's grave and the site of his death. Doug and I lie side by side on our rock-hard mattress as the drone of distant music and voices lulled us to sleep. We woke in the dark, early morning hours and waited for the sun to rise before getting dressed. Not wanting to wake the proprietors and other guests, Doug and I tiptoed through the dimly lit hotel and into the reception area. An enormously thick, metal chain secured with a padlock ran through the door handles, barring our exit and forcing us to turn around. We slunk back through the inner courtyard, edging our way past rows of bicycles towards a side door. Doug moved two electric motorcycles that were blocking it and made sure that the door locked behind us. As we walked through the quiet village, we passed the same street sweepers we saw our first morning there. Then we exited for the last time through the east gate. Holding hands, Doug and I darted across the already busy highway and headed towards several roadside businesses in search of something to eat.

We entered a small restaurant through its roll-up garage door and ordered our first noodle breakfast—our first of many. Doug had his prepared the traditional way—rice noodles swimming in a light meat broth with chopped green onions and small, gristly pieces of meat. Being a vegetarian, I made a few adaptations—a bowl of rice noodles drizzled with peanut oil and soy sauce topped with chopped green onions and some sort of fermented vegetable that ten weeks later I was still unable to identify. I watched as other diners ate their breakfasts. It seemed counterintuitive to be eating a steaming bowl of soup when it was so hot and muggy and not yet 6:30 a.m., but who was I to question generations of Chinese culture? Doug and I carried our bowls to a small plastic table and wooden stools that seemed more appropriately suited for children. We set our bowls on the table and sat down. Our butts were only about one foot above the ground and our knees rose up awkwardly in front of us. I took a cue from the locals and planted my feet wide apart in a very unladylike manner, picked up a pair of chopsticks, and started in. I added some chili peppers and after a few bites deemed the dish not only palatable but delicious. By week five neither of us wanted to eat them ever again, but now back at home... what I wouldn't give for a bowl of those savory noodles! Part of it is purely nostalgia and the other part is because they were just so consistently, tantalizingly delectable.

The din of street traffic and locals slurping their breakfast noodles was interrupted by a barrage of loud bangs. I was so startled that I nearly fell off my stool. Heart pounding in my chest, I stuck my fingers in my ears and turned my attention to the street where a hubcap-sized roll of firecrackers was exploding. The wind had blown the thick smoke into the open-air restaurant as the last of the firecrackers went off. The local patrons didn't even seem to notice. We had turned our attention back to our breakfasts when a second and then a third roll was ignited. Firecrackers were easy to find, cheap and plentiful and by the end of our first week, Doug was buying them nearly every afternoon and igniting them the next day. It would be another four weeks before we understood the significance of the firecrackers. After finishing our noodles, Doug and I walked out into the drifting smoke to look for a cab. Bits of shredded red paper billowed about our feet and the smell of sulfur burned our nostrils as a taxi pulled up to the curb.

Once in the back seat, Doug showed the driver our GPS device and with his finger indicated the place that would be our official starting point. We decided to begin our walk from the edge of Dali City. The cab driver looked briefly at the screen and pulled out into traffic. Doug took another look at the device to monitor our location. Our hope was that it would still be of use despite the fact that GPS navigational devices, through no fault of their own, aren't one hundred percent accurate in China. For reasons of national security and to protect sensitive sites, the Chinese government intentionally skews maps of the country. Controls are so tight that in 2004 the government made all private mapping and surveying activities illegal. The resulting offsets can be anywhere from a quarter to one whole mile. Even though we were clearly traveling down highway 324, the device reported that our exact location was somewhere in the middle of Erhai Lake. Fortunately, our entire journey would be spent walking along two well-marked highways. As long as we didn't venture too far off them, neither of us anticipated any serious problems.

Doug and I were surprised to see how industrial the edge of Dali City was. It was nothing like Ancient Dali or the part of Dali City we had seen while searching for the old police station. We got out of the cab and retrieved our backpacks from the trunk. Despite wanting to keep its weight down to fifteen pounds, mine weighed twenty-two pounds when it was loaded with water. I paid the driver, who folded the bills, stuffed them into his pocket, pulled out his cell phone and asked to take our picture. We posed for him and then Doug waved him over to us for a group photo. The three of us huddled together while Doug stretched his long arm out and snapped a shot with his cell phone. I offered the driver one of our postcards in the Chinese fashion—held out with both hands—and he received it in kind. He read both sides and then looked up at us with an expression of disbelief. Grinning, he gave us the thumbs up gesture before getting back into his cab to look for his next fare, leaving us alone on the highway. After eight months of planning and waiting, we were finally ready to take our first steps towards Hong Kong. Four day after leaving Los Angeles, we were ready to begin our walk.

Doug and I looked at each other, said "Ready?" and very unceremoniously began walking. I don't even remember if we took a picture to commemorate the moment. It was 7:30 in the morning; we were at an elevation close to 6,000 feet and enjoying temperatures in the low eighties. My clothes were clean, my hair freshly washed, and my feet were used to the good life. For the next several hundred miles we would be walking along highway 324 until it became the 320.

The 324 was a fairly quiet road and we walked along its shoulder against traffic. Large cement blocks that had been painted white marked each and every kilometer. The highway number and kilometer distance were painted in large red numbers. Much to my satisfaction, I noticed they were the perfect height and width for sitting. A small post that rose a few inches out of the ground marked every tenth of a kilometer. These were usually bare cement with red numbers painted on them in ascending order. They were also the perfect height for tripping over. These were hazards I would have to avoid. I am woefully uncoordinated. I rarely wear heels because I'm prone to stumbling for no reason, and at any given time I have bruises on my legs from walking into things. The last thing I needed was a clumsy accident. Roughly 10,600 of these menacing little posts lie between Hong Kong and me.

In the outskirts of the city, any unused or open space no matter how small was being used as either a place to dump garbage or as a vegetable patch. Even a narrow strip of dirt only a foot or two wide and a few feet long had little squash plants or corn growing in freshly tilled and weeded soil. Every so often a huge truck would blow by and leave the plants quivering in its wake. Within minutes we saw our first rice paddies. Some of them were mere eight by ten-foot plots with sturdy green shoots in perfect rows standing in murky brown water.

Less than an hour in, Doug needed his first bathroom break near a mechanic's garage. I could smell the oil and grime from the street. Halfway up the short, grease-stained driveway, a man came out to meet us. "Mǎtǒng?" Doug asked, using the Mandarin word for toilet. The man pointed to a corrugated metal shack back by the side of the road and Doug headed for it. Before he reached the door, the man came running back out of his business waving a roll of toilet paper, the tail of it fluttering in the wind. Doug took it from him, stepped in and pulled the creaking door closed behind him.

I stood at the edge of the driveway admiring the rice paddy across the highway while Doug took care of business. A few minutes later, he emerged and returned the roll of toilet paper to the man who was tinkering with something in his garage. Doug came back down the driveway but stopped before he got to the end. "Micae, you have got to see this. Come look," he called to me as he stood once again beside the mǎtǒng. I recoiled slightly and, sensing my unwillingness, he reassured me, "It's not gross, I swear. It's genius!" he beamed. Steeling my nerves, I walked up to the shack and reluctantly pushed the door open with the tip of my trekking pole. I realized I had squeezed my eyes shut in anticipation of something disgusting and cautiously opened them bit by bit until the interior of the shack came into focus. There in the dim light above a pit of unknown depth was a metal folding chair. The center of the seat had been welded out. I didn't touch it, but I could tell that there was not a sharp edge on it. It had been burnished smooth and glinted in the rays of sunlight that shone in behind us. I let the door swing shut and looked back over my shoulder before stepping back out onto the highway. I saw the guy that had offered Doug the toilet paper. He was grinning, clearly proud of his handiwork. Had I known that this was by far the cleanest and only "Western" public toilet I would see for the duration of our walk, I would have at least tried to avail myself of his facilities. Alas, I had no idea what was in store for us.

Incidentally, this was the easiest experience we had asking for a bathroom for our entire trip. So many other times when we said the word mǎtǒng, we were met with looks of confusion. Quite often Doug would resort to miming pulling his pants down. Sometimes he would have to do this several times before his meaning was understood. I, however, fell back upon the tried and true *pee-pee dance*. It worked every time. Of course, now I realize that part of the problem was that the Mandarin language has completely different words for toilet depending on what kind of toilet it is: a public toilet, squat toilet, pit toilet, urinal, the ladies' toilet, or the men's toilet.

Shortly after Doug's bathroom break, a pickup truck passed us at the bottom of a hill. The driver pulled over, opened the tailgate, patted the bed of the vehicle and waved Doug and I over, ready to have us climb into the back. Feeling pretty confident after successfully busting out the word mǎtǒng and actually being shown to a bathroom, we crossed the highway to meet him. "Wǒmen zǒulù cóng Dali dào Shenzhen." Doug explained that we were walking from Dali to Shenzhen and retrieved a card from the side pocket of my backpack. "Wǒmen gěi," *we give* I told the stranger as Doug handed him the card. He read it and looked at us with an expression of disbelief that morphed into a smile. He gave us the thumbs up gesture, closed the tailgate of his truck and drove away. Doug and I watched him zip up the hill and disappear from sight.

We continued to walk for several hours and even enjoyed a few minutes of gentle rain. Every so often on the hillsides, Doug and I spied a lone, grey gravestone perched up high. Some of them were small and unassuming while others were grand and more ornate. I liked the idea that a person could be buried seemingly anywhere or in a specific spot for no other reason than it had a pleasant view. When I was a little girl, I told my father that when I died I wanted to be buried in a little grove of trees that stood beside the freeway. "You can't be buried just anywhere," he told me, and I remember how disappointed I was. I thought it was unfair and a waste because it seemed like such a lovely little spot to spend eternity.

Feeling hungry again, we stopped at a restaurant for lunch. Ordering for both of us, I requested something vegetarian and left it at that. A few minutes later, the waitress returned to our table with our new favorite dish, savory scrambled eggs fried with tomatoes and served with rice. One of the words I made sure to learn in Mandarin was the word for spicy, "là". I had even asked our Mandarin teacher Vivian to write the word in Chinese character for me. I showed my card to the waitress and pointed to the word. A moment later, she brought me a small dish of crushed red pepper and other spices, poured hot water over it, added a little oil and stirred it with the tip of a chopstick. I ordered this with every meal for the rest of our trip.

Thirty minutes later, our feet hit the ground again. Less than a mile and a half down the road, we saw a Buddhist temple across the street. We walked up the steps and through the front gates, took off our backpacks and leaned them up against a wall. Three separate buildings made up the complex. The inner courtyard was paved with stone tiles and pots with ornamental plants set on cinderblocks.

To our right and left were common rooms and a kitchen, and directly across from the gates was the temple itself. Hearing voices coming from a room off to our right, I poked my head in and found several women sitting at a table. "Wǒmen kàn ma?" I asked for permission to look around. One of the women stood up from the table and led us into the temple. Inside it was dim and cool and the air was still and musty. Little dust motes swirled and dipped in the pale light. The room had a very distinctive pleasant scent like the smell of an old book—gentle floral and vanilla notes nearly masked by the smell of cellulose breaking down in the paper. It's one of my favorite scents. If it were a perfume, I'd wear it. Before us stood two Buddha statues with altars beneath them. To the right, a male monk sat in the hazy light reading from some white papers, rhythmically tapping a slab of wood with a dowel. The beat was steady and unwavering. I put a five kuai note in the donation box and then Doug and I stepped back outside into the sunlight.

As we stood in the courtyard, our eyes adjusting to the light, another woman approached us and started speaking in Mandarin. Not understanding what she said, I handed her one of our postcards and told her to read it. "*Qǐng kàn.*" She took the card and handed it to a female monk who wore a blue robe and had a shaved head. After reading it, the monk beckoned us with her hand and led us to a kitchen. She pointed to the table and stove, and then mimed eating. Doug and I were still stuffed from lunch. Lamenting the fact that neither of us had learned the translation for "*We are full,*" Doug instead pointed back up the road, mimed eating, and then held his stomach to show that we had just been well fed.

Next, the monk led us to two upholstered chairs that sat under the eaves of the roof, inviting us to sit down and enjoy the cool, quiet shade. Moments later, she returned with a tray in her hands. It held an enormous Asian pear, some tamarind pods, longan fruit and wrapped candies. I took a couple of the tamarind pods and the Asian pear. The monk smiled, shook her head at me, dumped the entire contents of the tray into my lap and walked away. Doug and I couldn't believe it. This is exactly what Hippolyte was talking about. It was what Peace Pilgrim talked about. *People just give.* We stayed a few more minutes, said our goodbyes, put our packs back on and left, astounded by our good fortune and the generosity of strangers.

CHAPTER THIRTEEN

Making Camp

We left the temple with our pockets full of candies and tamarind pods. Soon, an enormous hill loomed before us and it began to rain so we got out our umbrellas. Months before our trip began, Doug devised a method that allowed us to use them hands-free. He cut four-inch sections of foam rubber tubing to encase the umbrella stems, which were then secured to our backpack straps with elastic laces and cord locks. Within seconds, they were up and we continued walking.

By the time we summited the hill, the rain had stopped. Four large boulders, either strategically placed or too cumbersome to move, sat in a turnout. Claiming one apiece, we took off our backpacks and had a seat. I turned my back to the breeze so my sweat-soaked shirt could dry. Across from us were two more hulking rocks and what looked like a six-gallon plastic water container. We sat with our backs to the road and looked at the valley that stretched out in front of us. On the opposite mountainside, there was some sort of quarry. The hillside had been stripped bare; there wasn't a tree to be seen. Huge machinery that seemed to defy gravity somehow clung to the hillside. I couldn't imagine what was stopping all of it from cascading down in an avalanche.

While taking in this scene, we were startled by a woman who appeared to be in her 80s as she emerged from the rim of the steep valley below. A bundle of sticks nearly as big as her entire body was strapped to her back. Releasing the strap, the wood fell to the ground as she wiped sweat from her face with the back of her hand and then sat on one of the rocks opposite us. I said hello and she responded with a slew of words that neither Doug nor I could comprehend. Sensing we didn't understand, she pointed to a small sapling tree I hadn't noticed before. It was laying on its side with its roots wrapped up in a piece of canvas. Doug and I gathered that she and her husband, who we could hear calling to her occasionally, were clearing the hillside below and planting the young trees. After a five-minute respite she rose, cleared her throat, and then hocked and spat. She picked up the plastic water container effortlessly, heaved it over her shoulder and headed back down the steep hillside. Before we left, I placed a few of the candies from the temple upon her rock and stepped back onto the shoulder of the highway.

Our walk continued up another steep hill that flattened out before taking a sharp turn to the left. It was here that we came upon a group of men sitting on a low wall. I think it was there to prevent people from missing the turn in the road and plunging over the edge into the valley below. Wanting to know how many kilometers to the nearest hotel, we pointed down the highway and asked, "Fàndiàn duōshao gōnglǐ?" They looked at us with blank faces. We tried a few more times, reducing the complexity of our query to just the one word for hotel, "Fandian?" which was met with more blank stares. "Our Mandarin sucks to the extreme," I said to Doug, and we continued along. In the coming weeks I would be reduced to pantomime. I'd place my hands, palms facing each other, against one cheek. I'd feign sleep while making snoring noises one only hears coming from cartoon bears.

A mile further down the road, we came across a small village and a series of connected buildings that appeared to be the center of town. In one store, a woman stood behind a glass display case full of candy, pens, cigarettes, and soap. Inside her unlit shop, cramped rows of shelves were stocked floor to ceiling with everything from bicycle tires to insecticides.

Five women gathered outside in conversation. One had the most beautiful and unearthly shade of hazel eyes I have ever seen. They were piercing and could be seen from a distance. A young man wearing spandex cycling apparel sat on a bench in the shade of the building. An expensive looking racing bike was parked beside him. Again we asked, "*Fàndiàn duōshao gōnglǐ?*" He understood us immediately and told us there was a hotel in the next village eleven kilometers away. Doug looked at our GPS device, which now indicated we were not on the highway but in fact somewhere in the depths of the canyon below. We had walked exactly fifteen miles since stepping out of the cab that morning. Satisfied with our first day's progress, we decided to stop for the night.

Doug and I found a suitable, flat piece of land directly across the street from the store and behind a waist-high wall. A large piece of foreign-looking machinery was parked behind it. Twenty feet beyond that, a deep canyon sprawled into the distance. It was a perfect place to set up our tent. Soft straw was spread out all over and would surely be more comfortable than the hard mattress we had slept on for two nights at our hotel in Ancient Dali. We felt lucky to find such a charming spot because nearly every flat piece of ground we passed all day was either used as a vegetable patch or strewn with garbage. Doug went back to the store to ask if we could camp in this dream spot.

Before we left home, our Mandarin teacher, Vivian, gave us the Chinese character translation for "Can we pitch our tent here and spend the night?" and we saved it in our phones. We showed it to the shop owner as the other ladies gathered around us. When we pointed to the place on the opposite side of the wall, they looked at us like we were absolutely out of our minds but gave us the go ahead. We could hear their laughter as we set up our tent fifteen or twenty feet from the edge of the ravine.

Once we had our tent erected, Doug went back across the street to buy some snacks and bottled water while I blew up our air mattresses and lay out our shared sleeping quilt. It was a tight fit and there wasn't room for much else. Our backpacks were outside in the vestibule area where they would remain dry if it rained overnight. I had left the flap of the tent unfolded and a woman came by to peer inside. She laughed and called to her friends, who took turns peeking into the tent while I lie on my side, sweeping my arm out to show them the expanse of our luxurious dwelling.

A few minutes later, I heard voices and footsteps around the piece of machinery, so I crawled out of the tent to investigate. Two women were attaching a large, tubular, cloth sack to the machine and tying the other end into a knot. They flipped a switch and the beast roared to life, filling the limp sack with air. The other women brought over large bags of dried vegetation, weeds and brush that they fed into the mouth of the machine. It ground the material up and spat it out the other end where it was blown into the long bags. When the bag was filled, the end was knotted and another sack attached. I imagine the end product would be fodder for pigs or other animals. Doug pitched in and helped the women lift the cumbersome bags and feed the contents into the machine. I kept my distance. The machine was deafening and seemed dangerous.

By the time they finished, a group of school children escorted by their grandparents had arrived, walking up the highway in their little uniforms—navy blue trousers and jackets with light blue or white shirts. I still had candies from the temple, so I passed them out. A small crowd gathered around me while I entertained them with a magic trick until one clever little boy blew my cover.

When the sun began to set, the town's one streetlight came on and the woman from the shop shuttered the windows and closed the door. She walked across the street with a cardboard box brimming with trash, stepped past our tent and dumped its contents into the ravine. She smiled as she passed us, left the empty box sitting in front of her store, and joined the stream of pedestrians who were walking home. After she left, I walked to the edge of the canyon. Down below, an enormous pile of rubbish fanned out for yards. No wonder they had looked at us so strangely when we had asked to pitch our tent there. We were right on the edge of the town's garbage pit. For some reason, despite the extreme humidity, it was odorless.

We climbed into our tent just as the sun was setting. I turned on my headlamp and opened my journal while Doug fiddled with the GPS. After a few minutes he turned it off, put it away and rolled onto his side. One minute later he was asleep. I continued writing as I listened to his steady breathing punctuated by the occasional passing car. I felt my eyelids getting heavier and heavier, so I closed my journal and lay down, pressing my back into Doug's. I whispered to myself, "One thousand and forty-seven miles" and drifted off into serene and untroubled sleep.

CHAPTER FOURTEEN

Behind Bars in Butte

The town of Butte was established in the early 1870s as nothing more than a bunch of humble gold and silver mining camps. In part populated by Irish who had emigrated to the U.S. and Canada between 1845 and 1855, Butte quickly grew into Montana's first major city and the largest U.S. city west of the Mississippi and east of San Francisco. Butte, while not quite a *company town*, was still very much dominated by Anaconda Copper Mining. A 1920 census report puts the population at 41,611, although some claim that it was actually closer to 100,000. Either way, the population had reached its historical peak. However, following World War I, the population would soon begin to plummet along with copper prices.

Before Prohibition drove them underground, Butte boasted hundreds of saloons and gambling halls and had a vibrant red-light district where over one thousand women worked on streets with names like Model Terrace, Fashion Place and Pleasant Alley. In 1933, with the end on Prohibition, the district reopened with the name Venus Alley. Even though the population by then had fallen to 39,000, it still attracted visitors. The last bordello closed in 1982. Today, Butte has a population of 34,000.

On April 19th, 1920, the same day Hippolyte began his journey from Seattle, Butte miners went on strike. Two days later, deputized mine guards fired shots into the crowd of picketers. One man was killed and sixteen others suffered gunshot wounds. Federal troops arrived on April

22nd to restore order and by May 12th, miners had returned to work.

Walking at a rate of thirty miles per day, it would have taken Hippolyte nineteen days to walk five hundred ninety-four miles from Seattle to Butte. He would have arrived approximately May 9th, just as the strike was entering its final days. One would think law enforcement in Butte would have enjoyed some peace and quiet, but they found reason to arrest my uncle. Once again, he was incarcerated for walking barefoot.

Eighty-five miles down the road, Hippolyte relayed his story and it made the news in the *Bozeman Daily Chronicle* on May 29th, 1920.

"TREKS THAT WAY FOR HIS HEALTH"

Anyone who sees a dark complexion man barefooted and bareheaded, but otherwise clad in a khaki suit will take his word for it that he is not crazy, but just traveling that way for his health, He is Hippolyte Martinet, a carpenter by trade, at which he is not using just now. He is engaged in trekking from Seattle to New York, eating on the proceeds of the sale of postal cards containing his picture and sleeping in the open on the bedding he carries in his pack.

Martinet figures that he is making 30 miles a day on the average. He left Seattle on April 19, and came by way of public roads, occasionally taking to the ties when the railroad presented a more inviting appearance. He says he has met with good treatment everywhere except Butte, where two unharnessed bulls picked him up and charged him with being insane. A doctor who was called to examine him declared him no more crazy than the policemen, and prescribed letting him go on his way. He went on his way with a deep-seated opinion that Butte was not a nice place to go.

It is Martinet's idea that he will reach New York sometime in August. From there, if his finances permit, he will go to Europe.

Nearly a year later, Hippolyte relayed the story again to a newspaper in Genoa, Switzerland. This time he provided more details of his arrest. An excerpt from the article reads:

> Evidently, then it was for this radically extreme simplicity in dress that Mr. Martinet had a peculiar where he was "pinched" and brought to jail by two husky policeman. They charged him with a great many names too long and legal to remember. Then they brought him socks and a pair of shoes and a hat—all with which our world roamer refused to associate. Finally they fetched a doctor—a sort of mental inspector—who performed a scrupulous examination of the prisoner. And the verdict was that "this man may appear insane; but you are all crazy."

While we were never quite sure what the grounds were for our detention, Doug and I would also have run-ins with the police...once when we were together and another time when I was alone.

CHAPTER FIFTEEN

Going Abroad

By first light, our packs were on and we were well into our second day before any of the shop owners had returned. The only indication that we had been there was an area of compressed straw left by our tent. As I put on my sunglasses, I thought about Hippolyte on his journey across the planet—almost always walking eastward, the warm sun rising in his face. Our morning meal consisted of the leftover snacks Doug bought the afternoon before and the giant pear given to us by the monk at the temple. In the cool of the morning, we munched on crackers and chips and passed the pear back and forth, heading southeast down the winding highway towards the village below. In my day-to-day life, I rarely take the opportunity to pause and appreciate the early morning hours; it's a shame because it's such a beautiful and lively time of day. The birds that woke us with their chattering had emerged from the protection of their bushes and darted about frenetically. Doug and I swore we could hear the mournful howls of a lone wolf somewhere in the distance.

I was excited to begin our second day of walking. It still felt so alien and unreal to be in China. I have friends who have talked about volunteering for Mars One, the global initiative with the mission to establish a permanent settlement on the red planet. I can appreciate that it's a huge and exciting adventure to be a pioneer in space, but I don't entirely understand the lure because there are still so many places I want to visit on this planet. It is so easy to get caught up in the ways we are different that it is easy for me to forget that, underneath our skin, we are the same. We all work, love, sleep and eat... and we all go to the toilet.

Our first day, we noticed roadside bathrooms that cropped up every few miles, mere feet from the side of the highway. They were convenient in their location and prevalence, so we never had to wait too long for one. At least Doug didn't. I consider myself an experienced traveler and I know that one has to abandon any illusion that things are going to be like they are at home. After all, that's really the whole point of travel—to be exposed to new and different things. However, there is no fast and steady rule that says that you are required to like and enjoy every aspect of it. As much as they demanded my appreciation, I was never going to warm up to roadside toilets.

Most of the roadside bathrooms we saw were a single mud and brick construction divided into two rooms by a wall. Each room had its own entrance marked with the symbol for male or female, two of the few Chinese characters that Doug and I were able to recognize. The separate L—shaped entrances led to small rooms with a cement trench that ran across the floor under the middle wall and into the other room. The trench was generally configured in one of three ways. A graded slab of concrete ran across the room so that all waste flowed down and out the backside of the building. Others were engineered with a trench that was graded so waste ran from one room into the other and out a hole in the other wall. The third and my least favorite configuration was a cement trench that directed all waste out along the front side of the building where it was visible from the street. I am sure that there is some logical reason for this design, but my delicate Western upbringing made it a challenge to walk past without shuddering. In the coming weeks, there were several occasions when Doug tried to assure me that a bathroom was "not that bad," so I'd peek my head in only to turn around gagging, lurching away as fast as possible, all the while cursing him, "Damn it... *ack*... Doug... *bleck*... I'm not... *urgh*... falling for that... *aarf*... again!" I took a forensic anthropology class in college, and years later I even witnessed an autopsy. I'm far more traumatized by the roadside bathroom.

The previous afternoon, I used the roadside bathroom adjacent to our campsite and hoped at all costs to never use one again. I walked into the structure and only too late realized I had forgotten to delete my brain's "bathroom experiences" default setting and reset it to "Asian squat toilet," which I had actually used before. As one does, I headed to my habitual stall of choice, mine being—not the first, not the last, but one somewhere anonymously in the middle. Expecting to find the bathroom empty, at the second of several waist-high, doorless partitions, I came upon a woman who was hunkered down, the voluminous and heavy folds of her skirt gathered about her as she squatted over the trough. I promptly turned on my heels and left. It was awkward and I was not prepared. I'm not one of those women who goes to the bathroom in packs and I have strict rules at home. I don't want to talk to Doug when he is in the bathroom and Doug knows not to talk to me when I'm in the bathroom. Yelling "FIRE" is the only permissible communication with me behind that particular closed door. As the book says, "Everyone Poops." I just prefer, no, I NEED privacy.

I went back in twenty minutes later. Some bathrooms have a big bucket of water by the door for washing waste away, but this one didn't have one. Thus, I used the stall that was next to the one the woman had been in and listened to the impossibly loud buzzing of flies emanating from the cubicle next door. Afterwards, I squeezed a generous blob of sanitizer into my hand and walked out, doing mental math and counting days and miles, wondering if I could possibly avoid using a roadside bathroom again.

The next morning when nature called, the previous day's foray into our campsite's bathroom was still fresh in my mind, so I got resourceful. I walked in the opposite direction of the public bathroom, and in the crepuscular glow of early dawn abandoned all modesty, faced the street, dropped trou, dug in my heels, held onto a sturdy bush with one hand and had my morning pee off the steep hillside into the garbage dump below. It was lovely, and I don't think that I used a roadside bathroom more than four times throughout the rest of our trip.

Only a few hours into our second day, Doug began to experience some gastrointestinal difficulties and needed to use the *facilities*. We saw several men sitting in an open room around a faded green, felt-covered mahjong table and asked about a bathroom. One of the men pointed across the street. When Doug reached the other side, he looked back at us and one of the men waved for him to continue on to a narrow path that led to a stand of trees which, as it turns out, was the proffered bathroom. I was prepared to walk further up the road and wait it out, but one of the men called to me and pointed to a couch against a wall opposite their table. I decided to take him up on his offer since my last seat had been a rock and I wasn't going to pass on comfort.

I settled into the soft corner of the sofa, leaned back into the vinyl upholstered cushion and sighed, warning myself not to get too comfortable. My host set a thermos down on the table in front of me. Next, he took a small glass from a shelf and carried it to a waist-high sack that sat in the corner of the room. He grabbed a pinch of something from the sack, put it into the glass, and came back to where I was seated. He set the glass on the table in front of me, poured hot water over it, and in seconds I smelled the delicate aroma of green tea. The glass was so hot that I couldn't touch it with my bare fingers, so I untied the bandana from the shoulder strap of my backpack and used it to pick up the steeping brew. I watched as the men continued with their game, laying down tiles and pushing chips into the center of the table, occasionally stopping to smoke a cigarette out of a water pipe made from soup cans that had been welded together. They took turns passing the pipe until the cigarette, placed filter tip down into the bowl, was reduced to ash.

After a few minutes, the man who brought me tea addressed me and pointed to the "bathroom" across the street. I looked, but there was no sign of Doug. I assumed that he was asking about him, so I busted out one of the few phrases I knew in Mandarin. "Tā bìng le—*He's sick,*" I said, jerking my head in the direction of the bathroom across the street. He said something else that I didn't understand, but he had a look of mild concern on his face. To put him at ease, I waved a hand dismissively in Doug's direction, cocked a butt cheek and made raspberry sounds as I waved my hand back and forth behind my rear. The men all nodded comprehendingly and went back to their game of cards. I was on my second glass of tea when Doug came across the street to join me. I patted the seat cushion next to me and he sat down. Our host grabbed another glass and a pinch of tea leaves, poured some hot water for Doug and then gave him a squeeze and pat on the shoulder before rejoining his game. “What was that about?” Doug asked. “Uh… I told them you had the runs,” I sheepishly admitted, only then considering that perhaps the admission was more personal than necessary. Doug rolled his eyes and shook his head, clearly exasperated with me. We sat for a few more minutes, thanked our hosts for the tea, and headed back to Highway 324.

CHAPTER SIXTEEN

Taking Candy from Strangers

After leaving our hosts, we walked a few more miles before coming upon a restaurant. We hadn't had a real meal in twenty-four hours, so we stepped inside for lunch. Two women were sitting at a table watching a movie on a wall-mounted television as they removed the fine, prickly hairs from the vines of a squash plant. We placed our order, sat at a plastic table, and waited for our food to arrive. Doug fiddled with the GPS while I tried to make sense of the movie. The characters were very young women working on the floor of a large factory. In the following scene, the women appeared in a cheerfully decorated dormitory furnished with bunk beds and colorful curtains. I thought it odd that they lived and worked in the same place. It wasn't until later that we learned this was actually quite common because we passed countless gas stations that had employee housing above them.

After our lunch of boiled squash stems (a vegetable that would be served to us frequently), we crossed the street to buy water. The shop owner, noticing Doug had sat down to tend to his feet, came over and set a large, ceramic-coated basin in front of him. He returned with a pitcher of water and invited Doug to wash. Doug was soaking his blistered toes when I noticed two young men struggling to tape banners to a wall in the stiff breeze. I went over to help. When we were finished, they began speaking to me in Mandarin. Because I did not understand them, I held up my index finger and a few seconds later returned with two of our postcards. They looked at the cards, smiled, and walked off. Doug was lacing up his shoes when they came back with two bags of tamarind candy and gave one to each of us. It was such a thoughtful gesture and we were so appreciative. Casting a lifetime of warnings and cautionary tales aside, Doug tore into his bag and claimed that his parents had been wrong all along, and in fact, strangers had the best candy of all.

It was only day two of our walk and we were already overwhelmed by the interest, enthusiasm, and generosity shown to us. Motorists were pulling over to take pictures with us or they would honk and give us the thumbs-up gesture out the window. One car full of people pulled over and gave us two bottles of water. It was extraordinary, wonderful and heartwarming. I think Doug was more surprised than I was. Earlier in the day, he paused, took a moment to gather his thoughts, and then proclaimed, "Wow, now I know what it feels like to be a hot girl!"

Over lunch, Doug calculated that we had walked sixteen miles. We agreed that was adequate progress and began our search for a hotel. At the edge of the next town, we walked into the first hotel we saw. A sign at the reception desk listed rooms from highest to lowest price as well as the hourly rate. The most expensive room, the Presidential Suite, was on the top floor and went for $1,300 a night. We opted for the cheapest (overnight) room available on a lower floor at the rate of $25.

Our room was definitely a splurge. It was one of the more expensive rooms during our entire stay in China. It had a western toilet, an enclosed shower and on the counter to the left of the sink, there was a selection of four different brands of condoms fanned out neatly on a little tray. An identical tray was on the bedside table. We soon discovered that condoms were almost always present in commercial hotels. One of the more prevalent brands was "Jissbon." In the larger cities, the interior of elevator doors was often plastered with Jissbon advertisements featuring the company mascot, Jissbon himself, an unrolled yellow condom wearing sunglasses and looking, for lack of a better word, cocky.

In the last decade or so, a shift in world order has seen the Chinese overtaking the world in myriad arenas. According to the results of a 2004 global internet survey conducted by the condom company Durex, this included the sexual arena as well. The following report was first published in the *Shanghai Daily.* Personally, I think it reads better as it appeared in the English language Chinese news website, *China Daily.* I suspect they used the same flawed translation app that was the impetus for our private Mandarin lessons.

> The Chinese have the most per capita sexual partners as 19.3, while with the most gloomy sex ardour. Each Chinese has on average 19.3 partners toping the sex league table where an worldwide average number is just 10.5, according to the world's biggest condom maker, Durex. It makes one doubt how the Chinese possess so affluent partners while with world low sex drive, ranked the last seven in the world, also revealed the Durex survey.

I'm not sure what accounts for the reported low sex drive of the average Chinese person; however, I can say exhaustion, mostly due to the heat, was responsible for our lackluster libidos. We were simply too tired to avail ourselves of even one let alone eight condoms. That night Doug and I bathed, washed our clothes in the sink, ate dinner in the hotel "restaurant" and were in bed by seven o'clock. We started calling ourselves Ma and Pa. "Good night Pa," I said to Doug. "Good night Ma," he answered back, kissing me chastely and turning out the lights. I have no idea how Hippolyte was walking thirty miles per day.

CHAPTER SEVENTEEN

Best Day of My Life?

The next morning, after hotel staff were dispatched to our vacated room to count condoms that clearly weren't complimentary, we checked out well rested, owing nothing. The previous day's walk had been very pleasant. It started downhill, flattened out and was effortless, almost leisurely. But on this our third morning, the highway snaked its way up a single mountain that sat nestled amid a range of equally imposing if not higher mountains that commanded our attention. The narrow highway we were on was the only man-made artifact as far as we could see in every direction. After over a mile of continuous and steep ascent in the burgeoning heat, I needed a little encouragement. I plugged in my earbuds and the first song to play, even though I had heard it on the radio dozens of times before, suddenly seemed to be about... me! It was all about not giving up and having the *best day of my life*. The next song was also about me and reminded me to hold on tight to my dreams. In fact, all the songs spoke directly to me in the same way that when you are in love every song on the radio seems to be written about you. I felt youthful and renewed, brimming with a kind of excitement that I hadn't known in years.

After five and a half miles of grueling switchbacks and steep hills that maliciously concealed even steeper rises behind them, we were finally at the top, and the view was... not at all what I had expected. I thought that surely the worst part was behind us, but there we were, looking down into a stone quarry; a cloud of white dust hung near the bottom. Just then, a gargantuan truck spewing black exhaust groaned and lumbered past. It left us choking on its fumes as it followed the highway that descended into the pit below.

It took far less time to walk into the quarry than it had to ascend the hills that led to it, and before we knew it, we were at the bottom of a man-made crater, grey and dusty as the moon itself. Truck after rumbling truck passed us on the narrow road. On both sides of the highway, masons negotiated business in plywood sheds or under tarpaulin canopies, but all labor was performed outdoors in the sweltering sun. Men sat beside mountains of stone, their hair, skin and clothes covered in a layer of dust as they used masonry saws, hammers and chisels to produce everything from blocks with perfect angles to ornate palace dogs and headstones like those we had seen perched on the hillsides along the highway. The noise from the saws was deafening and the grey dust blanketed everything in a thick layer of powder; every shrub and tree lining the road was masked in the same film that covered the sculptors. The air in the canyon hung perfectly still until a truck would blow past, stirring up more choking dust. I took the bandana off the shoulder strap of my backpack and tied it across my mouth as we continued our climb out of the quarry. The piece of thin cloth made it even hotter and more difficult to breathe, but at least it kept the dust out of my nose and mouth. In some places the road was so narrow that we had to step into the weeds to allow trucks to pass. I no longer felt like I was having the best day of my life.

I hated that canyon... and the quarry... and the bullying heat. It was nearing noon, the sun felt ruthless and cruel, and the lip of the canyon seemed so far away. I tried to walk while staring only at my feet, hoping that every few minutes when I did look up, I'd be surprised by our progress. Yet, every time I raised my eyes, the top of the canyon seemed to be just as far away, leaving me crestfallen. Sweat had poured from my back, down my legs and into my shoes. My socks were soaked. How I could be squishing with every step yet making so little progress was beyond me. The numbers that had been waking me up at night started to taunt me again. Self-doubt added its weight to my pack that I assumed looked as filthy as Doug's. My clothes were drenched and I was miserable. Earlier that day we put up our umbrellas for shade from the blistering sun, but they were blown violently inside out every time a truck roared by. I wanted out of that hateful chasm and I cursed my backpack, taking a mental inventory of everything in it and deciding what I could ditch and when.

We finally dragged ourselves out of the quarry and BAM! A big city appeared directly across the street. This was something to which we would never grow accustomed. The provinces of China we were walking through had no suburbs. There were no transitions to ease us from one surrounding to the next. One moment we would be in the midst of the most bucolic and charming countryside with hills and green fields and then BOOM! We'd step into a world of concrete, tall buildings, traffic and honking horns. The same cities ended as abruptly as they began. We could stand in the shade of a twenty-story building and across the street from us see fields of rippling grass and weeds bisected by the highway that disappeared into the distance.

Taking a minute to look at our GPS, we saw that there were several restaurants in town. The first and closest one was closed, as were the second and third. Hungry, hot, tired and thirsty, we decided to continue walking, stop at the first restaurant we saw, and eat whatever they served. Thankfully within a few minutes we found a place... the place we were meant to be.

Doug can get angry when he's hungry, or as he calls it, "hangry". When he told me that he was so hungry he was "ready to eat the ass end out of a hobby horse," a charming colloquialism from his tenure in the Navy, I knew he meant business. This is how we ended up at a hot pot restaurant despite the fact that the temperature hung in the 90s and our clothes were still drenched with sweat. I was so hungry that boiling hot soup sounded like the most enticing thing in the world. We entered a spacious room through a sliding glass door. There was a sofa to the left of the door, and we asked permission to leave our backpacks next to it. The restaurant was operated by an older couple, their adult daughter, and her toddler. Because we were so filthy dirty, I was relieved to discover we were the only people in the establishment. Best of all... there was air-conditioning.

We asked for something meatless with a veggie broth and the daughter, with her son on her hip, led us to a glass front refrigerator and pointed to an assortment of vegetables, meat and tofu. After making our selections, she led us to where our food would be cooked, served, and eaten. The table had a large metal bowl in the middle that was heated by a burner below. The grandmother poured a vegetable broth into the bowl, turned the burner on, and when the liquid came to a rolling boil, she turned the heat down and incrementally added other ingredients. While our lunch simmered, we drank glasses of hot tea. Something about the morning we'd had, the seven miles of climbing hills in and out of the quarry, the dirt and the tortuous heat, made our lunch the best meal I can remember. In between mouthfuls I paused long enough to say "This tastes sooooo good." Remembering the Mandarin phrase, Doug announced to the owners, "Hěn hǎo chī!" and we went back to fishing out the last choice bits of vegetables and tofu from the bottom of the pot. The grandmother came back to our pot twice and added more.

We ate until we were completely stuffed. Had I been anywhere else, my inclination would have been to crawl off somewhere and have a nap. Instead, I resentfully eyed my backpack and thought again about everything I wanted to jettison. I consulted with Doug, who also wanted to lighten his load, and we decided that we should mail some things home. Spotting a jumble of cardboard boxes in a corner of the restaurant, we asked the owners if we could have one and were told to take our pick. We dug into our backpacks, each pulling out the items we were willing to part with. Into the box went my skirt, my dress shoes, dress top (that I thought I might wear in the evenings when we went out to dinner), heart rate monitor, buff, sun sleeves, prescription glasses, and windbreaker. Doug added his watch, the solar charger, one bag of tamarind candies and our freeze-dried camping food.

Once our box was full, we asked for directions to the closest international parcel service, and the daughter kindly offered to escort us there. It was a blessing she did because the office was several miles away and tucked inside a maze of alleyways that rivaled the markets of Marrakesh. Unfortunately, we could not ship anything electronic, so we pulled the solar charger, my heart rate monitor and Doug's watch out of the box.

We also learned it was prohibited to ship non-domestic food items, so we pulled out our dehydrated camping meals. Disappointingly, the only item poor Doug was able to ship home was the bag of tamarind candies, which had by now become a cherished souvenir. We paid the postage, got our receipt, and went back to the restaurant where we had left our backpacks.

Our side trip to mail our belongings consumed more time than anticipated and we were anxious to get back on the road; however, we just weren't ready to say goodbye yet. When I sat down on the couch, grandmother sat next to me and rested her head on my shoulder as I scrolled through the pictures in my phone and showed her Doug's blonde-haired and blue-eyed granddaughter. She was about one year older than her grandson, who was still eyeing us warily.

I didn't want to leave, but we had to keep to our schedule. We stood up, thanked them profusely, took some group photos and said our goodbyes. They were so kind that it made my heart swell. I hugged grandmother goodbye and kissed both of her cheeks. She hugged me back and said some things that I didn't understand. I decided that she was telling me to be safe and to watch out for cars. The grandfather held up a finger for us to wait and came back with four bottles of water. That was enough to push me over the edge, and I left with my eyes brimming with tears. This family had shown us such kindness. It was so hard to say goodbye knowing that we would never see them again. Before we walked out the door, I pointed to the web address on the card we had given them and did my best to let them know that our group photo would be posted there that night.

The city limits ended abruptly, and we were once again in quiet countryside. Doug and I walked for several more hours until the sun began to set behind us. I didn't realize how tired I was until we stopped to allow a train of tethered ponies to pass. When we stepped back onto the shoulder, my feet suddenly ached and burned. It seemed like providence when a hotel actually found Doug and me. Ahead of us, a man stood at the side of the road. As we neared, he pointed over his shoulder and said "Fandian." Doug and I made an immediate and hard left and found ourselves in our new accommodations.

The man led us to a building and opened the door. Immediately to the right and behind a plywood door was a plywood room only a little larger than the twin-size bed that was pushed up against the back wall. An equally small room with a twin-size bed was down the short hallway. Back outdoors there was a tiny pedestal sink and beside it a shed housing a shower and squat toilet. It all cost only 60 kuia, which was just under ten dollars. Sweaty and exhausted, we were more than happy to hand over the money.

That morning we had both put on freshly washed clothes, but as I looked down at my shirt and my pants and thought about the quarry we had walked through earlier that day, I couldn't bear the thought of putting them on again the next morning. "Xǐyījī?" we asked hopefully, and were shown to a washing machine. After we showered and changed, we loaded our clothes into the machine and added some soap. Twenty minutes later when we opened the lid to have a peek, they were swishing around in murky brown water. When the cycle finished, we hung them up to dry.

We asked if there was a restaurant nearby, and the owner told us *no* but offered to drive us to one on the back of his motorcycle. Three adults on one motorcycle was no big deal in China. Already we had seen families of four and five go by on scooters. Doug politely declined his offer. Because it was evening, a meal seemed in order, but neither of us were hungry after the huge lunch we had eaten. So, like a 1960s sit-com couple, we went to bed early in our separate beds. As I drifted off to sleep, those song lyrics about this being the best day of my life and holding on tight to my dreams cycled through my head. I realized how quickly a day can turn itself around if you give it time. Even the numbers were beginning to seem less scary.

CHAPTER EIGHTEEN

One Drop

The part of me that is African was long ago diluted with Belgian, French, English, Irish and Scottish. Yet it's still there, somewhere in my DNA. I'd like to explain how that feels, but I can't. The Germans probably have an eight-syllable word for that obscure sensation, but it's not in my lexicon. I don't know that I will ever be able to describe what it feels like to know that there is a very small and invisible part of me that connects to a history, experience and strength that I know isn't rightfully mine to claim. I identify as white, I am perceived by others as white, and nobody would mistake me for anything else. For my entire life I have benefited from white privilege.

I've spent countless hours meditating on Hippolyte and the complexity of our family history, ethnicity, and how our black ancestry had been kept secret. A male cousin did a genetic test and discovered that our ancestors came from the region of West Africa that is now Benin, Mali and Togo. I did an internet image search for people of that area. I pored over photos of bare-breasted women with infants on their hips and women with jars of water or trays of food balanced on their heads. One photo in particular made me stop and stare. My eyes met with those of an older woman from Mali, her face long like mine. Her hair is wrapped in an ornately woven piece of cloth; a rust-colored shirt or dress hangs off one shoulder. I try and read her expression, but I can't, at least not completely. In the way she holds her head, her chin elevated, I see pride. I also see mistrust and something else I cannot name. Who was she? I think of my relatives that may still exist there today—my very distant cousins with whom nine or more generations ago I shared a common grandparent.

My great-great-great-grandfather left behind his entire family in Belgium; yet, I don't think of them in the same way I contemplate the family that was left behind in West Africa. Although I surely have distant relatives in both places, the circumstances of their departures were so vastly different.

One ancestor embarked upon an adventure. The other was brutally kidnapped. My three times great-grandfather most likely stayed in contact with his parents and learned of their passing and the births of nieces and nephews. My relative that came from Africa likely never knew what became of his or her parents, and the parents, in turn, likely never knew what became of their child. What could be worse than never knowing what became of a beloved family member? What could be worse than missing your parents, counting the years that have passed, thinking, "He would be in his eighties by now. Is it possible that he's still alive?" Not being able to ask, "Where are you? Are you well?" It would be an unbearable heartbreak not knowing whether to project these entreaties across the ocean... or towards the heavens. I'm comforted by the fact that my family knew what became of Hippolyte. It's easier to look at photos of him when I know what happened—that he didn't just disappear and leave his family with questions that would never be answered.

In some pictures, especially early on in his journey, his complexion is fairer and his hair is short and tame. In later photos, his skin tone seems more olive or Mediterranean. A year and a half into his walk, his complexion is much darker, no doubt because he was walking without a hat. It's in these photos that his ethnicity might be questioned. This leads me to wonder why he chose to walk without a hat in an era when all men wore hats as part of their daily ensemble.

Was Hippolyte worried about his ancestry being discovered? Was walking hatless part of a conscious and intentional ruse, a covert way of hiding his ethnicity? Perhaps he thought that if he walked without a hat, people would assume that his dark complexion was due to sun exposure rather than his black ancestry. That would certainly be safer.

Even in the Northern states, having ambiguous ethnicity could pose a risk. Sometimes how one perceives himself isn't as relevant as how he is perceived by others. For example, despite having American, Dutch and Thai ancestry, Tiger Woods is recognized as "the black golf player," and although his mother was white, Barack Obama is known as the United States' first black president. Both have been assigned the minority status of a stigmatized ethnicity while the rest of their ancestry is all but completely ignored.

People of mixed ancestry have been historically assigned to the minority ethnicity until no discernible trace remains and they are assumed to be Caucasian. Nearly a century ago, enough people with African ancestry were passing as white that legislation was enacted to prevent these people from concealing their ethnic heritage. People were legally bound to full disclosure if they had any non-Caucasian ancestors, if it was possible that their veins coursed with anything other than European blood—even one drop.

The One Drop Rule, as it came to be known, is a historical and colloquial notion unique to the United States. It was eventually codified into law in 1924 by Virginia's Racial Integrity Act. It's also known as the "one black ancestor rule," the "traceable amount rule," and the "hypodescent rule." The Racial Integrity Act required that the racial composition of every person be recorded with the Registrar of Vital Statistics. Unless descended from absolute Caucasian European ancestry, one was labeled as "colored." Willfully or knowingly providing false information about one's ancestry was a felony punishable by up to one year in prison.

The ultimate purpose of the Racial Integrity Act was to ban interracial marriage. No marriage license would be granted until both parties could prove they were both white. The 5th clause of the act stated, "It shall hereafter be unlawful for any white person in this state to marry any save a white person." The act did allow for a white person to marry a person of Native American ancestry provided it was 1/16th or less. This became known as the "Pocahontas Exception." The exception was made at the insistence of members of the "First Families" of Virginia who claimed they were descendants of Pocahontas, the Native American woman who is said to have saved the life of John Smith by placing her head atop his when her father threatened to execute him with his war club. Other than this exception, the Racial Integrity Act was quite simply a law created to keep the white race "pure". Violation of the 5th clause was punishable by up to five years in prison. All but eight states adopted similar statutes outlawing interracial marriage.

The Racial Integrity Act was overturned in 1967 by the landmark Supreme Court Decision, Loving v. Virginia. In 1958, Mildred Jeter and Richard Loving traveled ninety minutes to Washington D.C. to get married and then returned to their home in Central Point, Virginia. Two weeks later, acting on an anonymous tip, the police raided their home hoping to find the couple having sex, which was also illegal. Instead, the police found the couple sleeping. Mildred pointed to the framed copy of their marriage certificate on their bedroom wall. The certificate was all the evidence needed as grounds for their arrest. Mildred spent several nights in jail. At their arraignment, the Lovings pled guilty and were each sentenced to a year in prison, a sentence that they were told would be suspended for twenty-five years if they left the state. Mildred and Richard moved to Washington D.C., both leaving behind family in Virginia. In 1964, frustrated by their inability to travel together in Virginia, Mildred contacted the ACLU, who filed a motion on her behalf with the Supreme Court of Virginia. The court upheld the Racial Integrity Act, but Mildred appealed, taking the motion all the way to the Supreme Court of the United States, where she won. Their marriage was recognized by every state and they could finally travel to Virginia without fear of being arrested.

It's uncertain if Hippolyte and the mother of his two sons had been married or if theirs was a common law relationship. Anti-miscegenation laws in Louisiana might have prevented it if she were of purely Caucasian ancestry. Hippolyte's own grandparents were denied their wish to be married but later granted it during the Reconstruction Era. Their marriage was later nullified when anti-miscegenation laws were reinstituted all across the South. These laws were once again repealed, thanks to Mildred and Richard Loving. It's little wonder that I have found so many conflicting accounts of Hippolyte's ethnicity. In a more detailed copy of the 1920 Census Report for the state of Washington, his race is listed as white, his mother's birthplace is listed as Belgium, and his father's is listed as France.

By the 1930's, in the Northeastern part of the United States, a sufficient number of African American tourists had endured challenges difficult enough to generate the need for a guidebook addressing their unique travel experiences. In 1936, a New York City mailman named Victor H. Greene published *The Negro Motorist Green Book*. It was a compilation of resources geared for African Americans in order to make travel safer, more convenient and enjoyable. Early editions only covered New York, but subsequent pressings expanded to cover most of the United States, parts of Canada, Mexico, the Caribbean and even Bermuda. In 1920, however, no such resource was available to Hippolyte. I'm not naïve enough to think that a dark-skinned, shoeless, wandering man was welcomed everywhere. My traveling uncle was most likely perceived as a vagrant or beggar. I'm sure he got his share of sideways glances, doors shut in his face and dogs set after him as if he were a common hobo.

Hobos, less disparagingly known as itinerant workers, had already developed a secret method of communication called "The Hobo Code." It was a system of symbols often written in charcoal or chalk that communicated information such as where one could safely sleep, get a free meal or free medical care, what parts of a town were dangerous, where the police were aggressive, where authorities lived, which towns were dry, and even where dangerous dogs or armed people lived. The "Hobo Code" was vital for men who made their living moving from town to town accepting whatever work was available. The symbols were rudimentary. A cross meant that one could get a free meal provided they listen to a religious talk. A teardrop within a circle meant that water was safe to drink, and my favorite symbol, a very simplistic cat image with ears and whiskers meant, "Kind lady lives here". A circle with two parallel horizontal lines was a dire warning and meant, "Get out! Hobos not welcome here".

Hippolyte had two things working against him. One, he was backpacking barefoot. Two, he had an ambiguous ethnicity. I suppose that the only way that someone would have known for sure that Hippolyte had African ancestry would be if he admitted it, but why would he? The Tuskegee Institute reports that between 1868 and 1968, 3,446 blacks were lynched in the United States. In 1920, fifty-three black people were lynched. Three of them, twenty-three year old Elias Clayton, twenty-two year old Elmer

Jackson and twenty year old Isaac McGhie were lynched in Duluth, Minnesota on June 15th, 1920, roughly one week before Hippolyte would have arrived in St. Paul, one hundred fifty miles to the south.

Six black men, including Isaac McGhie, Elmer Jackson and Elias Clayton were arrested and jailed after being accused of raping and beating a nineteen-year-old girl named Irene Tuskin. A doctor who examined her the next morning found no evidence of rape or physical violence.

When a false rumor spread that Irene had died as a result of the assault, McGhie, Jackson and Clayton were torn from their jail cells, beaten and hung from lampposts. It was reported that a crowd of 10,000 gathered and watched. The rope was procured from a hardware store near the jail. When told what the rope was intended for, it is said that the owner of the hardware store told the mob that it was "On the house." Afterward, the body of one of the boys was cut down and left lying face down in the street. This was done at the request of the photographers so that all three bodies would be in the frame. Cars turned on their headlamps to illuminate the scene for a photograph which would later become a souvenir postcard. Dozens of men lean in so as to be included in the photograph. One man stands on tiptoe. All of them are wearing hats and heavy overcoats and have blank expressions on their faces with the exception of one man who grins. In total, seven men were indicted for the rape of Irene. Five of the charges were later dismissed and in the end, only two, Max Mason and William Miller, were tried. Miller was acquitted while Mason was convicted and sentenced seven to thirty years in prison. He served four years and was released under the condition that he leave the state. There were thirty-seven indictments for the lynching mob, twenty-five indictments for rioting and twelve indictments for murder in the first degree. Only three people were ever convicted and even then, it was only for rioting. Irene Tuskin died in 1996 at the age of ninety-four.

My calculations have Hippolyte arriving in St. Paul somewhere around June 22nd. I think about him walking through this part of the country so soon after this horrific event, the chill in the air made even icier by a climate of hatred and bigotry. The story of the lynchings made headlines throughout the country. Less than five miles away in Superior, Wisconsin, the Chief of Police declared, "We are going to run all idle negroes out of Superior and they are going to stay out." In fear, many black residents fled Duluth as well.

It's all the more ironic that while in St. Paul, Hippolyte was the celebrated guest of the Naturalist Society and a banquet was held in his honor. Months later, Hippolyte would recount the story for a French newspaper. My translation of this excerpt of the article reads:

> At St. Paul, Minn, the Globe-Trotter was especially well-treated. The Naturalist Society invited him to a banquet held in his honor, on which occasion he described the purpose of his undertaking and his general views on natural modes of living. There the newspapers gave him attractive publicity and the community as a whole offered him sensible and generous hospitality.

I have so many questions about this event. Where was it held and what was served? How many people attended and who were they? I've searched for a Naturalist Society in Minnesota and have had no luck. It could be that *Naturalist Society* was an inaccurate French translation. I have tried multiple variations on the theme with no success. In my mind, I can see Hippolyte sitting at a long table with his backpack behind him and his dog laying at his bare feet. Perhaps they offered one of Hippolyte's favorites, raw onion juice in warm milk—a remedy for respiratory problems.

I thought about the generation of my family that perhaps sighed with relief when their children were born fair enough of complexion to "pass" and not have any document labeling them as mulatto. In the 1880 census, both my great-grandfather and Hippolyte are listed as mulatto. In the 1920 census, Hippolyte was listed as white. Whether he claimed he was white, or the owner of the house he boarded in assumed he was white, is a mystery to me. My mind always goes back to the horrific events of June 15, 1920, when three young men—boys really—were torn from their jail cells, dragged up the street and hung from a lamppost. Their shirts had been torn open and pulled down about their waists, the sleeves used to tie their arms at their sides as a crazed crowd of onlookers watched. Hippolyte must have been aware of this horrifying event. Did he feel the tension in the air? Was he concerned about his safety? Did his heart race? Did he walk faster?

CHAPTER NINETEEN

Banquets

A photograph commemorated our passage into Guizhou Province from Kunming. It felt like our first real milestone. We stood face to face and kissed on the empty highway, he in Kunming and I in Guizhou, Doug holding the camera out in front of us. We like that goofy kind of thing. I usually hate having my photo taken but never do when Doug is at my side. The best photos of me are always when I'm standing next to him—my whole face changes. It was still grey and misty after a spectacular thunder and lightning storm the night before. All night long, the lightening lit up the sky; it was never completely dark for more than two seconds. It was truly epic and something that I, a resident of Southern California, never get to see. While walking through the American Midwest during the summer months, I'm sure that Hippolyte saw his share of magnificent lightning storms. I hope he was shown hospitality. I'm sure that a dry spot to lie down upon and a mere cold sandwich may have been just as satisfying as the banquet he attended in St. Paul.

The storm blew in not more than two hours after I had pointed at the ominous and foreboding clouds in the distance and asked the hotel owner if he thought it might rain. He looked to the clear sky in the opposite direction and with his hands indicated that the wind was pushing the clear weather towards us while chasing the storm clouds away. Confident in the man's forecasting abilities, Doug hung our freshly washed laundry in their courtyard while I kept company with some local women who sat street side as they nursed their babies. One little boy climbed out of his mother's lap and stood holding onto her skirt, staring at me with wide eyes. With reassurance from his mother, he took two tentative steps towards me. I held out a finger for him to grasp before he spun around and climbed back up into the safety of her lap. He turned to look at me again, buried his face into her neck, and then came tears. He was wary of me for the rest of the evening. Just days before, a shop owner pulled out his phone, leaned across the counter and handed his grandson to Doug. When the baby realized he was with a complete stranger, no less a bearded, bespectacled, bald and white one, he also burst into tears. The man took a quick picture and Doug handed the poor kid back. Usually the Pied Pipers of babies, Doug and I were both epic failures in China.

We asked where we could find a restaurant and the hotel owner led Doug to a kitchen and pointed to tables in another room across the hall. His wife came out and gestured for Doug to follow and led him past the courtyard, through an agricultural building and into a vegetable garden where a dozen or so chickens patrolled the area. The late season, twenty by forty-foot garden was a wild tangle of vines and corn stalks. She pointed at each different vegetable and, if Doug nodded, she picked it and put it in the metal basin she carried on her hip. That night we dined upon rice, some type of mottled green squash and one of my new favorite dishes—long beans.

After dinner, Doug and I went up to bed. On several previous occasions when we were shown to a room, doors were swung open with a flourish to reveal twin-sized beds covered in matching pink comforters festooned with red hearts and interlocking gold wedding bands, a nice change from the knock-off Hello Kitty that was the predominate theme in most family-run hotels. That night, instead of the honeymoon room, we were escorted to the "jilted and bitter former lover" room as evidenced by the poem written on the plastic door that led to the bathroom. Printed in calligraphy on wispy, white clouds, the poem titled "Most Sincere Love" read, "I watched into the church for the wedding you put your heart. I love you, my favorite trace of the sweetest." After such a tender and earnest beginning, it quickly degenerated into something that made the *screech, screech, screech* soundtrack from *Psycho* play in my mind. "I hope you have a lot of hardships if we do not separate. Will reunion the road again if we do not..." The final words faded in an almost threatening manner into indecipherable text, delivered like a parting shot muttered under one's breath. Whoever this poor girl was, I don't think she's heard the last from him.

Exhausted, Doug and I climbed into bed and turned out the lights. When the rain began to fall, we discussed the pros and cons of retrieving our clothes from the line in the center of the courtyard. In the end, we decided to leave them out in the torrential rain. The worst thing that could possibly happen was that our garments might actually get cleaner. We had long ago quit peeking at our clothes as they swished around in the washing machine. It didn't matter how much we rinsed them out before putting them into the machine; by mid-cycle the water always resembled rich, chocolaty milk. In the morning, we went to retrieve our clothes and found that someone had kindly hung them on an eight-foot-long, rolling rack and dragged the whole thing halfway up the stairwell.

After an early morning start, we stopped for a late breakfast at the first open restaurant and were met by the cook and three other men. They were seated around a table full of empty beer bottles. Two of the men had a good buzz going while the third, clearly having the time of his life, was bleary-eyed drunk. We ordered food and were quickly joined by drunk guy, who dragged a chair across the floor and sat at our table talking to us excitedly as he chain-smoked while we ate. I was more than a little annoyed with him until I gave up altogether and decided to succumb to his enthusiasm. We gave him one of our postcards, which prompted the rest of his party to pick up their beers and join us. Then more glasses were brought out, drinks were poured, and glasses emptied. When we asked for the check an hour and a half later, the cook, who early on had joined in the revelry, wrote "1 US $" on a slip of paper. We protested, but he was adamant, so Doug rifled through his wallet and found several one-dollar bills. He handed his crispest single to the cook who grinned and took it from him. The other men gathered round to look at it and then opened their wallets, pulled out colorful notes of different denominations, and thrust them toward Doug. They bought every plain old, boring green dollar bill that Doug had, plus one five-dollar bill. We were happy to oblige. Doug and I were having a hard time getting cash from ATM machines. Many required a six-digit PIN versus the standard four digits in the U.S. I guess that's what you get when you have a population of 1,382,323,332 people.

Because our GPS told us the nearest hotel was twelve miles away, we decided to take our leave. We took several group photos and drunk guy is front and center in every one of them, the proud owner of the only five-dollar bill that Doug had on him. It was a fun and boisterous meal, made even more enjoyable by the company and kindness of strangers. We left with that feeling you get when you are the guests who regretfully have to be the first to leave a happenin' party.

Two hours later we stopped at a roadside store for water. It was a rustic building. Actually, it was a shack and the freezer containing beverages and popsicles was powered by an extension cord that ran to a house two hundred feet up the dirt driveway. We stood waiting for a minute or two and even called out, but all was quiet. We were still in a region of China where every home had a dog chained up in the front yard. They were always on the shortest leads, some only three or four feet long. One dog was tethered to a fence by a rope so short that it couldn't even lie down. Without exception, every dog we passed snarled and lunged and snapped its teeth even when we were at a distance. I can usually recognize when a dog is all bluster. These canines meant business. Many were confined to metal or wood cages at the edge of driveways. Trapped amid days-worth of feces and bones that had been gnawed clean, they lunged at the bars as we passed. If only they knew how much we wanted to free them. It was a cultural difference that Doug and I struggled with. Back home, dogs are more than just pets. They live in our homes and sleep in our beds. They are family members. We love them and mourn when they die. In rural China, dogs serve a purpose. They are functional. They are protection and sometimes they are food. It was hard to process. I'm not sure that it is intentional cruelty. I think it's just a different perspective because the people we met were thoughtful, kind and generous in ways that were as unfamiliar to us as their barking and snarling dogs.

I decided to alert the shop attendant to our presence by walking a few feet up the driveway into canine territory. In an instant, his dog served its purpose and began to bark. I retreated to the side of the road. A twenty something year old man, clean shaven and wearing a bright blue shirt, came trotting down the hill to serve us. Doug frequently bought frozen treats and this time was bold enough to try the green pea ice cream pop. I passed and bought three waters—one to drink then and two for the road.

I gave him one of our postcards and after a ten-minutes rest we were back on the highway. Later we came upon a sign that alerted us, much to our chagrin, that the next six miles were a steep downhill grade. Within forty-five minutes, my knees were so sore that I wanted to groan with every step, and we still had several miles left. Twenty minutes later, a person on a motor scooter pulled to the side of the road in front of us. The driver, wearing a bright blue t-shirt, was the guy from the roadside store. He approached us carrying a plastic bag with four bottles of water and two containers of instant noodle soup. I was astounded by his thoughtfulness and felt a huge smile spread across my face. There was no containing it, and I literally felt it in my chest... in my heart. The coup de grace was that the soup was vegetarian! How did he know? Ninety-five years later, people repeatedly validated Hippolyte's credo.

Mercifully, the miles-long hill we had been descending flattened out for a short while before rising again. Tinny sounding bells chimed in the distance and Doug and I turned to see twenty or more goats nimbly making their way down a sheer hillside followed by a woman who was equally surefooted. They quickly caught up with and then passed us as we hobbled along. Our GPS indicated there was a hotel at the top of the next hill on our right but we only found a trash strewn dirt lot. My knees still throbbed and now pain shot up and down my shins. It was becoming bad enough that I was prepared to clear a space in the trash wide enough for us to pitch our tent. However, our GPS teased that another hotel was potentially two more agonizing miles ahead of us, so we dragged ourselves to the three-story building that our GPS was pinging on.

Doug was a sweaty, dirty and disheveled mess and I knew I looked the same. We poked our heads through double doors that were open to the street and saw two women sitting at a table. "Fandian?" we inquired as we both mimed sleeping. We were instantly told in a loud and commanding voice, "no" by the older, scowling woman. "Yes," the younger of the two women countered sweetly as she stood to greet us, smiling as she led us out the back of the building. Before guiding us up a flight of stairs, she reached to take my backpack from me. "Bu. Mei" I told her, saying both words because I was not able to remember which one meant "no" and which one meant "not". My backpack was always soaked with sweat. Earlier that day I set it on the ground, and when I picked it up a few minutes later, it had left a wet spot on the concrete. I winced as she swung it over her shoulder and carried it to the third floor. My legs burned more as I reached the top of each stair flight. We were forever on the third floor. It happened with such consistency that I began to wonder if the Chinese considered it good luck.

From the landing, we had a view of the courtyard and what was once a lovely tiled swimming pool. Now the water was green and stagnant and visibility was zero. Dragonflies buzzed and skimmed across the surface and every once in a while something from below the surface caused little ripples in the water. Beyond the wall was unblemished countryside. She opened the door for us and I was relieved to see mosquito coils on the table next to the television. This time our accommodations were in a themeless room. The only thing familiar about it was the tan linoleum that we had seen in almost every hotel room so far.

We showered and changed into the outfits that had almost spent the night out in the driving rain. It was my turn to do the laundry, so I bundled up our filthy clothes, went downstairs into the lobby, and asked if there was a xǐdíjī—*washing machine*. Again, the older of the two women indicated loudly and adamantly that they did not, at which point younger sister stood up, smiled, and gestured for me to follow her. She led me outdoors to the washing machine and, embarrassed, I put our filthy and sweaty clothes inside. She produced a box of detergent and dumped one scoop of the white powder onto our clothes, took a second look inside, added another scoop, shut the lid, and pressed the start button.

I returned to our room to write in my journal and update the website while Doug went to the lobby. Soon, three floors below, I heard the eruption of laughter. An hour later, I finished my entry and went downstairs to find Doug at a table surrounded by laughing people, open beers and a plate of fried peanuts. No longer crabby, older sister was sitting right next to Doug and smiling bigger than anybody else in the room. Everyone scooted over and she grabbed a chair from a nearby table so I could join them. Doug went to the refrigerator and brought me a beer while older sister pushed the plate of peanuts over to me. Doug and everyone else at the table had already eaten their evening meal. I munched on his leftovers, more beers were opened, and two hours later we went up to bed, utterly exhausted. As I drifted off to sleep, I thought about Hippolyte and the banquet thrown by the Naturalist Society. I felt like we had been guests at two banquets that day.

CHAPTER TWENTY

Indiana

When I told people that Doug and I were going to finish the walk for Hippolyte, many of our friends wanted to know if we also planned to walk without shoes. My answer, always proffered quickly and often before the last word of the question had left their lips, was always a resounding and emphatic "No". Walking barefoot sounded painful and dirty; besides, Doug and I both experienced episodes of plantar fasciitis that caused severe heel pain. I wouldn't consider doing it without orthotics let alone without shoes. While some women can lay claim to shapely legs, beautiful hair or a flat stomach, my feet are the one part of my body I feel confident about, aesthetically speaking. I wasn't going to do anything to mar my crowning glory.

The first few days, our legs were sore. Mine were so sore that one morning, I found myself unable to stand again after using the squat toilet in our hotel room. Because the floor was dirty, using my hands to push myself up was out of the question. I surveyed my surroundings and saw a way out of my predicament. I duck-walked, groaning with each agonizing step across the floor and towards the wall-mounted sink. I grabbed on to both sides and pulled myself up, but not before pulling the sink part way off the wall. The soreness in our legs quickly subsided and soon they were easily able to carry us seventeen miles a day. We often felt that we could have gone further if it weren't for the fact that our feet ached. In our defense, we were walking on asphalt and concrete. Hippolyte was most likely traveling on considerably softer dirt roads. Even so, we were in awe that he consistently logged thirty or more miles a day. The day we managed to pull off twenty-four miles left me with nasty blisters and necessitated a welcomed day off for recovery.

Footwear had its pros and cons. The occasional pebble worked its way into our shoes or sandals and delayed us multiple times a day. We calculated that over the course of our trip, we each spent at least two hours standing beside the road, teetering on one foot, index finger searching and probing for whatever rock was trying to bore its way into our flesh. That and a few epic blisters were the only cons to walking with shoes.

The pros to wearing shoes were evident daily. Occasionally we saw broken glass and other undesirable detritus alongside the road. Doug was still photographing roadkill and so far had amassed an impressive catalogue. Cat, dog, bird, bat, snake, chicken, goat—it was all there. Occasionally I'd see something up ahead on the road, and as I neared I would start my chant, "Please don't be a dog, please don't be a dog, please don't be a dog." Often, I would get up to it only to realize that it was nothing more than an oddly shaped pile of water buffalo dung. After I had been duped a few times, I let my guard down and approached what I thought was a pile of bovine poop. As I closed in, a cloud of flies lifted off of a freshly run-over cat.

We shared the road with living animals as well. Aside from water buffalo, we were passed by gangs of disorderly goats who walked in weaving pairs and triads. The mules and cattle walked like us, in single file on the shoulder of the road. On one occasion, we were forced to stop for several minutes while a surge of boisterous ducks that occupied nearly both lanes of the highway were herded to the lake for their evening swim. All ten thousand were controlled and escorted by one woman who carried an unthreatening switch that she flicked back and forth leisurely as the horde waddled down the road, leaving it, as Doug said, "slicker than a snot sandwich." All left their mark.

Then there was the human dung that we'd see on the side of the highway. These malodorous monuments were left by motorists unconcerned with modesty or safety, who had pulled over, dropped their pants and answered the call of nature right there by the side of the road. The dead giveaway was always the toilet paper stuck to the top of the pile, proudly fluttering in the wind like a banner. I came across this scene at least four times… a pile of human poop that some poor butterfly had landed in. The butterflies remained alive, all six feet stuck and preventing their escape. I wanted to rescue the poor things but couldn't bring myself to extract them. Like a coward, I'd walk past and think, *Oh, the indignity! A beautiful creature such as a butterfly, the wings of which I'm certain inspired man to create stained glass, is going to die, mired in a human turd.* Lest I succumb to a similar fate, I wore shoes and put to bed any such romantic notions I had entertained earlier, like walking the last fifteen miles barefoot.

One evening after checking into a hotel, my cousin Brian sent me a message. He said he had some surprising information about Hippolyte. Actually, he said it was a *bombshell.* I prayed it wasn't that my uncle planned to take a steamer from Hong Kong to Australia and walk through the Outback. Good news or bad, I was in a dither to know what the information was and begged my cousin to share it with me. I had to wait a day before he sent me scanned copies of two newspaper articles I had never seen before.

RACINE NEWS AND SENTINEL

YOU SEE IT IN THE MOVIES

(SPECIAL TO THE NEWS.)

COLUMBIA CITY, IND., JULY 29—

About two weeks ago, Manager Russell Pinney, of the Lyceum theater, ran a news weekly film and in it was a picture of H. Martinet, of Seattle, who is walking from Seattle to New York. Yesterday forenoon, while driving from this city to Princeton, Mr. Pinney met none other than Mr. Martinet, who was "hoofing" it headed east. He offered to give him a lift, but the fellow refused, but he did bring his pack to this city. Martinet was barefooted in his picture, but is now wearing shoes, as he says Indiana roads are too hard for bare feet. He left here for Fort Wayne by way of Arcola at 4:10 o'clock.

FORT WAYNE JOURNAL GAZETTE

Thursday July 29 1920—Indiana

Hippolyte Martinet who is walking from Seattle Washington to New York City passed through this city Wednesday afternoon at about 4 o'clock, His picture recently appeared in a film magazine and Russell Pinney, local movie manager, while in his auto near Pierceton Wednesday forenoon was able to recognize Martinet. Pinney took part of Martinet's pack to this city, to lighten the walker's load.

To my relief, the big news was that Hippolyte wore shoes while in Indiana. For some reason, the ground in the Hoosier state was too hard for feet that had already walked barefoot over roughly 2,200 miles. I researched Indiana soil composition and found multiple scholarly articles that dissected soil surveys and charted areas of dense bedrock where nothing can take root.

As mentioned previously, Hippolyte decided to walk barefoot simply because shoes were too expensive. My running shoes have a suggested lifespan of between 300-500 miles, even if they are only used for walking. Covering a minimum of thirty miles a day, Hippolyte would only get between ten and sixteen days wear out of a single pair of modern shoes.

The two articles that Brian shared with me offered possible answers to the mystery of how the Naturalist Society knew about my uncle. Perhaps a member of the Naturalist Society saw Hippolyte in a newsreel at the movies or in the film magazine. The newsreel would have preceded the first talking movie, "The Jazz Singer", by seven years, so there is no chance that I would have been able to hear his voice. Though, what I wouldn't give to see film footage of Hippolyte, to see how he carried himself, to see him in motion.

CHAPTER TWENTY-ONE

Sharing the Road

Doug and I usually kept some distance between us as we walked along the shoulder of the highway. The distance wasn't intentional. It just always seemed to work out that he was a hundred yards or so ahead of me. I walked slower and often stopped to adjust my backpack, pull a rock out of my sandal or take a picture. Even though we always started out side-by-side, I ended up lagging behind him. But every hour and a half or so, Doug stopped and waited for me to catch up, and we'd spend a minute or two resting and discussing the astonishing things we had seen. There was always something to share. Our presence proved just as intriguing to all manner of locals, human or otherwise.

Walking through the countryside one morning, mountains in the distance and hillsides tiered with verdant green rice paddies in the foreground, I came upon a farmer using a long stick to prod his water buffalo out of a pool of muddy, brown water where it had been cooling itself. I paused and watched as it slowly and methodically climbed up the embankment. Its horns were so huge and broad that it seemed a miracle it was able to hold up its head. As we passed one another, the water buffalo, chewing its cud, gave me a precursory glance, looked away and then jerked its enormous head back in my direction to have a second look at me. Yes, it did an actual double take. If he had just taken a big mouthful of water, he might have sprayed it halfway across the highway. Mere feet from me, the massive animal came to a halt right there in the road; its jaw stopped moving and hung open mid chew as he surveyed me from my shoes on up with deep brown eyes that reflected curiosity tempered with mistrust. The farmer waited patiently, his stick held loosely at his side. I froze while the beast stood motionless and stared at me. It was nearly six feet tall at the shoulder and weighed close to a thousand pounds. The shaggy ears that twitched and flicked away flies became unexpectedly still. I extended a hand and took a cautious and slow step forward. The behemoth, suddenly skittish and agile, trotted away on surprisingly nimble feet.

These are the observations and experiences that Doug and I shared during our brief roadside respites—all of the exotic things we were witnessing that we'd never see back home. We'd also look at the roadkill photos Doug had shot for what we joked would be the world's least marketable coffee table book ever.

The morning of our eighth day, we got a late start and weren't on the road until after 8:00 am. The previous afternoon, we had again been stunned by how abruptly countryside ended and city began. On the nights we spent in cities, we'd fall asleep and awaken to the ceaseless sound of honking cars. Doug and I much preferred the quiet and relaxed pace of the countryside where cars yielded to farmers who herded their goats or cows down the center of the two-lane highway and semis veered onto the shoulder to avoid mountainous piles of water buffalo dung that sat towering and imposing in the middle of the road.

We often had the highway to ourselves for twenty minutes or longer without seeing a single motorist. Most of the traffic had been diverted to the G-80, one of Southwest China's newer superhighways that had turned parts of the 320 into ghost towns. In between the larger villages and towns, many houses and small motels stood in ruins, their roofs collapsing, windows broken, and doors either missing or hanging crooked by one hinge. Our hope was that they would be suitable for camping in, but to our disappointment, they were always filled with trash, rusted old bed frames and decaying furniture. Clearly it had been years since a car full of passengers had stopped to spend a night on its way north to Shangri-La or south to Kunming.

Occasionally, motorists would give us a short tap on the horn as they whizzed by. But that morning there was a steady stream of honking traffic that made me wish my earplugs weren't at the very bottom of my backpack. In the days before, the cars we saw usually carried only the driver. Sometimes, there might be a single passenger, but rarely two. This particular day, every car was filled to capacity—two people in front and three people in the back. There was no end to them. Three separate times that morning, I watched cars slow to a stop in the middle of a lane only long enough for all occupants to get out, change seats and drive off. Fifty yards up the road, Doug had stopped walking and was waiting for me. I quickened my pace and broke into a trot, anxious to catch up to him and discuss what we had just seen.

"Did I just witness not just one, not two, but THREE Chinese Fire Drills… in CHINA?" I shouted, such was my disbelief. "I know! What was that?" Doug asked, equally baffled. We laughed as a steady stream of cars, all the same make and model, converged upon us from both directions. Neither of us had any answers, so we resumed our journey.

It didn't take me long to fall behind Doug, and soon he was a hundred yards ahead of me. Now and then, one of these cars would pass him and the driver would crane his or her neck to gawk at the stranger, at which point the car would slowly drift onto the shoulder of the road. As the car approached me, the person in the front passenger seat would reach over and gently take hold of the steering wheel with one hand, easing the car back into its lane to avoid hitting me. This continued ALL DAY.

Eventually we came upon a vehicle that was stopped not on the side of the road but in the middle of the lane, empty of all occupants, who were now in the nearby roadside bathroom. Doug strode right up to it and took a picture of the text printed on the back bumper so he could translate it later. We saw the same text on almost every identical car that passed us that day. We estimated there were at least several dozen driving up and down the highway in a circuit. Some cars went by doing no more than 15 mph, the driver gripping the steering wheel and looking straight ahead but the eyes of every passenger on us. It felt completely innocent but where I come from, the *slow roll* is a threat.

During lunch, Doug translated the text from the picture he took, and we learned that the cars were part of a driving school fleet. The next day the highway, was swarming with even more of them. When we finally got to a hotel that had a television and cable, we tuned into the English language Chinese news station and learned what was behind the sudden explosion of student drivers. With literally only a few hours warning, the Chinese government, in a move to address the country's pollution problem, imposed a moratorium on the purchase of new cars. Beginning at midnight, only 125,000 new cars would be sold in Yunnan province per year on a lottery basis—125,000 cars per year for a population of forty-six million people. Furthermore, twenty percent of those cars had to be electric. Within minutes of the announcement, thousands of frenzied people rushed out to their nearest car dealership and bought absolutely any available car on the lot before the clock ran out. In the coming weeks when Doug and I were passing through large cities, we saw car dealerships that were all but empty. The few lonely cars that sat in the lots were those that had not been sold before the midnight deadline. They would sit there until the lottery for new car buyers began. The moratorium also coincided with the end of the college semester, so students immediately enrolled in school to learn how to drive their new automobiles.

I wish I had been there to witness the buying frenzy rather than merely hearing about it on the news. With stakes so high, it must have looked like a Black Friday stampede at one of our superstores. In this case, people would be throwing themselves onto the hoods of cars rather than duking it out in the aisles over flat-screen televisions.

CHAPTER TWENTY-TWO

New York

Hippolyte arrived in New York City on or about August 15th, 1920. On August 29th, he made page two of the *New York Tribune*. In a photo included with the article, Hippolyte stands barefoot, in cuffed pants, wearing a collared shirt and waist-length coat with wide lapels. His hair looks... tame. The article is brief and reads:

WALKED BAREFOOT FROM SEATTLE TO NEW YORK

> Hippolyte Martinet, whose name is as weird as his get-up, hikes it all the way from the Pacific in exactly four months. We've been wondering if his goal was the Grand Central Palace.

Although I have no record of Hippolyte paying a visit there, the thirteen—story Grand Central Palace would have been an interesting stop. Located on Lexington Avenue between 46th, and 47th, it was New York's principle exhibition hall for forty years and hosted the first Industrial Aeroplane Show in 1911—a mere eight years after the Wright brothers made four brief flights at Kitty Hawk. Later it was host to the Westminster Kennel Club dog show as well as auto, boat and flower trade shows until it was demolished in 1964 and replaced by 245 Park Avenue. Initially the home of the American Tobacco Company, 245 Park Avenue now houses office space for myriad businesses, most notably Major League Baseball, JP Morgan Chase and Heineken.

While the tone of the *New York Tribune* article was mocking and a little discourteous, *The Evening Post* was respectful and gave thoughtful attention to the who, what, when, where, why and how of my uncle's story. It was certainly more enjoyable for me to read. I'm not sure if the quotes were verbatim, but they give Hippolyte a voice and help me better imagine who this man was.

BAREFOOT WALKER SEES CITY'S SIGHTS

Here From Seattle After Marching 99 Days
Health Restored by Outdoor Life,
Former Carpenter Plans Return to France

After walking barefoot from Seattle to this city in 99 walking days, Hippolyte Martinet is to-day seeing the sights of New York. At 11:00 o'clock this morning he visited the Stock Exchange and addressed more than a hundred members, attendants and stock runners in the lobby of the Exchange Building. Later he ascended to the members' balcony and viewed the trading from that vantage point.

It was on this balcony that Martinet was found by a representative of the Evening Post. He is about five feet seven inches in height. His face was burned bronze color from the sun, and his brown beard was tinged with golden lights that contrasted oddly with the darker color. His unshod feet were as brown as autumn woods. He wore long khaki colored trousers and a heavy coat of the same material, the collar made of corduroy. Beneath it he wore a blue flannel shirt of warm material.

Walked for His Health

"There is nothing remarkable about this exploit," his speech somewhat marked by a pronounced French accent. "I am a carpenter by trade and working in Seattle shops affected my health. I went to a doctor and he told me that I was threatened with consumption unless I live constantly in the open air.

"Eighteen years ago, I came to this country from France. Since then I have lived alone and I have never married. It occurred to me that if I walked to New York City, I might accomplish a double purpose: restore my health on the trip, and take ship from that port to Europe to see if my old home is still standing despite the ravages of the war.

Sold Cards For Expenses

"Before I left Seattle at 5:20 P.M. on April 19, I had a couple of hundred picture post cards taken of myself that I might sell on my trip and thus earn my way. I took no food with me and my pack merely contained a sleeping bag and a map of the country. The cards kept me alive and I did not sleep beneath a roof on my entire trip here."

Here Martinet halted to receive the handshakes and congratulations of a delegation of Stock Exchange members who had missed his initial recital of his trip. When they had departed, leaving him clutching handfuls of cigars, the pedestrian took up the chain of his narrative.

Two things in this article immediately drew my attention. The author commented twice, in succession, on the color of Hippolyte's skin. First, his face is described as "burned bronze color from the sun" and in the very same sentence, the author describes the odd contrast between the color of his face and the golden highlights in his brown beard. The second thing that caught my attention was that Hippolyte told at least one whopper of a lie. He wasn't born in France and to my knowledge hadn't lived in France. He was born in Louisiana. I can only speculate as to why he fabricated this part of his story. Perhaps while in the North he thought it better to pass himself off as an exotic Frenchman rather than a Southerner. As for his statement about never marrying, that may be true. I have never seen any proof that he and the mother of his children were in fact wed.

Two months later on Saturday, November 13th, 1920, the news of his arrival in New York was reported in the *Steven's Point Daily Journal*, a Wisconsin newspaper.

HIKED IN HIS BARE FEET

Hippolyte Martinet hiked barefoot from Seattle to New York City.

It took but 90 walking days for Hippolyte Martinet to walk barefooted from Seattle, Washington to New York City where he visited the stock exchange and addressed more than 100 members, attendants and stock runners in the lobby of the exchange building.

"I am a carpenter by trade and working in Seattle shops affected my health" Martinet said. "I went to a doctor and he told me I was threatened with consumption unless I (lived or was) constantly in the open air. His pack merely contained a sleeping bag and a map of the country. I did not sleep beneath a roof on my entire trip."

A third article reports that it took Hippolyte a mere ninety days to walk from Seattle to New York. My curiosity piqued, I did the math and calculated that it actually took Hippolyte 118 days. On April 16th, 1920 while at the Sather Hotel in Seattle, he wrote a letter to his brother-in-law, Prosper, telling him that he planned to begin his walk on April 19th. Whether journalists miscalculated or somebody intentionally fudged the numbers, I'll never know.

In 1921, a French newspaper article described his foot journey across the Midwest as well as his experience riding in an open car through the streets of New York.

Because Chicago showed him cold shoulders, the bare-foot traveler did not tarry long at that spot. From that point, to New York he abandoned his nap-sack-perhaps to make himself feel light-hearted—and covered the distance on average over 50 miles each walking day.

Madison (Wisc.). Detroit. Cleveland. Philadelphia, Trenton (N.J.) and numerous other cities, received and treated him quite cordially. And when he arrived in New York City, August 15, 1920, he was driven in an open car thru the streets, collecting a crowd of people at City Hall, which kept the Knickerbocker cops busy for hours. At Coney Island he attracted circus-attention, and left with bulky proceeds from the sale of the post-cards—a photograph of himself—which he sells to appreciative audiences.

As Neptune is a god whom our "Walking Wonder" is not inclined to serve, he worked his way over on the S.S. "Finland", leaving New York on the 3rd of October, 1920 for Antwerp.

I'm not sure what was responsible for the delay in reporting, but on May 24th, a year and nine months after his arrival in New York, the *Philadelphia Inquirer* published this article on page sixteen. By the time their story hit the newsstands, Hippolyte had already walked to India. Four months later, newspapers would be writing about his passing.

AS A BOOTLEGGER

Mr. Hippolyte Martinet, an American, has just set off on a walk round the world. Prohibition may explain the first half of his journey, but why should he want to come back? —London Punch.

I'm more than willing to excuse the fact that they were so late in sharing his story, as they were the only publication to broach a subject that I often wondered about—prohibition. Was Hippolyte a drinker and if so, how good did his first beer taste after three years of living in a dry country? Hippolyte spent over a month in New York. I have no idea where he lived or what he did while he was there.

Although it was reported that he took the SS *Finland* across the Atlantic, a document titled "List of Aliens Employed On The Vessel As Members Of The Crew" registers Hippolyte as a crewmember on the SS *Philadelphia* on the 27th of September 1920, bound for Southampton. The *Philadelphia* has an amazing and colorful history. Built in 1888, the British-constructed passenger ship was originally named *City of Paris* and was the fastest ship on the North Atlantic route for three years. The ship's first westbound voyage was completed in under six days. On a trip to Liverpool in 1890, the starboard propeller shaft broke, causing the engine to race to such a degree that it shattered into pieces. Fragments from the engine pierced the hull and bulkhead, flooding both engine rooms. *The City of Paris* was towed to Queenstown for repairs, which took a year to complete. During this time her speed record was broken. Once overhauled and in the water again, she regained her status as the fastest passenger liner to cross the Atlantic. In 1898, during the Spanish-American War, she was chartered for service by the Navy and renamed the USS *Yale*. Three years later, the ship was renamed the SS *Philadelphia* and she returned to commercial service. By 1913, the SS *Philadelphia* was beginning to show her years and was downgraded to a second and then a third class liner. In 1918, the vessel was recommissioned as the USS *Harrisburg* as a troops transport during the Great War. At the war's end, the *Harrisburg* was returned to her owners and rechristened the *Philadelphia;* for nine months she resumed sailing from New York to Southampton. In 1922, now thirty-four years old, the *Philadelphia* was sold to new owners for use in the Mediterranean. Considerably worse for wear and badly in need of repairs, her crew mutinied in August of 1922. The *Philadelphia* was received in the Bay of Naples but deemed unfit, and customs officials refused to allow her to leave port. The ship's crew, described as "Bolsheviks" and members of the "Industrial Workers of the World" (a labor union established in 1905), ransacked and burned her. Too young to have served in the Spanish—American War and too old for service in The Great War, this was likely the first time Hippolyte set foot on a ship. I entertain images of my uncle standing on the stern of the SS *Philadelphia,* watching the New York skyline become fainter and fainter, the Statue of Liberty fading into a dot, but these images are unrealistic, if not theatrical. He was then a working crewman on what may have been his first trip abroad.

CHAPTER TWENTY-THREE

Communication Breakdown

In December of 2005, I traveled to Cambodia. I flew into Siem Reap, famous for its 900-year-old temple complex, Angkor Wat. This was before the tiny airport was remodeled, back when naked children ran across the landing strip to watch passengers disembark. Inside the small arrival lounge, chickens strutted around the baggage claim looking like they too, were waiting for their luggage to come off the carousel. After checking into a hotel, I walked to a restaurant. Its hand-painted sign advertised *No Dog No Cat No Worm No Rat*. I sat outdoors and while I waited for my food to arrive, I struck up a conversation with a couple from Sweden. They were on a month-long holiday with their four-year-old daughter. The previous year, they spent an entire month in Thailand. One afternoon while dining al fresco, their then three-year-old daughter saw a Western fellow walking towards them and called out to him with a precocious lilt, "Hey sexy man! You want massage?" They decided then and there it was time to pack up and go home. It was a phrase she had heard Thai women direct at Western men over and over again. Cognitively, she was at that stage when languages are learned effortlessly and without being taught explicitly. Her three-year-old brain was like a little sponge.

Three weeks into China, my brain was also like a little sponge in that it felt soggy and wet. Contrary to my expectations, Mandarin wasn't getting any easier for me. Doug fared a bit better, but even so, the simplest exchanges were often a challenge. Our Mandarin teacher taught us that the word for hotel was *fàndiàn*. Regardless, we regularly struggled to find accommodations. Countless times we asked for directions to a hotel and were led eagerly into a building, offered a seat at a table and handed menus. We would thank them, leave and continue our quest. A few hundred feet up the street we'd ask for a fàndiàn and be led into a building, up three flights of stairs and into a room with two beds and a bathroom. It was baffling. We couldn't figure out what was happening. Months later, back home, we learned fàndiàn could also mean *restaurant,* which is also known as a cāntīng.

If our initial request for a fàndiàn was met with looks of confusion, we'd pantomime sleeping and repeat *fàndiàn, f*àndiàn. Frequently, our pronunciation was corrected with a nearly imperceptible difference in vowel sound or tone. Eighteen miles down the road, using the new inflection, our pronunciation would be corrected again. In one instance, we were told that the word was pronounced fànd*iànna.* It worked like a charm... for two days. On day three... blank stares. We were flummoxed.

The fourth and last night we camped, we went to sleep without eating. We rose early the next morning and walked at least four hours before arriving at the outskirts of a tiny village. Doug first came upon the L—shaped building that sat at the top of a hill. On the driveway, a young woman washed a mass of dishes, pots and pans in an enormous plastic tub the size and depth of a kiddie pool. Many restaurants did their dishes this way. Under the eaves of the roof, an older woman, probably her grandmother, sat in a chair while four or five pullets chased after blowing bits of Styrofoam that scuttled across the driveway.

Doug inquired, "Cāntīng?—*Restaurant?* Chī fàn?—*We eat?*" and mimed putting food in his mouth. The young woman smiled, left her dishes waiting, and showed us inside to one of two tables in the middle of the room. Grandmother came indoors and poured tea for us. There were no menus, which was typical of restaurants in rural areas. They either served one thing and one thing only, or you asked them to prepare a specific dish. A minute later, the young woman led us into the kitchen and pointed to the glass front refrigerator. We selected a few vegetables and asked for eggs and rice too. She nodded and we went back to the table to enjoy the beautiful view of the hillside across and the valley below, lush and green, tiered with rice paddies. We had a lovely lunch that was delicious on its own but even more enjoyable for not having eaten in nearly twenty hours. Sated, we asked for the check and the young lady waved us off. We insisted on paying, but she declined. It took us a few minutes and our language app to deduce that we hadn't been dining at a restaurant but rather someone's home. We were mortified and our embarrassment was very evident. We gave them one of our postcards, took several group photos and asked them to look at our website later that evening, as I planned to post our group photo there. We left with a gift of two large plastic bags filled with nectarines. I still cringe with embarrassment thinking about this day.

Our communication difficulties in part were due to the fact that we were in rural regions of China where Mandarin wasn't always spoken. It took us a lot longer to figure this out than it should have. It wasn't until I returned home and did some deeper research that I learned China has fifty-six recognized ethnic groups and eight major dialects—all of which can be mutually unintelligible. Currently there are 297 living languages in China. I have no idea how many of them we heard. Months after arriving home, I met a neighbor who was from China. When I described our language challenges, she told me that it is quite possible that two villages separated by only twenty kilometers will speak completely different dialects. There you go.

Without fail, people would see us and begin speaking Mandarin or one of the local dialects. Regardless of what they said, we would respond with, "Women zǒu lù—*We are walking.*" Unfortunately, this led people to believe we actually understood them, and in rapid fire they would continue chatting away at us. At this point, we would add "Wǒmen shuō Hànyǔ yīdiǎn diǎn—*We speak Mandarin just a little bit.*" I eventually began punctuating yīdiǎn diǎn with my thumb and index finger to indicate just how small the quantity really was—the gap between my fingers gradually narrowing from one inch apart until they nearly touched. Sometimes the person simply smiled and walked away. Others repeated what I said and laughed, which I chose to interpret as "Well, aren't you adorable trying to speak Mandarin?" Often they spoke to us as though we understood what they were saying, even though we were clueless.

In these instances, I would just smile and nod. I decided to assume they were saying something nice and see where that got me despite several awkward experiences prior to our trip to China.

Years before, I traveled in Northern Vietnam with friends. We were there for almost two weeks and not once did we see a single person who carried even a single extra pound. It's not all genetics; it's lifestyle too. They walk more than we do, they ride bicycles, they eat a completely different diet and they understand portion control. In the evenings, people walked down the street delicately licking ice cream cones that looked as though they'd been scooped with a melon baller. The servings were half or even one quarter that of our small or toddler-sized cones. Even when something in the U.S. is not *super-sized*, the portion is still far larger than anything you would find there.

One of my traveling companions had put on a few extra pounds after retirement and sported a bit of a belly. One early morning, we were touring a lake by boat, accompanied by our guide. Another boat piloted by two men in their eighties pulled beside us. Both men were shirtless and sinewy; their knobby knees were the widest part of their thin legs. Looking at my male companion, one man said something that caused his friend to laugh and respond with something they both found equally amusing. Then they paddled away.

Simple curiosity compelled my companion to ask our guide, Viet, what the men said. Viet answered my friend very directly and without reservation, "They said that it looked like you are either in your eight month of pregnancy or that you are the happy Buddha." I nearly laughed out loud until I remembered the five-word conversation I had just the day before. We checked into a hotel and a female employee was showing me to my room. She paused as she was ascending the stairs, gestured to my stomach and asked, "You have baby?" "No," I answered somewhere between a groan and a sigh of exasperation with myself, not her. "Oh," she responded and put her hand in front of her mouth as she giggled coyly. Once in my room, I handed her a tip, closed the door and caught a glimpse of myself in the mirror. I could understand how my little belly roll could be mistaken for early pregnancy, but my rule of thumb is to never ask a woman if she is pregnant, not even if her legs are in the stirrups and she's crowning. I just... don't... do it.

A few days later my friends and I were sitting in a parked van when three women approached us from across the bare dirt parking lot. They walked up to the unrolled passenger side window where my male companion was seated. Standing on her toes so she could have a better look inside, one of the women made a comment at which point they all broke out into raucous laughter and promptly walked away. When they were out of earshot, my friend asked our guide what the woman said. Again, without missing a beat, Viet reported, "She said it looked like you were gestating twin bear cubs." I'm not sure which impressed me more, the colorfulness and creativity of that epic burn, or Viet's superlative command of the English language. He knew both the clinical term for the period of time from conception to delivery and the word for the progeny of a bear.

I can only begin to imagine the communication challenges Hippolyte must have experienced. Sometimes, even when we were communicating in Mandarin with someone who clearly understood us, Doug and I were met with looks of confusion. One afternoon as Doug and I walked down a particularly desolate stretch of the highway, a motorcyclist slowed and then rolled to a stop to get a better look at us. We exchanged greetings and Doug asked him in Mandarin how far it was to the next hotel. Still straddling his bike, he gave us simple directions and then said something else. It ended with the word *ma*, so we knew it was a yes/no question but understood nothing beyond that. As per usual, when people said things to us we didn't understand, we responded with, "Wǒmen zǒu lù cóng Dali dào Shēnzhèn—*We are walking from Dali to Shenzhen.*" Using perfect English, he responded with incredulity, "Are you suuuuuure?"

CHAPTER TWENTY-FOUR

Doubt

The first two days of our journey had been so much fun and relatively easy. It was all so new and exhilarating. I felt restless but not in the uncomfortable, fitful and troubled sense. I was restless in the best way possible. I felt charged and excited about where we were and what we were doing because it was so purposeful and meaningful to me. With every step, I was paying tribute to my uncle. Even better, the people we met daily confirmed exactly what he espoused. We were enjoying ourselves immensely, and I think a smile was plastered on my face the entire time. Strolling up and down a few mountain passes did nothing to prepare us for the third day, the day of the stone quarry. That was the day that serious, legitimate doubt kicked back in and I foolishly chose to entertain again, the idea that I might not be able to finish the walk; however, both reality and destiny are malleable. Circumstances give us the clay to hold in our hands, but it is we who shape it. We can knead it and work it and mold it into something breathtakingly beautiful or, with minimal exertion, we can roll the lump back and forth between our palms and make a turd. Either way, both scenarios have their beginnings in the same lump of earth.

One of the biggest mistakes I consistently make is envisioning myself failing. It's so unnecessary and self-defeating, but it's a habit I struggle to break. Even before we began the walk, I contemplated my inability to complete a walking journey of 1,065 miles. Then about eight days into our walk when I calculated we had whittled a four-digit number down into triple digits, Doug broke the news to me. We had miscalculated the distance from Dali City to Shenzhen. Rather than having roughly 937 miles left, we instead had 1,072. This news was particularly disheartening coming on a day when the temperature had risen to such a degree that Doug declared it was "hotter than two rats fu**ing in a wool sock." Our phones told us the actual temperature was 96 degrees but that the "real feel" was 104. I wouldn't say that I was crestfallen, but in that moment my hands started kneading and molding. My clay was starting to take shape. We walked another seven miles in the sweltering heat before we were back to where we had started eight days earlier, still 1065 miles from Shenzhen.

I began every morning questioning myself. "Can I do this? I don't think I can do this. What am I doing? Can I quit? I can't quit! We've bragged to too many people about this trip. What would they say? What would they think?" I couldn't bear the thought of facing, as a failure, all of the people I told about this journey. Ego and the desire to save face got me through the first 200 miles. Three baby swallows helped me get through the rest.

One early afternoon, Doug and I stopped for a meal at a small restaurant. Seated outdoors, we waited for our food to be served. Two noisy mud swallows were perched on a power cord that stretched between a wall of the building and the fence opposite it. The birds screeched and called, bobbing and jumping in earnest. I looked from them across the courtyard. Their mud nest was up under the eaves of the roof, just to our right, plastered to the side of the house. Peeking out of the hole were the heads of their newly feathered babies. One of them climbed onto the opening of the nest and gripped with its tiny feet. It teetered awkwardly, regained its balance and stood motionless. The parents screeched and bobbed some more and, in an act of faith, it leapt from its nest. It fell a few inches, opened its wings, and flapped frantically. A few ungraceful and gawky wing beats later, it landed on the branch of a small tree fifteen feet away from us. Had it failed, it would have fallen onto the concrete patio eight feet below. One by one, its nestmates emerged, believed their wings would carry them, pushed off and flew. They literally took a leap of faith.

The phrase "leap of faith" was coined by the 19th century Danish philosopher, Soren Kierkegaard, who explained that there was a chasm that separated human reason from faith and that believers in God must make a "leap of faith" across that abyss if they are to find salvation. I think Kierkegaard may also have been watching fledgling birds when he made that connection. I decided to take my own leap of faith and abandon my morning ritual of self-doubt and instead have trust that my own two legs and mad determination would get me to Shenzhen. I battled doubt again after I got home. It snuck back in and tried to make my goals seem impossible, not for anyone else, but for *me.* That chasm got wider, deeper, darker and scarier. It tried to undermine my confidence, but I won and now, you hold my book in your hands. I was terrified to begin this writing project. But, then I remembered what my friend LeeAnn Owens always says, "Sometimes you gotta kick ass, even if it's your own."

CHAPTER TWENTY-FIVE

Antwerp to France

After departing New York, the SS *Philadelphia*'s next stop was Southampton England, where Hippolyte disembarked. From there it continued on to Antwerp Belgium, which was Hippolyte's next destination. Port to port it was an eighty-mile walk across England. Perhaps like the *Philadelphia Inquirer* suggested, having had enough of Prohibition, the prospect of a drink was irresistible. I can clearly envision him striding down the gangplank with his impossibly long, signature gate. Once back on dry land and out of a dry country, he stops at the first pub he sees. As he raises a pint to his lips, his backpack, slung loosely over his shoulder, falls to the floor.

In the United States, the National Prohibition Act, also known as the Volstead Act, didn't officially take effect until January 17th, 1920. Washington State, however, in an effort to save grain, enacted wartime prohibition on January 1st, 1916. Assuming Hippolyte didn't break the law, once in England it would have been roughly four years since he'd had a drink. However, before departing across the Atlantic, Hippolyte spent approximately six weeks in New York City. At the time, the metropolis had a population of roughly 5,620,000 and as many as 100,000 speakeasies—some not much larger than a closet. By my calculations, that equals one speakeasy, or blind pig, for every fifty-six people. It wouldn't have been hard for my uncle to find a drink had he been so inclined.

From London Hippolyte boarded a ship and sailed to Antwerp, the homeland of his grandfather and namesake, Pierre Hippolyte. I have no idea if Hippolyte searched for family while he was there. I wonder if he was curious about his relatives in Hamme-Mille, the town where his grandfather was born. It lay forty-six miles south of Antwerp—a mere day and a half walk.

The 1916 Olympics were cancelled due to World War One. In 1920 when Antwerp hosted the Summer Games, doves symbolizing peace were released, and the five-ring Olympic flag representing the unity of the five continents debuted. The war to end all wars left 20,000,000 wounded and took the lives of 11,000,000 military personnel as well as 7,000,000 civilians. The U.S. took home ninety-five medals. Two of the medals were in swimming by Hawaii's Duke Kahanamoku, who popularized surfing, a sport Hippolyte's niece, Mary—or Sis as her family called her, would enjoy with her husband, Jim Bailey. Somewhat famous in Hermosa Beach, California, they were local fixtures known for riding tandem on redwood longboards, sometimes with their dog Rusty hanging ten on the nose of the board.

Hippolyte's next destination was 109 miles to the south in Arras Pas de Calais, France. This leg of his European tour would have taken Hippolyte roughly four days. Only six miles from the front lines of combat, it was shelled almost continuously for three out of the four years of conflict. It sustained significant damages and two thirds of the city's 155 buildings were destroyed, including all of its historic structures. Monuments such as Arras City Hall, the Belfry and Arras Cathedral -whose construction began in 1030—were reduced to rubble. Efforts to rebuild the city began immediately after the war. With the goal of making the city look exactly as it had before, archives and photographs were consulted so that the exteriors of all buildings could be replicated (to then modern safety specifications) and placed in their original locations. Reconstruction was finally complete in 1934. This Herculean effort provided Hippolyte with employment and means to wait out the winter so he could avoid walking in freezing temperatures and later the scorching heat.

In February of 1921, Hippolyte wrote the following letter to one of his sisters. He had three: Marguerite, Marie Louise and Blanche. This letter was written in his native French. I always assumed Hippolyte spoke

French Creole but my friend, Fatima Mooney, who translated the letter for me remarked that his spelling and grammar were flawless. Because Hippolyte typically wrote to Blanche in English and mentions his sister Marie Louise therein, I believe he was writing to Marguerite. The letter reads as follows.

> Arras
>
> February 4th, 1921
>
> My Dear Sister,
>
> I am always at Arras in the middle of ruins. I am fed in the canteens and I sleep in the barracks quite like the soldiers. There is no way to do otherwise because everything is destroyed. Although the climate is rather cold, I am doing well and I even got fatter and especially, I am happy in France.
>
> I will stay here for a month and a half and then it will be full Spring and I well set out to visit France.
>
> If, then my dear sister, you want to answer me, answer me soon when you receive this letter and receive my best wishes.
>
> I want to tell you my dear sister, my intentions at this moment. Although, I have only seen a small part of France, I am enjoying this country. So, if in my walk though France, I found a place that I love better and where I can find a peaceful situation, I will stay in France.
>
> Otherwise, I will come back to America where I expect to find myself back towards the end of the year.
>
> I am going to send you postcards from Arras and the region. About the postcards, I received those sent by Marie Louise and I thank her. When I am on the road, I will keep you informed about my life by writing you time to time.

After a six-month hiatus, weather permitted Hippolyte to resume walking, and he penned a letter to his sister Blanche informing her so. Casually written in coherent but somewhat broken English, he wrote:

Arras Pas de—cals France
4, 6 1921

Dear Sister Blanche

Your recent letter was duly received, contents noted, was glad to learn that all doing well & same, in fact I sure did strike thing good here. Started to work Oct 20th up to April 2nd without lost a single day, but we do not get much pay, however I'm all right financially, therefore will tour France on a hike, begaining Friday April 8th will stop in the big town Paris for 10 days or so, I will have lots of things to look over, also to have some post card made of myself, will send some then, but in the mean time sending views of the devastated region, also three card was sent me by a friend. I'll pay him a visit on my hike.

Now coming to bad health. Also getting old they both very costly things to tryfel with at that rather danger, believe me I have acquired some experience on this hike, therefore I'll suggest that you go and get a through physical examination by a good doctor. Now whatever you may do, don't take his drug write me as soon as you get posted on your ill, and I'll do the suggestion for you to get well. You may also tell Honorat if he would like to get going at 50 write me, I myself don't feel like a boy at 43 but like a airplain. I have a 1000 & 2 thing to tell you but not the time to write so much, wrote to Uncle Nonone to send my Batiester as yet no reply, best regard to all, affectionate

Bro, Hippolyte Martinet

on the road.

Hippolyte further endeared himself to me with his comment about feeling like an airplane at the age of forty-three. I wonder if he was talking about his overall improved health, the excitement over his impending departure, or both. I beam when I think that at forty-three, after receiving what amounted to a death sentence, my uncle found within himself his own personal fountain of youth. I realized that when Hippolyte wrote the letter, he wouldn't actually be forty-three for another nineteen days. Maybe he was mentally preparing himself for a numeric increase in age by claiming it before time forced it upon him. I did this before turning thirty, forty, and fifty, and I'm sure I'll do it when I'm on the cusp of sixty.

Two parts of his letter baffled me. I have no idea who Uncle Nonone was. I've searched and was unable to find his name in our family genealogy. Batiester is yet another mystery. I had no idea what a batiester was or why he needed one. Because Hippolyte was prone to the occasional misspelling, I tried various permutations of the word *batiester,* which didn't yield any helpful results. The closest I could surmise was that perhaps he was referring to a baptismal document necessary for obtaining a passport. The French word for baptistery is *baptistére* and seems the most logical fit. If so, maybe Uncle Nonone was his godfather. (When Hippolyte crossed the Atlantic, he did so as a "Citizen's Seaman" and was able enter Belgium without a passport.)

From this point on, the only letters I have are between Prosper and Hippolyte. To my knowledge, Hippolyte never wrote another letter to Blanche and she never wrote another to him. I've considered the possibility that his last letter caused a falling out. Maybe she was angered by his overbearing suggestion that she take his medical advice over that of a doctor. It's also possible that she was just too busy raising five children who ranged in age from one to nine years old.

CHAPTER TWENTY-SIX

Blisters and the Heat

Between the two of us, Doug was the first to get blisters, only his never worsened and quickly healed into protective callouses. My first blisters appeared a few days later in the arches of my feet after putting in a twenty-four-mile day. We hadn't intended to walk that far but did so out of necessity. After walking seventeen miles, we went to what our GPS told us was a hotel.

"Is this a hotel?" we asked.

"It is," we were told.

"Do you have rooms available?" we inquired.

"We have rooms available."

"We would like a room, please" we requested and were promptly denied. Confused, we asked again. "This is a hotel?"

"This is a hotel," we were assured.

"And you have rooms available?"

"We have available rooms." Our hopes rose again.

"We would like a room please," we reiterated. We held out money just in case she thought we were indigent, but the woman up and walked away.

"This is a hotel, you have available rooms, but no room for us?" we blurted out to her retreating figure.

"*Yes*" she said over her shoulder, in English before exiting to the street.

In print, our discourse seems pretty straight forward, but the problem is that in Mandarin there aren't single words for the concepts of yes or no. It is considerably more nuanced and the words used for those two concepts will vary depending on context. What makes communication even more challenging is the fact that many of the people we were conversing with wouldn't even nod or shake their heads to indicate affirmative or negative. Confused, exhausted and a little embarrassed, we left. That is how we wound up walking twenty-four miles that day. Even though we fell short at least six miles of what Hippolyte walked regularly, it was the most we had walked in a single day, and I was proud of our achievement—even if it wasn't by design.

Denied, deterred, but not dejected, we continued down the highway. Eventually we came to a lone, multi-story building on the side of the road. The door was open, so we poked our heads in and asked if it was a hotel. Our luck had changed. It was, and the owner told us the rate was twelve U.S. dollars a night. We were ecstatic. He led us up three flights of stairs, unlocked the door, looked at our surroundings and made a noise that was the Mandarin equivalent of "meh" and re-negotiated his asking price down to seven dollars. We gladly handed over the money and the man left.

I took off my shoes and socks to allow my blisters to air out and then collapsed on the bed. Doug headed to the bathroom to take a shower and when he opened the door, a blast of gag-inducing odor poured into the room. The squat toilet had apparently been installed without the standard gas trap that prevents sewer gasses from coming back up the pipes. When Doug finished with his ablutions, I took what may have been the shortest shower of my life. When traveling in countries with untreated water, I'm diligent about not letting shower water get into my mouth. I shower with my lips sealed tightly and breathe in and out of my nose. When I'm finished, I immediately dry my face and mouth lest I contract giardia or some other intestinal parasite. That evening, I took my shower in short bursts that lasted exactly as long as I could hold my breath. I shampooed and then ran to the bathroom door, popped my head out, took a few deep breaths, held the last one in, and darted back into the tiled torture chamber to rinse and condition. I darted back to the door again for a few more breaths before heading back in for a final rinse. The latch on the bathroom door must have broken during my frenzy because it would not remain closed for more than a few seconds. Without warning, it would pop open and a cloud of odor would roll out as thick as San Francisco fog. We propped our backpacks against it to keep it closed but the odor still crept into the room. I considered sticking my foam earplugs up my nostrils for the night but decided against it. *Just live it. Just experience it* I told myself. You will never be back in China in this hotel, on this day, after having walked 24 miles. *Just be in the right here and the right now,* I convinced myself. So, I put my ear plugs not in my ears, not up my nose, but back in their pouch and listened to the layered noises—the echoes of a child's voice in the hallway, the honking of horns outside on the highway, the nasal singing of a woman on someone's radio and the gurgling belching noises made by the stinky squat toilet.

The next morning I ditched my shoes and began walking in my hiking sandals. Those first blisters eventually healed, but then I developed massive blisters that covered the balls of my feet. I applied mole skin, but it did little to help. The damage was already done and they worsened over time. I began each day in agony. The balls of my feet felt as though they tearing with each step, but after fifteen minutes or so, the pain subsided into a manageable but ever-present sting. If I stopped walking for more than a few seconds, I was back to square one until I hit that fifteen-minute mark. When I took my socks off at the end of each day, I was genuinely surprised not to see blood.

Blisters that had healed into dry pockets of skin developed blisters underneath. Eventually, they became so bad that twice we were forced to take two-day breaks so my feet could recover. I spent most of the time lying in bed, occasionally getting up to hobble to the bathroom. The blisters were so impressive that I posted pictures of them on Facebook. They were the size of silver dollars and had a greenish hue. Doug's sister is a nurse and commented that they looked infected. The next morning I enlisted Doug's help. He pierced one of them with a needle and a putrid liquid trickled out. When the blister was completely drained, I trimmed and removed the thick pockets of skin. Underneath, the flesh was moist, pink and translucent. I thought about Hippolyte walking without shoes. I bet he didn't have any blisters. Had the bottoms of my feet not been raw, exposed flesh, I might have considered walking shoeless, but they looked as if only an onion skin layer of flesh stood between the muscle of my foot and the outside world. The skin would eventually heal and blister again in a cruel and tortuous cycle that I just couldn't break despite the precautions I took.

Our biggest challenge, even more daunting than the blisters on my feet was the temperature. This coastal southern California girl was not cut out for that kind of heat. Back home, a Chinese man bragged to me about Chinese laborers building railways in Africa. They get the job done while the locals succumbed to heat stroke. It was so hot that there were days when I truly felt on the cusp.

The nights were nearly as hot as the days. Finding accommodations with air conditioning was always something to celebrate. But just as often, we were happy enough to find a place with a ceiling fan or even just a place with a shower and toilet. One afternoon we walked through a town and instead of being met with smiles and looks of interest, people pulled their heads back in their windows and pulled curtains closed, children ran indoors and people looked at us with suspicion. That night we rented and slept in what we believe was the town's jail. The room was up three flights of cement stairs and past a large, locked metal gate that was bolted securely to the wall of the stairwell. Another barred metal gate was in front of the door that once unlocked and opened, revealed our room for the evening. It measured roughly seven feet by seven feet and its one window had bars on it too. There were two wooden platform beds. One occupied the wall opposite the door and the other was against the wall to the right of the door. There was room for only one of us to stand in the only unused space at a time. Woven bamboo mats lay on top of the beds in lieu of mattresses. Fortunately, our air mattresses were in our backpacks. We used them frequently, even when we weren't camping. Once, Doug rapped his knuckles on a hotel mattress and it made a dull knocking noise that made me get up to answer the door.

The bathroom was down the hall and had a squat toilet and a pipe that came out of the wall for a shower. Unfortunately, there was no running water. Doug had to lug a five-gallon bucket of water up three flights of stairs so we could flush the toilet and have a sponge bath. Back in our room there was a socket in the room for a light but alas, no bulb. There was also an old yet very sturdy-looking fan that was bolted to the low ceiling. An inch-thick layer of dust quilted the blades. The contraption had two speeds; one painfully slow, roughly one rotation every five seconds and the other one so maniacally fast that we feared it would come flying off of its fairing and decapitate one if not both of us. In the end, we left it on high. It was too darn hot to consider any other option. The next morning we woke to our 3:30 am alarm and were impressed to see that it was still a whipping and wobbling blur and very much still attached to the ceiling. We dressed, one at a time with our backs to the walls of the tiny room. Neither of us wanted to lose a hand to a fan blade whilst raising our arms to put on our shirts.

There were a few times it was so hot, I truly felt like I was at risk of heat stroke. One punishingly hot day, when the heat was visible as an undulating shimmer on the highway, we trudged up a particularly steep pass and into the first open business we saw—an appliance store—and asked if there was a hotel near. The store was packed with washing machines and air conditioners. The man pointed to the stairs at the back of his store and led us to a room with an A.C. unit on the wall directly above one of the two twin sized beds. Most hotel rooms had two or more twin sized beds. I selfishly claimed the one below the AC unit for myself. I cranked it up and then walked straight into the bathroom and without undressing, stood under the showerhead and turned on the cold water. After I peeled off my wet clothes I went and lay down on the bed in an empty room. I could hear Doug's voice off somewhere else. I lied there for at least three hours and still felt miserably and sickly hot. Doug tried several times to lure me out of the room and tried to convince me that it had cooled down since our early afternoon arrival. He'd comment on how cool our room was but I was still sweating and nauseously hot. I'd get dressed but the second I stepped out into the hallway, the heat hit me like a wall and I did an about face and laid back down on the bed. Eventually I got up and followed the voices to the fourth floor where I found Doug, the owner of the store, his partner, and their in-uniform policeman friend all sitting around a table drinking beer out of short glasses. Eventually a beer was poured for me and I relished it even though it was warm. For dinner, we ate peanuts. By the end of the evening, the table was full of empty beer bottles and cigarette butts. The next morning I woke up early and wrote a message for the owner to thank him and his friends for their hospitality. I consulted the language App in my phone and transcribed the message in Chinese characters. I pray that my message wasn't lost in translation because I meant every word of it. Truly, I will remember their kindness for the rest of my life.

When we went downstairs, we found the owner asleep on a couch. The front doors of his store were wide open. Out on the street, we crept past families who had moved their beds or sleeping mats onto the bit of sidewalk in front of their homes and slept outdoors. We were as silent as possible, stepping lightly, not even speaking until we got to the edge of town where we were less likely to wake sleeping dogs and leave a raucous chorus of barking in our wake. We paused for just a moment to watch bats dive and swoop as they gorged on the clouds of tiny insects that were attracted to the halo light of street lamps. Before the sun was even a distant glow on the horizon, they'd be gone, back to wherever they lived, their stomachs full from the six to eight thousand insects they typically consume in a single night.

CHAPTER TWENTY-SEVEN

France and Switzerland

After leaving Arras Pas-de-Calais, Hippolyte walked 112 miles southwest to Le Havre, a harbor town in the Normandy region on the right bank of an estuary of the Seine. Founded in 1517 to ease traffic on two other French ports that had become silt-packed and impractical, Le Havre was France's first major slave-trading port. During the seventeenth and eighteenth centuries, 399 slave-trading expeditions returned to this "haven," as the name of this town translates. Most of the slaves were sent on to the Caribbean, but some were sent to the Mississippi Delta and Louisiana. I wonder if Hippolyte was aware of Le Havre's history and that there was a slight possibility that one of our relatives could have passed through the very harbor he was visiting.

A strategic port during the First World War, of the 6 million British soldiers that were mobilized, 1.9 million of them passed through Le Havre. Had the arrival of these English soldiers been staggered throughout the war—one ship arriving per day—on average, 1,219 soldiers would have marched through Le Havre for each day of the 1,558-day war that ended on the eleventh hour of the eleventh day of the eleventh month in 1918. Six thousand soldiers who called Le Havre home were killed in combat. Although several ships were torpedoed by German submarines just outside the port, Le Havre, further to the south from the war front than Calais, was otherwise almost completely spared from destruction. Hippolyte's foot tour of this seaside town occurred a little less than two months before Japan's twenty-year-old Prince Hirohito's historic visit to Le Havre. His six-month tour of Italy, France, Netherlands, Belgium and the United Kingdom was meant to be symbolic of Japan's new status as a world power.

Hippolyte's next destination was Paris, 130 miles to the southeast. He was headed there at the time of year Paris is most famous for, the spring, best enjoyed after a French winter. It's possible that he followed the Seine to the City of Lights, where Paulownia trees would be budding with lavender-colored flowers and parks and gardens were coming into bloom. It was here that one of my favorite photographs of Hippolyte was taken. He is photographed head on as he walks barefoot down the middle of the Champs-Élysées, the Arc de Triomphe visible in the background, and what looks like a Ford Model T keeping a cautious, respectful distance. He used this photo to make new postcards (opposite page).

> Sauntering along for-oh, just a couple thousand miles. Hippolyte Martinet photographed in Paris while strolling from Antwerp to Monte Carlo. Not long ago he walked from Seattle to New York.

Although he was received warmly by the press, the police were less welcoming and, mistaking him for a beggar as he tried to sell his postcards, evicted him from Paris—but not before he wrote a letter to Blanche's husband, Prosper.

> Paris April, 24. 1921
>
> Friend Prosper,
>
> A very lonesome after-noon for me in this great gay Paris for this reason it's raining and rather cold. In fact this immoral life don't appeal to me at all, how ever as beauty she the most wonderful city of all that the eyes can see, to give you an idea I have mailed a few also postcard. In the mean time I'm waiting for postcards of my own. Therefore will send some also an address where you'll may write that is to say I leave Paris April 28 useless for me to go in detail, you may read the newspaper clipping & be very well posted on my coming hike. Please mail at once to said.
>
> With best wishes to also regard to all,
> Friend I'm Hippolyte
> 4-2 Rue St Marri
> Paris

H. MARTINET U. S. A., Globe-Trotter

Le retour à la nature pour la régénération } Humaine
Une langue universelle pour l'harmonie }

Admittedly, I know very little about the country's geography. I looked at a map and tried to deduce what route Hippolyte would have taken east from Paris towards Switzerland. I imagine that northern France was bucolic and lovely in 1921. I conjure images of rolling, green hills swathed with grape vineyards and scattered with grazing sheep. While I am aware of the destruction sustained in the cities, I could never envision the devastation the countryside suffered. In reality, roaming off the beaten path could have been deadly.

After World War I, the French government assessed damages sustained across the country. Some areas were so devastated and dangerous that they were declared too environmentally damaged to be occupied. Strewn with the bodies of dead soldiers and animals, unexploded munitions and barbed wire, these areas were labeled "Zone Rouge"—*Red Zone* and entry was strictly prohibited. All together, these non-contiguous Red Zones covered more than 460 square miles. Six villages had to be entirely relocated. During the last century, these abandoned hamlets have reverted to thick forestland. They now look primeval, almost begging to be explored, but to enter one of these ghostly regions is to risk life and limb in the most literal sense.

In the northeast of France, near the borders of Belgium, Luxembourg and Germany, is Verdun, the site of the longest battle in history, where an estimated 750,000 died in 303 days of combat. The site of the Verdun battle is arguably one of France's bleakest Red Zones and strikes a harsh contrast to others that have been reclaimed by nature. The ground in Verdun is still covered with the bones of fallen soldiers, unexploded shells, and barbed wire. Arsenic remains in the soil in such abundance that, 100 years later, trees no longer grow and animals die.

Other areas have been *cleaned*, labeled Yellow Zones, and returned to civilians for agricultural use. Even so, farmers still accidentally plow over shells and blow up their tractors. Some lose their lives. The unearthed bombs and other munitions are carefully removed and collected every spring in what has become known as the Iron Harvest. An estimated 300 million tons of undetonated munitions remain in northern France and Belgium. Even though crews work to uncover and dispose of the unexploded munitions, it is estimated that they would have to continue working for between 300-700 years to discover and dispose of them all.

I'm sure Hippolyte was aware of this hazard and chose a safe route through the country. Because he occasionally followed the rails as he crossed the United States, it's possible he did that in France as well. However, railroad tracks were strategically bombed because they were used for military transport. Through research I learned that France boasts a network of beautiful canals, some dating back to the 17th and 18th centuries. Constructed when France and Spain were enemies and passage through the Straits of Gibraltar was a month-long journey rife with pirates, the canals enabled France to transport goods between the Atlantic and the Mediterranean. In the 19th century, the canal system was expanded in response to the Industrial Revolution and the sudden need for efficient transportation. Eventually, railroads rendered the canals uneconomical. Impractical in the monetary sense, they would have provided a safe, alternative route. These waterways remain today and many of the smaller canals are used solely by pleasure crafts.

It seems both logical and possible that he followed the Seine 130 miles southeast to Paris and then walked along the canals as he headed east towards Switzerland. At least that's what I would have done. Every picture I have seen of these waterways makes my feet itch and my shoulders miss my backpack. Spanned by centuries-old, arched stone bridges, they have a picture postcard allure that is utterly captivating. Laid out to avoid changes in elevation, the canal routes are blissfully flat. Tree-lined towpaths parallel them as they pass churches, abbeys and fields of sunflowers. Following this route, it would have taken him only four and a half days to walk to Paris, not nearly enough time to enjoy their rustic charm.

In a letter written on April 6th, Hippolyte mentioned that he would be paying a visit to a friend who had given him some cards. While he did not mention the name of the town, and because I'm told he was there, I suspect it was Damas, roughly 223 miles to the southeast. That's the only reason I can imagine Hippolyte would pay a visit to this seemingly anonymous town.

I referred to my map again and was unable to locate Damas. I conducted an internet search and discovered that two towns in the same region bear the name Damas. Damas-aux-Bois had a population of 457 in

1921; as of 2006, its population had fallen to 268. The second, Damas-et-Bettegney, had a population of 394 in 1921 and by 2006 had increased its population by exactly one. Armed with this information, I stood hunched over my map of France, scanning it quadrant by quadrant with a magnifying glass and still couldn't find either Damas.

The mystery of the two Damas begged to be solved and so I was compelled to go to my local travel store to search their travel books. I headed straight for the F section and found several different books on travel in France. I turned to the index and thumbed to the Ds and, sadly, Damas was nowhere to be found in any of the four books I consulted.

Left to my own imagination, I tried to envision what these tiny towns might have looked like and, more importantly, what kind of vibe they had. It's in small, anonymous towns like Damas that dogs are elected mayor. Lest anyone think I'm being disrespectful to the French, dogs, cats and beer-drinking goats have all been elected mayor in the U.S. My own mother lives in Idyllwild, California which is governed by Mayor Max II, a Golden Retriever. And just so nobody thinks I'm being disrespectful of my own country, Saucisse the Dachshund got four and a half percent of the vote in the 2001 mayoral election in Marseille, France. Saucisse is the French word for *sausage.* However, if you search the internet for the word, the first result is for the dog. Despite losing the mayoral race, he went on to have a wine named after him and a short career in French reality television. Not bad at all for a wiener dog that was found in a dumpster.

After Damas, Hippolyte headed east to Switzerland and visited Lausanne and Geneva, the French-speaking parts of the country. His visit there found its way onto page six of *The Pittsburgh Press* on Saturday, September 10th.

> GIRLS. THIS IS FOR YOU—Hippolyte Martinet, American, this week passed through Switzerland. He is walking around the world in his bare feet. That's the natural way to walk, and Hippolyte has no foot troubles.
>
> Savages invented shoes for ornament. The heel was added to keep the feet from slipping in a stirrup. Soldiers set the styles, so all men adopted heels. Like most foolish things, once started, it couldn't be stopped.

If nature had intended us to walk on shoe-heels, she would have made them out of bone or callous and grown them on our feet.

Heels, especially high French ones, throw the spine out of plumb and may cause serious nerve disorders.

The same article was picked up by *The Ogden Standard, The Salt Lake Telegram, The Reading Times, The Wisconsin State Journal* and the *Bismarck Tribune.*

He then crossed the border back into France for a visit to Vichy. Hippolyte must have received the documents required for his passport in Vichy, the town famous for its healing waters. I know this because my uncle had yet another encounter with the police. Some aspect of his appearance must have piqued their suspicion. They suspected he was a Russian spy and apprehended him. Upon producing his passport, he was released; however, I believe this encounter, compounded with other experiences, left my uncle with an unfavorable opinion of the French despite his initial impression.

From Vichy he walked 308 miles to Marseilles and then another 111 miles to Nice, where he addressed another letter to his brother-in-law Prosper.

Nice France July 7 1921

Friend Prosper

Your letter to hand contents noted you can't realize the great joy it was to me to read a letter from home in this lonesomeness of traveling. In fact I may say that France a wonderful country and believe me I am in a position to state the fact I did hiked down and across at that going up again over the French Alps on to Switzerland, Italy, Egypt, South America, Australia, China and then am back to U.S.A. no place like. All this simply suggestion. Nonetheless my fool ambition. I'm also anxious to get out of France for this reason, it's not interesting at all with the people, that is to say they're stupid don't appreciate such a sport therefore I hope to find hiking more pleasurable in other countries. I did live fairly well of the contributions of my post card thus far at this writing I'm badly disappointed here waiting for seven days for a passport same is due here by this time yet thus far nothing yet believe me one can't get over a state line in Europe without official papers by the way I did wrote two or three letters to Uncle Nonone begging him to send me some official statement from my home but thus far never had a reply had he done so same would be of great help to me for goodness sake. When ever you write give me some news & not so much that all is well one single statement of that suffice, I myself don't say much because a very poor writer but don't forget by the time I do get out your way will have some chewing on the rag to make you sick and tired off.

I'm enjoying the best wish you all same also regard to all
Very truly yours friend
Hippolyte Martinet
PS If you would write immediately address
H Martinet Globe Trotter
Rome Italy

True to form, Hippolyte's letter is a confusing jumble, parts of it nearly indecipherable. In one sentence he relays where he has been while simultaneously listing potential future destinations. Other parts of his letter are ambitious, opinionated, blunt and non-linear in a way that is completely familiar to me. I understand being overcome with excitement as unordered ideas loosely translated into phrases come tumbling out of my mouth, leaving my audience perplexed. It's a personal trait that used to embarrass me, but now I say with pride, "Yep, I'm a Martinet alright.

Hippolyte in Geneve

CHAPTER TWENTY-EIGHT

Paparazzi and Police

In early June we put in a nineteen-mile day and checked into a hotel. We hand washed our hiking clothes, hung them out to dry over our trekking poles and went downstairs for dinner. The first floor of the hotel was a restaurant that had been empty and quiet when we checked in. Now it was packed with men who chain smoked cigarettes from homemade soup can water pipes. An enormous, bluish-grey cloud hung over the entire room. Doug and I claimed the only free knee-high table and, like everyone else sat down on miniature stools. The place was everything in a dining establishment I usually try to avoid—hot, loud, crowded and smoke-filled; yet that day, we felt pretty darned lucky that we landed in the most happening joint in town. Men crowded every table. It had a Friday mood—boisterous and jovial. The only woman in the place besides me was the waitress who, with a calm air, darted back and forth serving at least thirty patrons. She delivered beer, trays of sunflower seeds and the occasional plate of food and steaming rice. Every now and then, she went to a bookcase that was lined with small, brown ceramic jugs, grabbed one and left it with a group of locals.

She took our order—a couple beers and some dinner—and quickly returned holding a tray crowded with two large bottles, short serving glasses and a dish of sunflower seeds. Noticing we didn't have a bottle opener, a man at a neighboring table came over, grabbed one of our beers, and lifted it to his mouth as he prepared to use his teeth to uncap it. In unison, Doug and I shouted, *Noooo*! We were having twin visions of his teeth crumbling at our expense. A man from another table scolded him, took the beer out of his hands, aligned the cap with the edge of our table, and with one hit of his fist, deftly opened the bottle *tssssssk aaaaah!* We filled our wee glasses, toasted each other and emptied them in one satisfying gulp. I sighed and got more comfortable on my brick-sized stool.

By then I was used to the weird reversal of fortune in which I was virtually ignored while men poured drinks left and right for my boyfriend. Before I knew it, another glass was put down in front of him along with one of those jugs. One of his many hosts, uncorked it and poured two generous fingers of Chinese moonshine whiskey. At least I assumed it was whiskey because it was brown. Seemingly oblivious to me, the man and Doug did shots while I sat there like a wallflower having fallen victim to some unknown cultural protocol.

Truthfully, I was glad to be left out because I once tasted Laos moonshine and assumed the Chinese version was of similar caliber. Roughly eight years prior, I purchased two small bottles from a distillery alongside a tributary of the Mekong River. The liquid ran from the still in a thin stream down a split piece of bamboo into a wooden bucket. The draw for me was the intricate pattern of woven reeds that encased the bottle. I bought two and shipped them to myself via sea mail in a cardboard box along with other curios and trinkets. A month and a half later, the package was sitting on my doorstep. A corner of the box was wet and when I bent over to pick it up, I caught a whiff and cursed whatever neighborhood tomcat had apparently marked it as his own. Disgusted, I carried the stinky and dripping box to my kitchen sink. Upon opening it, I realized I had needlessly maligned a cat. One of the whiskey bottles was broken. I wasn't smelling cat urine; I was smelling Laos whiskey. It's potent stuff in more ways than one.

Doug had been in the Navy for twenty-five years and was no stranger to alcohol. However, he was unaccustomed to his new *hot girl* status, so I kept my eye on him while an ever-increasing group of locals joined the game of *Get the Western Guy Drunk*, a game I'd seen play out several times since our arrival in China. While Doug was being plied with drink, I decided it was a good time to update the website and began composing on my phone. When I finished, I opened my VPN app, which enabled me to connect to the internet through a server in another country. A VPN is useful when one wants to access sites that are blocked by an agency, institution or government. Engrossed in retelling that day's adventure, I was oblivious to my surroundings. As I held my phone in front of me, a man at the next table leaned over and with a weathered hand pointed at the VPN icon on my phone. He said something in Mandarin that I couldn't understand, but his tone was clear and I interpreted it as, *Oooh, you're sooo busted.* I momentarily cringed and then peered up to see the face that belonged to the accusing finger. His eyes met and held mine for a few unblinking seconds. I pressed the power button on my phone until the screen went dark, turned my back to him, tucked the condemning device deep into the waist of my pants and did my best to conceal the incriminating bulge with my shirt tails. Then I took a long draught of the beer labeled "Polar Arctic Fresh," just like the ice water feeling in my stomach.

I was fairly certain that using a VPN in China was illegal, but didn't know what penalty it carried. My fear was compounded by a radio podcast I had listened to earlier that day. It was a story about a young man from Minnesota who spent eight months in a Chinese prison after accidentally kicking a soccer ball into a businessman's briefcase. While Doug was still getting the *hot girl* treatment, I panned the room. My eyes stopped on a tall, stern-looking man seated on a small dais flush with the wall in, of all things, a barber's chair from an era long ago. From time to time, I would glance in his direction. He rarely moved and never smiled. He didn't eat, drink, or speak to anyone. The part that made it surreal was his haircut. It was styled exactly like Spock from *Star Trek*—those precision bangs, bone straight and glossy, nary a fly away on his perfectly coifed head.

By the time our dinner arrived, I was too anxious to eat more than a few bites. I was still nervous about the man who pointed at the VPN icon on my phone. Who was he? Who was the Spock guy, and what kind of trouble could I get into for using a VPN? My appetite was ruined either by paranoia or legitimate fear, so I pushed my nearly full plate in front of Doug. As soon as he finished our dinners, I signaled it was time to go. We retreated upstairs to our room, much to the disappointment of his new drinking buddies.

Our newly-found fandom could have easily gone to our heads. We were fawned over by nearly everyone… the operative word being *nearly*. A woman wearing a traditional ethnic minority headscarf stopped and waited for me to catch up to her one morning as I ascended a particularly steep hill. "Canada?" she asked in English with a huge and hopeful smile. "Měi guó rén—*American*" I answered enthusiastically, mirroring her expression. Her face fell like a soufflé. Doug wasn't immune either. One afternoon, three teenagers on a motorcycle pulled up beside him and stopped. "What is your name?" the boy driving the motorcycle asked in English. Doug answered in Mandarin, "Wo shi Doug—*I am Doug*." Without missing a beat, the boy responded with a very unflattering parrot of Doug's reply. A second later, Doug was standing in their dust as the three of them sped off laughing hysterically. Leave it to teenagers to put us in our places.

In retrospect, I'm grateful to these people who helped keep our egos in check. It was a reminder that not everybody would be enamored with us. Two days after we left the whiskey bar hotel, Doug and I stopped at a farmers' market and sat down for something to eat. As we snacked on one of my favorite street food dishes—fried baby potatoes sprinkled with salt, chili peppers and chopped parsley—I checked my email, holding my phone in one hand as I typed with my thumb. Neither of us noticed the four policemen in dark navy uniforms armed with rifles across their chests… until they were standing right in front of us.

By this time in our journey, Doug and I were used to what we called the *Chinese Paparazzi*. People frequently approached with their cell phones wanting to take photos with us. Because of this, when the armed officers approached, we weren't alarmed in the least. Naively and perhaps arrogantly, we assumed they were simply curious. The officer pointed at me and then barked a few words neither Doug nor I understood. "Women shu hanyu idan dian", I said with a smile which melted off my face the moment he deftly pulled the driver's license from its slot in my phone/wallet folio, which rested unprotected in my open palm. He walked away with it and stood with his back to me. The faces of the two men from the whiskey restaurant—the one who had pointed to my VPN app and Spock the bouncer—looked judgmentally at me every time I closed my eyes and the hairs on the back of my neck stood at attention. One of the armed police officers stood in front of us while the other two stood behind. It was clear we were not free to leave. I swallowed the bite of potato that was still in my mouth and felt it land *kerplunk* in my stomach... where it sat like a rock. My mouth felt suddenly dry but the idea of drinking water made me feel nauseous.

The officer who had taken my license removed the radio from his utility belt and placed a call with an air of urgency. There was no chance I was going to understand anything he said, so I turned my attention back to my phone, hit the power button and watched the screen turn dark again. I pushed the remainder of the potatoes toward Doug. They seemed suddenly unsavory, just like my meal in the whiskey restaurant. Doug, perhaps wisely, continued to eat what very well might have been our last meal that wasn't served on a metal prison tray as we sat amid the needless triangulation of security. After a few minutes of talking, the man who had taken my driver's license strode towards us. With one word he commanded, "Follow." It felt like my heart stopped for a few seconds and then raced to make up for the lost beats. As ordered, we stood up and put on our backpacks. My insides turned to water and I tried to hold my hands steady as I buckled my hip belt. Doug and I fell into line behind the officer who was still holding my driver's license. We walked in near silence as the other officers followed behind us with their hands on their rifles. "What's happening?" I asked Doug, trying to sound as casual as possible. "I don't know," he answered. He was either unconcerned or, like me, doing his best to look calm and, more importantly, innocent. Had Doug not been with me, I most certainly would have burst into tears. What had we done wrong? And more importantly... what was going to happen to us?

It was less than an eighth of a mile walk to the police station, so we were there in minutes. A few curious onlookers from the market followed while keeping a respectful and casual distance. The officer who held my license gestured for us to sit on a stone bench and wait. As instructed, we sat, having no idea what we were being brought in for or what was going to happen next. My alarm increased as the details of that radio story about the guy from Minnesota spending eight months in a Chinese prison ran through my head—crowded jail cells, forced labor, rats that swam up out of the room's ONE communal toilet. I felt like I had electricity running through my legs and made a conscious effort not to tap my foot or do anything else that would make me appear nervous. I planted both feet firmly in front of me as I weighed my options and the potential consequences. As casually as possible, I took out my phone and hit the power button. Thirty-five agonizing seconds later, it came to life. I turned on my VPN so I could post a status update on my social media account. Trying to type as fast as I could with my thumbs while maintaining an appearance of calm and disinterest, I told anybody who might read my status what province we were in, what highway we had been walking along, which cities we were nearest, and that we had been taken in by the police. I added that if I didn't update my status in the next few hours to PLEASE, PLEASE, PLEASE contact the U.S. embassy. I moved the VPN app to my game folder, shut my phone off and put it away. By this time, the crowd of curious onlookers across from the police station had grown and was milling about, waiting for something to happen.

Thirty minutes later, a police car pulled into the parking lot. Two women got out and walked to the bench where we were seated. They did not carry rifles but had holstered handguns on their utility belts. We noticed that one of the women had more colored bars pinned to her chest and more chevrons on her sleeves than the men who brought us in. She smiled and then spoke to us in English. "Hello, please come with me," she said, and we followed behind her and her partner as two of the officers from the marketplace brought up the rear. She pulled a ring of keys from her belt, unlocked the metal, barred door in front of us and held it open as we followed her into the narrow hallway. Behind me I heard the rattle of keys and turned around to see the officer who still had my license pull the barred door closed with a *clang*, lock it, and walk away. The group of onlookers who had been standing across the street moved like an amoeba onto the police station driveway. I was seriously worried. My heart raced, my insides churned, and my knees felt weak.

The officer who had addressed us in English led us into a room and I heard the door shut and lock behind us. We were offered a seat on a sofa and given short glasses of hot water to drink. There was an open window across from us, but it too had bars over it. She asked us to produce our passports and when we handed them over, one of the other officers briskly left the room with them, locking the door behind her. My heart raced even faster as either completely paranoid or entirely realistic scenarios ran through my mind. Neither Doug nor I knew what to expect. A few seconds later, I heard the clang of the barred metal door that we had passed through earlier, but this time it hung reverberating in the air like a struck tuning fork and gradually faded into silence.

That silence was interrupted by the policewoman with the most chevrons on her uniform. "Where are you from?" she asked with a smile and friendly tone. The other officer stood behind her, staring at us with a blank expression. "California," Doug and I answered in unison. What followed can only be described as the most friendly and congenial interrogation imaginable. I began to relax for an instant but then contemplated the possibility that we were being set up and played for fools in a good cop/bad cop scenario. She asked when and why we came to China, what our professions were, where we had been, where we were going, the names of the last town and hotel where we stayed and what street it was on. Doug and I read each other's minds. We said we didn't know what street it was on because we couldn't read Chinese characters. Of course, we knew exactly where we had stayed the night before, but we didn't want to get anyone in trouble because we knew for a fact not every hotel was licensed to rent to Western tourists.

Doug pulled up a map on his cell phone and we did our best to seem confused as we pointed at different streets. Thirty minutes and countless questions later, the officer returned with our passports and my driver's license. Our interrogation was concluded with a warning to keep our passports on us at all times and to always stay at hotels. I tried not to squirm in my seat thinking about the tent, camp stove, air mattresses and camping quilt in our backpacks. We were escorted back to the parking lot. All of the men who brought us in had disappeared. I assumed they went back to their beat, patrolling the market. I have no idea what possessed me, but I asked for a group photo, to which the interrogating officer consented. She repositioned us with our backs to the street so that the police station wouldn't be in the picture. Every other officer at the station pulled out their cell phones and we spent the next couple of minutes taking group shots. With the show clearly over and nothing else to see, the crowd of disappointed onlookers dissipated. We headed back to the highway, free for the time being.

GLOBE-TROTTER
H. Martinet U. S. A. Globe-Trotter
Le retour à la nature pour la régénération
Une langue universelle pour l'harmonie
Humaine

CHAPTER TWENTY-NINE

Wild Man!

After Nice, it was a short fourteen-mile jaunt to Monaco, where Hippolyte visited Monte Carlo. In March of 1921, just a few months before my uncle's arrival, Monte Carlo hosted the Women's Olympiad. It was a five-day event organized by Alice Milliat and Camille Blanc in response to the International Olympic Committee's decision not to include women's events in the coming 1924 Olympics.

Hippolyte left Monaco and crossed into Italy, beginning this leg of his barefoot journey at the top of Italy's boot. While many travelers wire home for more money, Hippolyte would instead, on occasion, send money home. Thus, it was in the American Express offices in Genoa, roughly 114 miles across the border from Monaco, that Hippolyte's very presence caused a commotion dramatic enough to command an interview and lengthy newspaper article. The article was written by famed sports writer Frederick George Lieb, who roughly two years later coined the phrase "The House That Ruth Built" after Babe Ruth christened the New York Yankees stadium with a home run on their opening day, April 18th, 1923. Excerpts of this article appear in previous chapters.

> With a frightened face and a fearful pace the pretty tender stenographer from London ran breathlessly into the Foreign Exchange Department of the American Express Company at Genoa, where Paris was just getting off the telephone line on which Zurich was impatiently trying to get on, and disturbed

the steady buzz of the sunny morning rush with her sudden ghastly appearance.

"...Wild man...!" she managed to blurt out, as she dropped in a fainting condition into the Chief's swivel chair. Water to revive the scared maiden was handy, but not needed: for the hustle and bustle that ensued was sufficient to wake up even the mummy of an Egyptian princess. The Travel Man abandoned his routes, the Foreign Trade Man his markets; the Tariff Man lost sight of his duties, and the Traffic People followed the train of the Office Parade that was headed by 100% of the Office Boys.

And the "Wild Man," who had now come thru the Foreign Exchange Department, which leads onto the front terrace—the sunniest spot of the old palace occupied by the Italian headquarters of the American Express System at Genoa—to have his photograph snapped, proved to be the no less famous and curious object than Mr. H. Martinet, the U.S.A. Globe-Trotter or "Walking Wonder" that is embracing the world with his bare feet.

Walking all over its face—that's what this queer but interesting back-to-nature philosopher is doing to poor old Mother Earth. Like all other mothers however, Mother Earth seems to be treating tolerably the hard leathery feet of the man who started pawing her face at Seattle, Washington, on April 19, 1920—with bare head, bare hands, bare feet, and least but not last: with bare pockets; last but not, by any means, the least: with bear-health and a rigid constitution.

If it were not for his long bushy hair and his short grizzly beard, it would be hard to believe that our "Walking Wonder" was born 43 year ago. Even so, his 5-ft stature and mahogany tanned face and sturdy body, which had been developing so naturally in St. Martinville, La., U.S.A., since May 13, 1878, now appeared full of youthful vigor before the focused camera; and this robust man, with professional running corks firmly gripped in his rough hands, posed like an innocent country boy imbued with the spirit and zest of an Alaskan miner. But the true prototype of this walking American, confirmed somewhat by the fact that he is of French descent, is apparently reflected in his bold and brawny physique as that of a gallant Gaul that never used to worry about buff spats and white collars.

"That junk you've got round your neck may look classy, aw-right, aw-right," said the Globe-Trotter, turning to the Office Dandy who was squirming his neck inside of his high and stiff collar in order to peep over the crowd that gathered around the "Walking Wonder." "But," he continued with a French twang in his voice and with a clean bit of Yankee slang, "my friend, I feel ah...well, a whole lot more comfortable than any of you fellows. All day long yer harnessed up in your fancy outfit. At night you take off yer regalia and wrap y'self with yer pajamas. Ye throw off yer stifling shoes and immediately put on a pair of slippers. I don' wanna preach, y'know; but people sure do need more air and sunshine."

Even if this man did pretend to preach it seems he would be justified in many of his assertions. But he is practicing more than he is preaching. His only traveling implements consist of a strong knap-sack which he carries buckled upon his shoulders in military fashion. An olive-drab shirt, with the sleeves half rolled up, a pair of moleskin trousers that have never been pressed, and a cloth belt bearing "Seattle-New York" around his waist, complete the uniform of this tramping prodigy.

Evidently, then, it was for this radically extreme simplicity in dress that Mr. Martinet had a most peculiar reception when he walked into Butte, Montana, where he was "pinched" and brought to jail by two husky policemen. They charged him with a great many names too long and legal to remember. Then they brought him socks and a pair of shoes and a hat—all with which our world roamer refused to associate. Finally they fetched a doctor—a sort of mental inspector—who performed a scrupulous examination of the prisoner. And the verdict was that "this man may appear insane; but you are all crazy."

At St. Paul, Minn., the Globe-Trotter was especially well-treated. The Naturalist Society invited him to a banquet held in his honor, on which occasion he described the purpose of his undertaking and his general views on natural modes of living. There the newspapers gave him attractive publicity and the community as a whole offered him sensible and generous hospitality.

Because Chicago showed him cold shoulders, the bare-foot traveler did not tarry long at that spot. From that point to New York he abandoned his nap-sack—perhaps to make himself feel light-hearted—and covered the distance on an average of over 50 miles each walking day.

Madison (Wisc.), Detroit, Cleveland, Philadelphia, Trenton (N.J.), and numerous other cities, received and treated him quite cordially. And when he arrived in New York City, August 15, 1920, he was driven in an open car thru the streets, collecting a crowd of people at City Hall, which kept the Knickerbocker cops busy for hours. At Coney Island he attracted circus-attention, and left with bulky proceeds from the sale of the post-cards—a photograph of himself—which he sells to appreciative audiences.

As Neptune is a god whom our "Walking Wonder" is not inclined to serve, he worked his way over on the S.S. "Finland," leaving New York on the 3rd of October, 1920, for Antwerp. From here he walked across Belgium and France, passing Paris without unusual incident, and continued thru Switzerland on a daily trot of 64 kilometers.

In Vichy, the famous water-cure resort, the police concluding from Mr. Martinet's wavy hair, thick beard, and general savage appearance, took him into custody thinking that he had been sent as a Special Undesirable Ambassador from the Soviet government in Russia. Later, as they were escorting him out of the city with the appropriate ceremonies generally extended to uninvited revolutionary and bolshevist leaders, the Globe-Trotter produced his American Passport, which turned the officials into surprised apologists.

Such incidents, however, never discourage this strange and adventurous American. In Geneva, Lausanne, and other Swiss towns he received most satisfactory treatment and interesting consideration.

Italy, according to Mr. Martinet himself, seems to be one of the best places in which he has so far tramped. Italian hospitality, of the simple but northerly-unreserved type, has been his frequent experience during his walk from Milan to Genoa. He is now on his way to Florence; thence to Rome and Brindisi; then avoiding boat-rides as far as possible, he is planning "to take a walk" over to Hong-Kong; then—but, let us first hear how he will fare in the land of Chop Suey.

At a little country place in France, called San Joan, the striving pedestrian was invited for dinner by a kind-looking man who he met in the street. When they got into the house the countryman's wife was frightened into a fainting fit at the wild sight of the "Walking Wonder." The two men worked frantically over her with water and vinegar, and when they brought her back to her senses, she beat both of them out of the house with a kitchen utensil.

In the way of food, our experimental vagabond is not at all fussy—he eats anything and everything he can get hold of. He prefers vegetables; and his favorite dish, whenever he is able to obtain it, is composed of onion juice mixed into warm milk. Although he advocates the simple back-to-nature life, he preaches no "isms" or "shisms." He sleeps eight hours daily—making his bed on sand, gravel or rock if necessary. When he rises—before Old Sol at times—he immediately sets a quick pace and follows the quivers of his compass needle. He is never late on the job; as slow trams and creeping buses do not impede with his daily program.

With but a common school education, this walking observer has built for himself many useful opinions and some practical philosophies about life. "A man traveling has more chance for education through constant adventure and contact with human nature than a college professor," he wisely puts it. "I can tell how broad-minded a man is, or how little ...he has, by the way he takes interest in me or when ...me up on account of my shabby and unattractive appearance."

When Mr. Martinet returns from his world-promenade he intends to settle down, taking unto himself a nature-loving wife, and write a book narrating his curious experiences—especially treating "Man's Amusements."

One of the best bits of advice this walking thinker offers—enthusiastically and free of charge—concerns the health of people in general and, particularly, the welfare of men who are getting bald or gray hair: "You can't restore your hair or your health by using a lot of Pinkham's Pink Pills for Pale People. Neither is it necessary for you to take a walk around the world, nor live as I do now. But, by cutting out many artificial and unnatural habits, and substituting sane and clean ones, you can expect to get back health—and your hair, too, if you can manage to get heaps of sunshine everyday. Sleep about eight hours. Dress simply—wear light clothing. Eat plenty of vegetables—masticate your food thoroughly at all times. Drink lots of fresh water. Add 'member—you

> can't get too much sunshine (if you avoid sudden sun-burns)—either on your body or on your bright bald billiard ball."
>
> Thus our stalwart "Walking Wonder," gripping his running corks in his hands with a visibly nervous tension, started in a quick gait on a path that soon led him out of the stuffy city into the open road along the winding river. And as his straight and nimble figure was gradually diminishing on the perspective of the serpentine road, it seemed as if the cool and wistful autumn breezes were humming:
>
> "There is something in October
> sets the gypsy blood astir: We
> must rise and follow her, When
> from every hill of flame She calls
> and calls, each vagabond by name."

I loved everything about this comprehensive, light-hearted article. It even inspired me to try Hippolyte's favorite dish, onion juice in warm milk. Bless whoever made this for him because my eyes streamed with tears as I put part of a brown onion through a press. I poured the juice into some warm milk and gave it a try. The concoction burned my throat a bit, so I added some salt and freshly ground pepper and the mixture was only slightly more palatable. It might be an acquired taste. Perhaps I need to try it a few more times before I actually enjoy it. As I recall, that worked with Brussel sprouts… and beer.

I was especially entertained by the story of Hippolyte accepting a dinner invitation from the "kind-looking man" whose wife chased my uncle out of the house wielding a kitchen utensil. I'd love to know what this woman armed herself with: a meat mallet, an eggbeater, a wooden spoon or was it the ubiquitous cast iron skillet? While nobody chased Doug and me away with any sort of implement, we were refused lodging at several hotels. This was, on one occasion, achieved by simply ignoring our presence and a few times by shouting at us until we left. Initially, we assumed we were being judged on our disheveled appearances—and sometimes we were—though I can hardly blame anyone. However, more often than not, I assume it was because we had entered hotels that weren't licensed to rent to Western tourists. Regardless, I am certain there were times when unlicensed hotel owners took pity on us and gave us a room anyway, despite the risk to themselves.

The article managed to be comical without mocking my uncle or ridiculing his lofty endeavor. It's the only article about Hippolyte that even remotely points to his intelligence. Lieb acknowledges that my uncle is different, quirky even, but then actually refers to Hippolyte as a philosopher. I'm not sure everyone perceived him this way and I'm touched that Lieb elevated my uncle's status from "wild man" to deep thinker. Hippolyte wasn't just an aimless vagabond. He had a purpose.

Later in the article, Hippolyte relayed his intention of settling down with a mate. Lieb phrased it in almost biblical terms, "taking unto himself a nature-loving wife." My gut tells me that "nature-loving wife" were Hippolyte's words. I can sense his loneliness, and the romantic in me is sad that he and this woman never got to meet and spend the rest of their lives together. In the same vein, I think I actually missed Doug before I ever met him. My life was busy and satisfying, but when Doug came along, he filled a space I had almost forgotten existed. I can't imagine any aspect of my future without him. He makes every load bearable.

When I learned Hippolyte had given his backpack to a motorist to carry for him in Indiana, I assumed he would have been without his belongings for a few brief hours. As the article explains, Hippolyte didn't get his possessions back until he arrived in New York, approximately 791 miles away! If my uncle walked from 6:00 am until 8:00 pm at 3.5 miles per hour, he would have covered the fifty-mile-a-day distance he claimed and would have been without his backpack for a little over two weeks. I remember the day Doug and I dragged ourselves out of the quarry and decided to mail items home from our backpacks. Once mine was pared down, there wasn't one item in my bag I could imagine parting with. Even a couple pounds lighter, there were days I would have gladly handed it off. Like him, I could have traveled further and faster without it. However, I never could have accomplished fifty miles in a single day. The best Doug and I had managed was twenty-three. Most days, we were averaging a little over seventeen—the last quarter to half-mile or so usually spent wandering streets looking for unmarked, mismarked or non-existent hotels.

The Lieb article helped me feel closer to my uncle through shared experiences. Hippolyte commented, "I can tell how broadminded a man is or how little he has by the way he takes interest in me... on account of my shabby appearance." This observation hit home with me and I found myself excitedly saying, "Yes, yes!" after our return home as I pored over the article again. People in China took tremendous interest in us. Drivers pulled over on the highway, gave us bottled water and bags of fruit, and politely asked for group photos. Lagging behind Doug one afternoon, I summited the rise of a hill, came around a curve in the road and was greeted with applause. Ahead of me, Doug waited with a group of motorists standing beside their car. They continued to cheer me on as I walked up to join them. One of the men gave me a hearty pat on my shoulder and handed me a bottle of cold water. I was sweaty and disheveled, hot and exhausted, but rather than treating me like an urchin, I was welcomed with grins and enthusiasm. Since then, I've never experienced anything as rejuvenating. I couldn't help but return their smiles and enjoy the sweetest, coldest, most refreshing water.

When Doug and I stopped at restaurants, the owners or servers would invariably begin speaking to us in rapid fire Mandarin. Since our meager language skills were quickly exhausted, we usually resorted to handing over one of our postcards, which would be passed around the restaurant. Seeing their enthusiasm and interest, I would eagerly hand out more cards; every card I gave away meant one less ounce I had to carry on my back. After finishing our meal, Doug and I would pull out our money and ask for the check. More times than we could count, our money was refused. Eventually, Doug and I had to have a discussion. We even posed the question on our website and, despite feedback telling us otherwise, we agreed that in the future we had to pay for our meals before we handed out our postcards. We made this decision because we noticed a clear pattern. The people who had the least to give were the most generous. I know this was exactly what Hippolyte was referring to when he said he could "tell how little someone has by the way he takes interest in me."

Twice, motorists pulled over and offered us money. On one occasion, Doug was offered enough money to support us for two or three days. On another day, a man offered me a comparable sum. Both times we politely refused but gave the men cards and asked them to leave an encouraging message on our website.

Another day, we passed an open garage where a group of people were packaging loose tea leaves. They came out to meet us on the sidewalk, so we gave each of them a card. After reading hers, a young woman looked at me, gathered her thoughts, and said to us in English, "This is meaningful. I want to help." I loved her phrasing because it was so succinct and precise. Our walk was incredibly meaningful to me and it pleased me to no end that she understood me and took interest. We pointed to our web address printed on the bottom of the card and asked her to leave words of motivation and support. That's all we wanted from anyone.

Some people politely took our cards, read them, and walked off with little reaction. However, many people read our cards and then looked back at us with astonishment. College students always responded with keen interest and several times Doug and I had to turn down their generous offers of gallons of bottled water, energy drinks and other road provisions because it was too much for us to carry. I think what we were doing resonated with them. Many children in China live with their grandparents because their parents are off working in big cities. Some of these children see their parents once every two years. Maybe these youths appreciated our desire to honor an elder. I believe our walk also resonated with older men who perhaps recognized they were living their final years. Maybe like me they think that death truly comes not when you draw your last breath, but when people stop saying your name and invoking your image. It was these men who read our postcard, looked at me and smiled. I hope on some level they too felt honored by what we were doing. I also hope that somewhere, on some plane, Hippolyte is hearing his name.

One afternoon after putting in a good nineteen miles, I sat on the edge of our bed, freshly showered, hair air-drying into a wiry mess. As I bent over to put on my shoes, I groaned loudly. Hearing Doug chuckle, I asked, "What?" feeling a little self-conscious but too exhausted to really care. Doug reached over and touched my hair. "You're beginning to look like him!" "Like who?" I asked. "Like your uncle, Hippolyte," Doug answered, as if he could possibly be talking about anybody else. "Look," he said and held up a finger for me to wait as he pulled up our website on his phone. He found the photograph of Hippolyte, took my hand and led me to a mirror. I looked at the image of my uncle and then at my own reflection. I was a wreck. Despite wearing sunblock and a hat, my face was getting tanned brown, making the lines around my eyes stand out. The backs of my hands looked like leather and my hair, ravaged by the sun and humidity, resembled that of a troll doll. I then looked down at my bare feet. Even though I scrubbed them every night, they were still filthy. I had taped moleskin to my blisters and no matter how hard I tried, I could never completely rid the surrounding skin of the gummy residue that had now turned black.

Regardless, I asked Doug to take my photo. I sat on the foot of our bed while Doug told me where to place my feet and how to arrange my hands so I was posed to resemble Hippolyte in his portrait photo. He took the picture and showed it to me. My hair was thick and wavy like Hippolyte's, though I would have described my appearance as *feral* rather than savage. Ordinarily, I would have been mortified by my appearance, but instead of feeling ashamed, unattractive or embarrassed, I felt proud. I *was* beginning to look like him.

Me beginning to look like Hippolyte

Hippolyte

CHAPTER THIRTY

Missed Mail In Italy

Although I'm uncertain of his exact route, Hippolyte likely followed the Mediterranean coast until the curving waterfront of Genoa came into view. This city, occupied since the fifth or fourth millennium BC, would have beckoned Hippolyte to explore deeper into Italy, home to fifty-five UNESCO World Heritage sites, more than any other country in the world. Genoa boasts both Gothic and Renaissance architecture. Pastel-colored buildings line narrow lanes, inviting travelers to wander until finding themselves in any one of several Grand Squares. Trams, the first one built in 1909, take passengers from Piazza Portello up the steep hillside to the Palazzo Rosso. The Palazzo Rosso houses one of the most important art galleries in Genoa. From the rooftop of the Palazzo, one can enjoy a view of the city and plan a tour.

From Genoa, Hippolyte continued ninety miles south to Milan. Today it is a city equated with high fashion rather than being home to one of the most famous and familiar works of religious art. I've often wondered what my uncle's spiritual beliefs were. In a letter to his brother-in-law, he signed off with "God Bless." I'm inclined to think that even if he weren't a religious man, he wouldn't have passed up the opportunity to visit the refectory of the Church of Santa Maria delle Grazie to see the second most famous painting of all time, Leonardo da Vinci's *The Last Supper*. To see it now requires booking reservations two to three weeks in advance.

After Milan, it was another 190 miles to Florence. He might have visited the Duomo, but if he didn't, it would be nearly impossible to not see the iconic cathedral, capped with the terracotta-tiled dome. While in Florence, Hippolyte would have had the opportunity to see other famous works of art including Botticelli's *Birth of Venus* as well as *Annunciation,* painted by twenty-year-old Leonardo de Vinci with his master, Verrocchio. The Uffizi Gallery, built in the 1500s, displays both works. It has housed the art collection of the Medici family for the last several centuries.

One hundred and eighty miles further south, Hippolyte arrived in Rome, where he wrote another letter to Prosper.

> Rome 5th of October 1921
>
> Dear Friend-
>
> I have written to you from Nice (France) and to sister from Geneva (Swisse) and since I have been unable to hear from you, I am in Rome reaching here from Florence. Italy is a beautiful country and I have the best of experiences, since the World with my own eager eyes and when back home I shall have to tell the long long story.
>
> The experience I had while crossing the border of France into Switzerland, how the people received me and were glad to see me to their land. The difference between the two countries has been for me great experiences.
>
> Anyhow I am doing well, I do hope you well and happy.
>
> Do write to me. I will be glad to hear from you and do please mail me all letters to Alexandria Egypt—C/O The American Express Co.—I will proceed by tomorrow or after to Naples visiting Pompeii and then to Brindisi where I jump on a boat to Egypt. Hoping you well and happy, God bless you.
>
> I remain yours
> Very truly—
> Hippolyte
> C/O the Am. Exp. Co Alexandria Egypt

True to his word, Hippolyte passed through Naples, and his visit there was picked up by two newspapers back home. *The New York Herald* ran the story on page four on October 18th, 1921, and North Carolina's *High Point Enterprise* ran the same article on the 20th.

REACHES NAPLES IN WALK

> NAPLES, Oct. 18—Hippolyte Martinet, an American who is on a walking tour around the world, arrived here to-day on his way to Egypt. Martinet says he left Seattle, Wash, in April, 1920.

When I began traveling internationally, almost no one I knew, including myself, had email. It was years before internet cafes and Skype, which now allow me to send and receive instant communications from anywhere on the planet. Because I've almost always taken advantage of my long summer and winter holidays—often traveling alone for eight weeks at a stretch—I'm intimately familiar with the feeling of having fun and not wanting to go home while at the same time feeling completely isolated despite being surrounded by people.

Thus, I can almost feel Hippolyte's aching disappointment after going to the post office in hopes of receiving a letter from home and not finding one waiting for him, the one thing that might have helped him feel tethered as he walked from state to state, country to country and continent to continent. I see him standing in line, watching anxiously as the people ahead of him are served. When it's finally his turn, he politely asks for mail addressed to him. The postal worker leaves to search for an envelope and Hippolyte's heart quickens with the anticipation of seeing his name penned on an envelope in familiar handwriting. I can feel his heart sink when the postal worker returns empty-handed.

After Rome, Hippolyte ventured further south. He never made it home to tell his "long, long story," but I can easily imagine that he would want to share his sense of awe when standing before these centuries-old monuments. Their histories are fascinating. It sometimes took several centuries before they were completed. The men who envisioned and designed many of them never lived to see their dreams realized. These monuments are staggering in both their beauty and scale. They are symbols of history and religion, but because of the massive amounts of resources and labor that went into their construction, my perception is that they are also symbols of strength, wealth and man's perceived power. In contrast, the city of Pompeii pays homage to man's powerlessness, fragility and temporality.

More than any other place, I want to know what Hippolyte thought about Pompeii, the city that was destroyed August 24th, 79 AD when Mount Vesuvius, only five miles away, erupted at noon and continued to spew ash and pumice on the city below for eighteen uninterrupted hours. The next morning, the cone of the volcano collapsed, and a massive avalanche of mud and ash flooded the city. The lost city was eventually rediscovered and unearthed in 1738 when construction began on a palace for Charles of Bourbon, the king of Spain.

These casts of lovers and families, of parents with their bodies curled protectively around their own children, were so profound and impacted me so deeply that I was inspired to earn a degree in anthropology. They charted the course of my life for several years. What did Hippolyte feel when he saw them? Was he as moved as I was? Did he think about the sons he left behind? Did he feel guilty? While Hippolyte mourned the absence of mail, did his sons also anxiously await mail from their father? Did he write to them at all?

CHAPTER THIRTY-ONE

Camping

As we were planning for our trip, my goal was to avoid camping in China as much as possible for one reason only. I didn't want the extra weight in my backpack. However, I was converted after we camped the very first day of our walk, that sincerely enchanted evening when we pitched our tent near the edge of the village garbage dump. Afterward, I wanted nothing more than to sleep in the countryside. I will never forget waking up in the cool of that first morning when Doug and I swore we could hear the howl of a lone wolf, a haunting sound that would bewitch and delight us nearly every morning thereafter.

Unfortunately, suitable camping areas were rare, and even though our tent had a footprint of roughly forty square feet, we struggled to find an empty plot of land big enough to accommodate it. If an area wasn't strewn with garbage, something edible was planted in the spot. Even when there were no houses or people to be seen, there were always a few stalks of corn or exotic looking squash growing alongside the highway. These little patches were weed-free and clearly well-tended. We even saw vegetable gardens planted in the dirt on highway medians. Covered in road grime, these plants adapted to being blown sideways by semi-trucks and were somehow surviving and feeding people. It may be that the Chinese simply enjoy gardening, but I suspected there was a more compelling reason.

I have no idea what China was like before the Great Famine, but I think it is possible that the practice of planting vegetable gardens on any available plot of land, regardless how small, was in part a reaction to what the Chinese refer to as the "Three Bitter Years." It is estimated that twenty to forty-five million people starved to death between the years of 1959-1961. The famine impacted fertility rates and another forty million failed to be born, bringing the population loss to an estimated seventy-six million.

Today, the Chinese government says the cause of the famine was thirty percent natural disaster and seventy percent mismanagement, although immediately after the famine, the Chinese Government referred to it as "The Three Years of Natural Disasters." Outside sources blame institutional and policy changes that were part of "The Great Leap Forward," the social and economic campaign instituted by Chairman Mao Zedong, leader of the Communist Party of China. The goal was to rapidly transform the country from an agrarian economy into a socialist society where private land ownership was prohibited and mandatory agriculture collectives enforced. The cultivation of private plots was strictly prohibited and thereby punishable.

In an effort to ensure the country's economic advancement, millions of farmers were forced to walk away from their fields and join the steel and iron production effort. The farmers who remained in the field were required to adopt new farming practices. They began planting crop seedlings closer and closer together—first three times closer and then twice closer still. The belief that plants of the same species would not compete with one another proved untrue and resulted in stunted plant growth and substantially lower yields. Farmers were also ordered to adopt a practice called "deep plowing." Previously, standard practice was to plow to a depth of six to seven inches. The theory this time was that more fertile soil lies deeper below the surface. So, by governmental decree, farmers began to plow to a depth of three to six feet. In many areas, the most fertile soil was actually at the surface. In areas of shallow soil, rocks and sand were pulled to the surface while fertile topsoil was turned over and buried at the bottom. This practice also resulted in substantial decreases in yields. (The U.S. was in part responsible for a similar disaster, the Dust Bowl, which began in 1930 and ended in 1940. Bad farming practices, poor understanding of plains ecology and drought caused severe dust storms that swept from Texas to Nebraska, killing people and livestock.)

This time, the lower yields were blamed on the tree sparrow and other wild birds. The government responded swiftly with the "Kill a Sparrow" campaign and citizens were organized to eradicate the perceived scourge. Posters depicted patriotic children armed with slingshots doing their civic duty by killing the winged pests. Adults shot birds down from the sky. People gathered with drums or pots and pans and chased the birds from place to place until the frightened animals eventually fell from the skies, dead from exhaustion. They raided nests, crushing eggs and baby birds. Thousands of birds took refuge in various diplomatic embassies, the only place they were safe. In Beijing, the Polish embassy denied a request for Chinese to enter their premises to destroy the birds. Not to be deterred, mobs of people turned up with pots and drums, banging continuously for two days until the birds were dead. Employees of the Polish embassy used shovels to scoop up the masses of dead birds. Some species were hunted to near extinction. Sadly, it was not understood that grains were only a small part of the bird diet and that they also ate insects.

With no predators to keep them in check, the insect population exploded, and in a show of biblical proportions, swarms of locusts and other insects devoured nearly everything. Crop yields fell by seventy percent. Eventually, the Chinese government had to import sparrows from the Soviet Union.

Peasant farmers were expected to satisfy growing quotas. They were only allowed to consume what they grew after their obligation had been satisfied. But because of the newly adopted farming practices and rampant insect populations, it was nearly impossible for quotas to be met. Farmers were accused of hoarding and profiteering—activities that were labeled "counter-revolutionary." Many people survived by eating grass and tree bark. Peasants died of starvation at a rate three times that of the city-dwelling population.

Yu Dehong, secretary of a party official between 1959 and 1960, relayed, "I went to one village and saw 100 corpses, then another village and another 100 corpses. No one paid attention to them. People said that dogs were eating the bodies. 'Not true,' I said. 'The dogs had long ago been eaten by the people.'"

The repercussions are still felt today. Older Chinese who survived the famine, much like survivors of our own Great Depression, take frugality to extremes. No scrap of food is thrown away. Everything is saved and reused over and over. Again, in the 1980s, there were food shortages in China. Ration tickets were distributed, and every month a family of three would receive one ticket for seventeen ounces of meat, one for nine ounces of sugar, and one for seventeen ounces of oil. Fabric was also meted out. These ration tickets were given out at the beginning of Chinese New Year. The allotted fabric was usually enough to make one item of clothing. A neighbor of mine grew up in mainland China. I asked if I could interview her about the famine that ended seven years before she was born. She told me that as a child her parents spoke several times about the famine. She remembers seeing very real fear wash over their faces as they relived the horror of those three bitter years. When I was a child, my mother would encourage me to eat by telling me, "There are children starving in China," a tactic that now seems exploitative. I know that I have never truly felt hunger.

Regardless of who or what was responsible for the famine, Mao's reputation was untarnished. Even people who survived the famine still revere Mao. Right or wrong, blame was placed elsewhere. Despite the fact that it is no longer legally required to have a picture of Mao displayed in one's business, his portrait is nonetheless prominently displayed in many homes and businesses. Several times, either in restaurants or in our hotel room, Doug and I saw movies in which a young, handsome and saintly Mao walked through fields dispensing advice to humble peasants who grinned while clutching their hats to their chests, elated to be honored with a visit from their beloved leader. When Mao walks off, presumably to minister to another peasant, the farmer returns to his labors, his face plastered with a huge grin, singing as he works the soil with a crude implement.

As Doug and I journeyed through China, we watched as farmers coaxed water buffalo who pulled the same ancient-looking implements through calf-deep water. These plows were made from scrap lumber and dull, rusted blades or a simple, sharp stick for tilling soil; we were transported back in time. It could have been any century. The occasional car that passed us on the highway was our only clue that the year was 2015.

After camping on the rim of the garbage dump, it was less than a week before we found a place to camp again. Doug and I noticed a nectarine tree at one end of a garden plot beside a modest house. Because nothing would grow in the shade of the fruit tree, the level land beneath it looked like a perfect place to pitch our tent. We introduced ourselves to the residents and handed them one of our cards. Next, we showed them our query, written in Chinese characters, a request to camp on their property. After reading it, the husband looked at me and said a few words. From the expression on his face, I interpreted his utterance as, "Of course you can camp here." From what we were able to gather, they supported themselves by selling water to semi-truck drivers. I don't know how truck drivers in the U.S. maintain temperature on their brakes, but trucks in China are outfitted with tanks that spray water on the brakes and tires. We were often misted when trucks passed as we walked along the highway shoulder; depending on the time of day, it was either a blessing or a curse.

We stepped into their garden and set up our tent. Young plants grew in orderly rows across most of the one-acre lot. The plot looked like it could have been flooded and used for growing rice. Perhaps that backbreaking work was better suited for the young. Across the highway, a house sat up on a hillside. A dog in the yard barked at us as we hung our sweaty clothes to dry. Thinking the dog would stop barking if it couldn't see us, we retired inside the tent. For dinner, we ate our trail snacks—some almonds and a package of corn chips that tasted surprisingly like sweet corn.

As soon as it got dark, we put in our earplugs. This muted the noise a bit, but the dog continued to bark on and off for the rest of the night. We felt terrible because our hosts had done us such a kind favor and were rewarded by having their sleep disturbed. That is, we felt terrible until we realized that every hour or so, a train passed on the hillside above us and blew its horn. The first time it happened, Doug and I bolted upright, thinking we had mistakenly pitched our tent across its tracks and were about to be run over. As soon as the blare of the horn faded, we could hear the dog across the road resume its role as sentry. Still, we were tired enough to sleep at least ten hours.

The next morning, the dog finally took a break from barking to play with what might have been its only source of entertainment, a dirty rag that it tossed into the air, caught with its teeth, and then thrashed around. Occasionally he would let it fall to the ground, leap into the air and pounce on it with its front paws. With our belongings packed, we walked back up to our host's house to say goodbye and give thanks. I mimed washing my face and the wife directed me to the hose the truckers used to fill their water tanks. Before she went back inside she warned me, again through gesture, not to drink the water. While I washed up, I admired our mutual abilities to communicate so well without words. By the time I had dried off, she emerged with a large bag of nectarines and pushed them towards me.

Doug pulled out his camera and mimed taking a photo of them and they both nodded, giving us permission. The woman stepped back into her house and from the open doorway I could see her straightening her hair. She called to her husband, who buttoned his shirt at the collar as he walked inside, beckoning to Doug and I. The photo could have been taken outdoors in the drive where semis refilled their water tanks. Instead, in an intimate gesture, they invited us into their single room home. Doug took their photo as they stood in the center of the room—the kitchen area to the left, their bed on the right side, and the toilet outside and across the parking lot—presumably so truckers could use it as well. When I look at their photo now, the word that comes to mind is *dignified*. This couple had carved out a livelihood for themselves in their little plot beside the highway and below the train trestle, where they grew and thrived together like the corn and taro they tended beside the nectarine tree that had sheltered us for the night.

I thought about my own life and the value I find in the work I do. I thought about the work that we all do, no more or less important than that of anyone else. If you think about it, we all rely upon and sustain one another to some extent. And I thought about my own home with its multiple rooms and two bathrooms. In comparison, it seemed... obscene. Did I need so much?

CHAPTER THIRTY-TWO

"Little Albania"

In my day to day life, I am regimented and follow a precise schedule. When something interrupts the order that I try so hard to maintain, I become anxious and can be a real pill. However, travel has taught me the importance of flexibility. Unforeseen circumstances occasionally demand abandoning plans, and though sometimes I balk, to my surprise I have learned that change isn't always bad. Hippolyte's original plan was to go from Brindisi to Egypt, but he wasn't able for reasons unknown to me. I don't know how he initially reacted, but judging from the contents of his letter, it appears that in the end, he had no regrets. Had Hippolyte been able to follow his itinerary and taken a ferry from Brindisi to Egypt, he would have missed out on what's arguably the best hospitality in the world and what clearly turned out to be a cherished experience in a country called Albania. Forty-nine days after leaving Italy and still mourning the absence of mail in Rome, Hippolyte penned another letter to his brother-in-law.

Salonica Graece

11-23-1921

Friend Prosper

I was very disappointed in Rome for I fail to have a line from you at said address, but hope to find same at Alexandry Egypt, will sail from this port next day or so for Egypt, thus far doing splendid in my traveling having travel Belgain, France, Switzerland, Italy, Albany at this writing in Greace but no good to me the best of all was little Albania was welcome in there as a King not as a hobo. The only country I was taken care of by the Government—beside that sold more postcard than any other country.

Now to post you all on the future that's to say in case I'm successful as in the past will make Egypt, British India China Japan from Tokyo back to Seattle and then for a good rest with good folks I a lot of story to tell. You may read a story of my voage long before that time for this reason I met a young American writer in Italy & he wrote a very interesting story of my intired life on the road same will published in some New York magazine up to you to find the story. Can't give you the name of the magazine thus far. I and doggy doing fine with best wishes for you.

Your friend, H Martinet Globe Trotter.

PS the picture was taken as a present to me in the biggest town of Albany therefore would like to have them whenever I settle back home as a remembrance of said little country.

In his letter to Prosper, Hippolyte referenced an article written by an American journalist in Italy. This was the Lieb article. My forty-three-year-old uncle refers to Lieb, ten years his junior, as the "young American." I suspect the Lieb article may be one of the only articles written about him that he had the opportunity to read. Other pieces printed in local publications likely escaped his notice because he was always on the move. Some of the articles were found by my cousins years later when conducting their own research into our uncle's life. The town Hippolyte mentioned as being Albania's biggest was likely Durazzo and it is still one of Albania's largest cities and ports.

I was intrigued by Hippolyte's mention of being hosted by the Albanian government. I had no idea what he meant by this. I imagine Hippolyte being issued a document he could produce that would help him procure food. I did some research on "little Albania" and learned that the country is famed for its hospitality. The concept is so deeply ingrained into their culture that, in my opinion, it makes Albania one of the most remarkable countries in the world, and I think Hippolyte would agree.

Besa is a sworn oath to trust and have faith and goes back to the 15th

Picture taken as a present to Hippolyte

century. Combined with the Code of Lekë Dukagjini, the belief that one's household belongs to God first and then the guest, it makes Albania a country with unparalleled hospitality. There was a time in Albania when a traveler could knock on any door, ask to be accommodated for the evening and then be invited in for a meal and given a bed. In fact, the Code of Lekë Dukagjini explicitly states that every home should have a spare bed ready for whoever knocked, be they pauper or royalty.

King Zog of Albania was Europe's only Muslim leader. He began his political career as prime minister, then became president and finally declared himself King. He was brutal, had his political opponents murdered, stifled the press, and survived fifty-five assassination attempts. He was exiled twice, once in 1924 and again in 1939. I like to call King Zog *The Despot with a Heart* because, despite ruling Albania with an iron fist, he saved the lives of 2,000 Jews during World War II. In 1939 while exiled in London, he ordered Albanian diplomats throughout Europe to issue visas and passports to Jews requesting protection. He also ordered

Albanian border guards to ignore obviously fake documents and to allow any Jew entry into the country. Once they arrived, they were taken in by families and given jobs. In the town of Berat alone, thirty-eight families took in 600 Jews.

While under Italian occupation, the Albanian government defiantly refused to hand over lists of Jews. But later, when Italy capitulated and Albania was occupied by Germany, it was clear that Jews were no longer safe in the cities. Almost overnight, they were issued Albanian documents with traditional Albanian names. They were secreted into the mountainsides and hidden in plain sight where they worked as shepherds. Throughout the war, no Jew was ever denounced to the German occupiers. Those who couldn't be taken in by Albanian families in the mountains were admitted into hospitals. When German soldiers came in to search, doctors told them that the wards where Jews were hidden were under typhoid fever quarantine, prompting the German soldiers to leave without inspecting. Albania was the only country to have a Jewish population higher at the end of the war than at the beginning. Albert Einstein emigrated to the U.S. through Albania after a German magazine published a list of "Enemies of the German Regime" who had "not yet hanged" and offered a $5,000 bounty for his capture. Over 80 years later, Einstein is still one of America's most treasured public figures.

Every country has its jewels. You won't always see them mentioned in travel books. They are local secrets that tourists rarely get to experience because they simply don't know they exist. While in China, Doug and I met a young man who bore a strong resemblance to a handsome and famous Chinese actor. While visiting with him, we had no idea why every young girl who passed us did a double take. Had we been familiar with Chinese cinema, we certainly would have noticed. If he hadn't revealed this to us, we never would have known he was the doppelganger of one of the country's biggest heartthrobs. He would have been just another anonymous face in a sea of people.

While not exactly hidden, Albania's Burrnesha may at first seem cryptic, even secretive, as though they are trying to conceal their true identities. One could easily pass a Burrnesha and never know they were in the presence of someone so highly revered and respected within their own culture. The Burrnesha is seen as being *complete.* Outwardly, the Burrnesha look male despite the fact they are biologically female. For the Burrnesha, the transformation has nothing to do with gender identity or sexuality. It is an act of courage, sacrifice and altruism achieved by making a solemn oath in the presence of village or tribal elders.

The decision is sometimes made for her when she is an infant or young child. Occasionally, a young woman makes the decision herself to avoid an arranged marriage without bringing shame to her family or dishonoring the groom's family. Most women take the oath when the family patriarch has died and there is no other able male family member to provide for them. Forsaking everything that is female and committing to a lifetime of chastity, the Sworn Virgin can then and only then support her family.

Once the oath is taken, for all intents and purposes, the Sworn Virgin is considered a man. A male name is adopted, male pronouns are used and only then can the Sworn Virgin inherit property or money, vote, drive, conduct business, drink, smoke, play music, wear trousers and use a firearm. The Sworn Virgins wear men's clothing, do male work, socialize with men, and act as head of household. Sometimes a woman becomes a Burrnesha to replace a deceased, married brother. The Burrnesha becomes a father to his children, who will call him Baba, *Dad,* but is not considered a husband to the wife. If there is a blood feud, it becomes the Sworn Virgin's obligation to seek vengeance and spill the blood of the enemy family. Only rarely can the oath be broken.

At the outbreak of World War I, Albania descended into anarchy as various tribes and regions rebelled against the idea of central rule. Greece, in an effort to protect its own minority population, did its best to establish control in the southern districts. In response, Italy sent in troops. Serbia and Montenegro took control of the northern regions, but Serbia was soon chased out by the Austro-Hungarian army. One can only assume that under this kind of chaos, men died and families lost patriarchs. Factor in lives lost during the Spanish Flu pandemic of 1918 and it would make sense that under these circumstances, the number of Sworn Virgins would have grown exponentially. If this was true, I can't help wonder if Hippolyte encountered any Burrnesha. What would my forward-thinking uncle have thought of these heroes? I also have to wonder what one of Albania's Burrnesha, who make one of the most life-altering sacrifices imaginable for the sake of their family think of the man who had abandoned his sons. Today, it is estimated that between forty and several hundred Sworn Virgins exist, but since modern Albanian women have more rights and near equal social status, the Burrnesha are a dying breed.

After Albania, Hippolyte headed south into Greece where, in the letter he wrote from Salonika, he shared his travel experiences with Prosper. I think Hippolyte was so taken with "little Albania" that he said nothing about his travels in Greece. From Salonika, Hippolyte traveled by sea through the Bay of Thermaikos, passing Greek isles as he was transported from one country of antiquities to another. As beautiful and inspired as this leg of his journey sounds, my heart is drawn back to the country that welcomed my uncle as a king rather than a hobo.

CHAPTER THIRTY-THREE

Am I On Drugs?

For a portion of our walk through China, Doug and I had to take a daily pill to prevent malaria. Antimalarials need to be taken while traveling in a malarial region and for a month after leaving. The first time I took antimalarial medication was in 1992 when I went to India. I was prescribed a once-weekly rather than a daily pill. This particular medication has since been banned for use by the military in several countries because of its neuropsychiatric side effects. The effects can include dizziness, tinnitus, loss of balance, memory impairment, agitation, confusion, insomnia, vivid dreams, nightmares, olfactory, visual and auditory hallucinations, anxiety, panic attacks, paranoia, persecutory delusions, dissociative psychosis, anterograde amnesia, depression and suicidal ideation. Central nervous system events that require hospitalization occur in roughly one in every 10,000 individuals who take it. The milder events, such as dizziness, headaches, insomnia and vivid dreams occur in about twenty-five percent of the people who take this drug. The auditory and visual hallucinations occur in about thirteen percent of people who take it. I am in that thirteen percent.

Although it is still occasionally prescribed in the U.S. among the civilian population, I will never take it again. It gave me the most epically terrifying visual hallucinations. I awoke one night in my seven dollar a night hotel room in Bombay to find a man with a face like a camel standing beside my bed in eerie silence. I sat up terrified but afraid to move. How had this stranger gotten into my room when the door was padlocked from inside? I stared at him for what felt like at least a minute, rubbing my eyes, blinking and looking at him again and again. He supported himself with a crude, wooden crutch padded with tattered rags. I surveyed the man in his entirety. In the dim light I could see the loosely woven fabric of his stained clothes, the rubber sandals on his feet and his long, dirty toenails. Then he held out a hand, palm up. I wanted to scream but was unable. "Please go away," I tried to mutter as I pulled my knees up to my chest and covered my face with my hands. Ten seconds later I looked up, he was gone, and I was once again alone in my room. I got out of bed, ran to the door and gave the padlock a few firm tugs to make sure that it was indeed locked.

Weeks later in London and still taking the medication as prescribed, I awoke suddenly in my garret room and sat up in bed. From the corner of the room, a line of smoky, ethereal, oval shapes floated towards me. As they neared, they became clearer. Evil looking, menacing skulls, their mandibles mutely opening and closing, loomed nearer and nearer. They were even more frightening than the camel man. Each skull that drifted up and over my head disappeared through the wall behind me. I was so terrified that my body shook from head to toe as though I was being electrocuted. Again I shut my eyes, but this time I clasped my hands over my mouth to stifle the scream I wasn't able to muster. When I opened my eyes, they were all gone. Both of these hallucinations happened before I was aware of the side effects of this particular medicine. At the time, I considered the possibility that I was being drugged, but I was traveling alone and the hallucinations had happened on different continents. In my mind, the only logical answer was that I was going crazy.

The vivid dreams can be just as disturbing. In one such dream, I woke to discover that I had gotten a massive tattoo. I don't have anything against tattoos, per se. I like that people express themselves creatively, using their bodies as canvasses. They just aren't for me. That being said, I was mortified when I saw my backside was plastered with an Al Roker and Kermit the Frog tramp stamp. Al and Kermie's arms were thrown over each other's shoulders and they grinned widely as if in the throes of a hypomanic episode. I woke from my dream in a state of panic and confusion, my mind racing as I tried to sort out when it could have happened, whether or not I had been drunk, and how I could possibly get rid of it in a time before the advent of laser tattoo removal. With my heart thudding in my chest, I jumped out of bed, ran to the mirror, craned my head over my shoulder and turned in circles trying to look at my backside. Nothing. I don't think I've ever been so relieved in my life.

Because of the nightmares and hallucinations, I now harbor deep mistrust for all antimalarials and only take them reluctantly because I know what potentially lies in store for me. As a consequence, regardless of what oddity I may be witnessing while awake, my initial reaction is to chalk it all up to that little pill I take every day.

Once you've woken up to camel man, floating skulls and bad decision tattoos, the balance problems caused by this drug seem relatively benign. The first time I stumbled in China occurred while walking up the three flights of stairs to our hotel room, I attributed it to my poor coordination. I do this frequently on the stairs in my home. Seconds later when I stubbed my toe on the riser of a stair, I blamed it on physical exhaustion. With my very next step, I lurched forward and stopped my fall with my hands as my foot came crashing down on the step below. By the fourth time I stumbled, I blamed the antimalarials. Even I am not normally this clumsy. Then Doug nearly took a tumble and observantly pointed out that none of the stairs were even. I looked at the remainder of the staircase that rose in front of me and couldn't believe I hadn't noticed it myself. It wasn't just the risers that were different heights; the treads were also different widths from one step to the next. I don't think any two steps in that staircase were the same height or dimension. International building codes that dictate that stair risers be four to seven inches high and treads at least eleven inches deep are of little relevance in a place where additions to homes are made piecemeal by homeowners when finances and time permit.

We were only three weeks into our travels when time began to behave strangely. Something would trigger a memory and either Doug or I would remark, "Remember when we stayed at the place with the..." or "Remember the time we saw the...?" The odd thing was that even though it felt like the event had occurred months ago, what we were reminiscing about had only happened the week before. It was surreal. I think it was because we were seeing so many new and strangely beautiful things that our senses were overloaded. These experiences were piling up on one another until the only way our brains could process it all was to make it feel like it all happened months ago.

Other experiences in China made me question my sanity or sobriety. Some things I witnessed were so peculiar that they gave me pause and forced me to question whether what I was seeing was really happening or perhaps just a vivid antimalarial drug dream. On one such day, Doug stopped in front of a building that was typical for the region—a concrete cube. Bottom floors are typically used for business, while the actual living area is in the back or on the floor above. He waited for me to catch up. "Look at this," he casually motioned me over. There was no need for discretion or secrecy as we were alone on the sidewalk. The metal roll-top garage door was wide open and on the cement floor sat a five by ten feet mountain of black, human hair of varying lengths. Raising one eyebrow he asked, "What is this?"

While Doug can tell me the name and function of any obscure tool or piece of hardware, or machinery, I was the one providing answers that day. No, it wasn't a Howard Hughes type of collection; I was confident there wasn't a sister garage somewhere filled with nail clippings and empty Kleenex boxes to be used as slippers. I knew exactly what purpose this pile of hair served. I learned about it several years earlier back home when I went into a beauty supply store looking for a product to stop my brittle hair from breaking. A smocked sales clerk told me he knew exactly what product I needed. I followed him down an aisle under fluorescent lights that sinisterly highlighted and waited to capitalize on my every imperfection. There on the end cap he pulled a pastel-colored bottle from the shelf. This, he told me, was the product that I needed. It contained keratin and something extracted from actual human hair. "It's the best," he promised me. "It's what you need." "No. I don't," I assured him. Even five years before going to China, this is exactly what I had been envisioning when trying to understand how these products were manufactured—a pile of human hair sitting on a cement floor in someone's garage. I ran from the store nearly gagging. Back in China, I shuddered and walked briskly away leaving Doug to snap a photo.

Doug and I left our hotel one morning at 3:00 am. As we walked towards the edge of town to rejoin the highway, suddenly, fifteen feet in front of us, a cat bolted across our path. That was in no way remarkable. What made the scene extraordinary was the fact that it was being chased by the biggest rat I have ever seen in my entire life.

Several times, while traveling down the quiet two-lane highway we followed, Doug and I walked under massive, clover-leaf overpasses that went absolutely nowhere. The bridges that towered above us were incomplete and offered no way to get on or off and furthermore, there was no other road anywhere in sight to which they might eventually connect—we were in the middle of the countryside and nothing but fields stretched before us in every direction for miles. In one case, someone's three story, cube home sat underneath a clover-leaf and two walls of the top floor had been torn down to make way for a bridge column.

Stopping at a store one morning to buy a cold drink and enjoy some shade, we came upon a woman sitting outdoors under a canopy. She was engrossed in her work and using three different razors to shave one half of the pig carcass that was laid out on a table in front of her. At one end of the carcass sat an electric fan. Attached to the brackets where the blades were once affixed were plastic bags that whipped around and shooed the flies away. The woman dipped her fingers into a shallow dish of water and sprinkled it on the carcass. Then she picked up a straight razor, something I didn't think anyone used any longer. After she worked an area for a while, she ran her hand down the carcass, caressing the skin of the pig and then swapped the straight razor out for an old-fashioned safety razor. She felt again for remaining stubble and then reached for what looked like my pink razor. Lastly, she finished up with tweezers. The question begged to be answered—was this a vivid dream or reality? Well, even a vegetarian knows nobody wants to eat bristly pork, so I went with reality. However, the day the golden retriever-sized dog passed us riding on the back of a motorcycle traveling fifty mph, I shrugged and gave up on the game. It could go either way. Had he been driving and wearing a helmet, I might have been convinced it was a hallucination, but this was China and he was sitting on the back, paws over the shoulders of the man driving the bike, wind in his face, looking as happy as any other dog out for a ride.

CHAPTER THIRTY-FOUR

Enough Already

When I was twenty-four, I took my first international trip beyond crossing the border into Tijuana, Mexico for underage drinking. It was a few months after my father suddenly and unexpectedly died. I needed some distance from that and from another problem that had pushed me to my breaking point. I decided to travel solo because I needed to test myself, and I needed a chance to feel strong after being so utterly destroyed and weakened by the previous eight months of my life.

I flew to Germany and my first night there I went to a pub, sat at the bar and ordered a beer. "Ein bier bitte," I asked, feeling so proud of myself when the bartender understood me. A man sat down next to me and started a cordial conversation which I was happy to engage in. I nursed my one beer while he drank another and another and another. Without warning, he morphed into an angry drunk. His eyes glassed over, his face was no longer friendly and his tone was contentious. He got off his bar stool and stood uncomfortably close as he slurred an unintelligible message in my ear. The bartender said something in German and the man, now enraged, threw some crumpled bills at him and stormed out. A few minutes later I settled my tab and headed for the door, and there he was... waiting for me. I headed back into the bar and explained the situation to the bartender, who called a cab and instructed the driver to take me back to my room, a mere two blocks away, and to make sure that I got through the door before leaving me.

In England a few weeks later, I accepted an invitation for tea with a man I met at a tube station. After we finished our tea, we walked through a park along a meandering path, past shaded benches where business men and women who hadn't yet made partner ate their brown bag lunches. We stopped and sat on the grass at what I feel compelled to emphasize was a *respectable distance* from one another. Our conversation continued, we talked about where we were from and described our home towns. Eventually he laid on his back and I followed suit, staring up into the trees, enjoying the way the sunlight filtered through the leaves and onto the grass. The sound of the wind blowing through the trees muffled traffic noises coming from the nearby street and birds chattered and rattled around in the bushes behind us. Suddenly, a feeling of unease creeped over me. I turned my head and saw that he was in the middle of ... an auto-erotic activity. Apparently the wind in the trees had also muffled the sound of his zipper being pulled down. I jumped up and fled with him in *hot pursuit*. "That was meant as a compliment," he shouted as he chased after me, zipping his pants and tucking in his shirt, giving me the competitive edge. "Not where I'm from," I countered as I kicked it into high gear, broke into a sprint and jumped into a moving double decker bus that had only seconds earlier pulled away from the curb.

Two years later, I was in Bombay having dinner at a family run, casual restaurant. Landscape prints torn from a calendar were framed on the wall and at the back of the restaurant, above the handwash sink, the ubiquitous sign, "No comb. No hock. No spit" had been hung to maintain decorum. I had seen them at nearly every restaurant in which I dined. I had just finished eating when two well-dressed men came in, ordered a bottle of whiskey and sat at a table across from me. I had been traveling alone for close to three weeks and most of my conversations were limited to asking for directions or ordering meals, so when one of the men introduced himself and invited me to join them at their table, I gratefully accepted. While I drank seltzer water, they sipped their whiskey until the bottle was empty and they then stood to leave. One of the men invited me to accompany them to his home for dinner. I politely declined, but he insisted I join them. Not even one second after intuition kicked in and told me I was in peril, their hands were on me and they pulled me from my seat. I wriggled away and sat back down on the metal chair that was bolted to the floor, wrapped my legs around the pedestal and held on tightly to the table that was mounted to the wall, gripping it with both hands. They then grabbed me under my arms and lifted and pulled while I yelled for them to leave me alone. Frantically, I looked around the restaurant and asked for help but was met with blank stares and unsympathetic faces. Only then did I realize I was the sole woman in the establishment. For at least another eternal two minutes, I struggled to hold onto the table and chair while they grabbed and pulled at me. I imagined myself disappearing forever—murdered, raped, sold into the sex trade. All of that went through my mind as I held onto the table because I knew that my life depended on it. Eventually, they gave up and left. I sat there in disbelief, my entire body trembling. Then I remembered the man at the bar in Germany who had been waiting outside for me. Fortunately, my hotel was right around the corner. I waited a half hour before I pulled my key out of my purse, had a quick look outside and sprinted down the crumbling sidewalk, towards my hotel, through the front doors, up the stairs and into my room, which I secured from the inside with a padlock. I spent the night berating myself for being so foolish.

It wouldn't be the last time I'd be harassed or feel threatened by strange men while abroad or at home, for that matter. Like women everywhere, I take a number of precautions. I dress conservatively, don't carry a backpack or large purse, I don't walk alone late at night and I refuse ground floor rooms. Yes, some of these precautions curtail my freedom a bit, but most of the time, because of these measures, I don't experience any problems. Consequently, I get comfortable and I guess... fearless. I relax my defenses and that's when I find myself in dangerous situations again. Overall, I've been very lucky. So far, the only thing I've been robbed of is a bit of my freedom, self-confidence and my sense of safety. Even so, those are terrible things to lose. As Doug and I were planning our trip to China, I thought about how much easier and safer traveling with a man was going to be. I hadn't even left yet and already I had lowered my guard.

In China, aside from the brutal heat, being chased from hotels and the occasional run-in with the police, we had no complaints. China was magic to us. It was joy. There wasn't a day we weren't greeted with huge smiles and unchecked enthusiasm... people waving or giving us the thumbs up as they passed us on the highway... those observant and considerate folk who pulled over on the hottest of days to give us bottles of cold water. On a hot afternoon, after reaching the peak of a hill, we sat on a low wall at the end of somebody's driveway, and the lady of the house delivered slices of watermelon that came right out of her icebox... sweet and deliciously cold. It wasn't the first time we had been treated to watermelon. One morning we passed a man selling watermelon beside the highway from the back of his truck. Hours later and many miles down the road, Doug and I took a much-needed shade break. We took off our backpacks and left them beside the northbound lane of the highway, crossed to the other side, climbed over the guard rail and sat on a little curb, pressing our backs against the railing to keep as much of our bodies in the shade as possible. We had only been there a few minutes when we heard a vehicle brake and slow to a stop. I popped my head up, suspicious that someone might try to take our packs. It was watermelon guy, and when he saw us, he opened his tailgate and gave it a pat, an invitation to come sit down. We accepted and gratefully sat with our legs dangling, a mound of watermelon behind us. He inspected several, turning them over in his hands, thumping each with his finger before finally settling on one. He produced a large knife and cut it open right there; it was red as a ruby inside, sparkly with sugar and speckled with black, glossy seeds. After a few delicious slices, he waved us over to the cab of his truck so we could look at the console and see the temperature. It was 100 degrees. The weather app on my phone confirmed the temperature. The "Feels Like" temperature was 109.

I lost count of how many bags of nectarines were handed to us from car windows. Before I went to China there was only one way I had eaten nectarines—when they were plump, slightly peachy-colored but mostly blushing red. I had never eaten them as they do in China—firm and crisp almost like an apple, with a mellow sweetness and a hint of refreshing tart. That's how I shop for them now. We felt so welcomed by nearly everyone. Late one morning, a man who owned a restaurant literally dragged us in off the street. He pulled us in by our arms and sat us down fully prepared to feed us and put us up for the night. Through pantomime he conveyed to us his worry that we weren't eating and had no place to sleep. His gesture made me feel cared for and safe.

One morning, I summited a steep hill and found myself alone at the plateau top. Doug was already on his way down. Several yards ahead of me, at a turnout on the opposite side of the road, a man sat on an idling tractor under the shade of a tree. I considered walking across the road thinking I'd be able to see Doug on one of the switchbacks below, but something alerted my senses. I continued walking and when I was directly across from him, he called out to me. I knew it was me he was calling because it was just the two of us at the top of that hill. I have no idea what he said, but his tone conveyed everything. I kept looking straight ahead as I walked, doing my best to look assertive, confident and strong. He threw his tractor into gear, steered it onto the highway and pulled up beside me. His creepy banter continued. I crossed to the other side of the highway, hoping I could look down below and see Doug, but all I saw were empty switchbacks. No Doug. Not even a single car driving up the hill that I might flag down for help. He followed behind me, his tractor chugging. I spoke to him sternly in English, hoping my tone would be as clear to interpret as his was. He laughed and continued talking. I was suddenly scared. I looked down the hillside and, finally, Doug came into view two switchbacks below me. I grabbed the orange whistle that hung from my backpack, hoping Doug would remember the code we had devised while hiking on the Pacific Crest Trail. Three long blasts meant "Help. Come now. I'm in serious trouble." I blew three times and the man chuckled. We both watched as Doug continued walking, unable to hear my distress call. I blew three times again. The man whistled three times in imitation and laughed some more. I blew three times again and this time he whistled like a songbird. I got it. I was as powerless as a tiny bird. Now I was scared and *angry*. I yelled now in a deep voice that I prayed would both carry to Doug and let tractor man know I was not to be messed with. He laughed harder still and slapped his knee. My fight instinct lost out to my flight instinct and I broke into a trot and then a full-blown run down the center of the highway. The man drove faster, pacing me, laughing and mocking me with bird calls every time I blew on my whistle. Finally, as I turned onto another switchback, Doug came into full view and I blew continuously for another hundred yards until he finally turned around and stopped. Tractor Guy steered back into the other lane, accelerated, passed Doug and disappeared down the road.

I explained what had happened to Doug as we continued walking. Another switchback down the road, Tractor Guy was parked on the shoulder, waiting. We kept our eyes straight ahead and ignored him as we passed. A few seconds later we heard his tractor start again. My heart raced until I noticed the sound receding as he drove back up the hill. We never saw him again.

CHAPTER THIRTY-FIVE

Hippolyte In Egypt

At 11:00 a.m. on Monday, December 12th, 1921, Hippolyte arrived in Egypt and disembarked at one of the most ancient ports in the world. Some historians argue that the area, once known as Rhacotis, dates back to 1000 BC and was merely a building yard. However, other experts contend that it was actually a thriving city. Alexander the Great had the silt and sand-clogged harbor dredged and built a 1200 meter by 200 meters-wide bridge linking the island of Pharos—mentioned in Homer's Odyssey—to the refurbished port and then renamed the city after himself. Alexandria, as it has since been known, would become the intellectual and cultural center of the world.

I'm certain that upon arrival in a new country, Hippolyte would head straight to the post office. After months of disappointment, at last there was a letter from home awaiting my uncle. It must have made a wonderful Christmas gift. Soon after, he wrote a reply to his brother-in-law.

Cairo, Egypt

26 Dec 1921

Friend Prosper

Your letter to date Nov 8-21 to hand. I have made a note of the contents, the news being as pleasant that they put a better spirit into my heart than ever. I am going to proceed on my hike from

Egypt through Palestine India and Burma to Hong Kong and will then sail home with lots to tell. My note is brief, but I have got one of the military police here to write out my adventures, it would take me weeks to write what he has put down in a few lines. There is no city on earth like Cairo. Just now there are serious police disturbances here, therefore I am going to beat it out as quickly as I can. I am sending you some pictures and a document of which I wish you to take great care of as they will mean a lot to me if ever I get back & I know I shall. My next address is

"TO BE CALLED FOR"
"Globe Trotter"
c/o Commissioner of Civil Police
Basra Mesopatamia
Kindest Regards to all your friends
I am most sincerely yours
Hippolyte Martinet

P.S. I had a dandy dinner Xmas day with the "Tommies" on guard and some of the police at the Babal Hadid Police /// Cairo
HM

When I saw this letter, I immediately noticed that the handwriting was not his. The penmanship was cramped, tight and small. It was legible but looked like it was written by someone who held their pencil with a death grip. It was so unlike the graceful, relaxed, looping script I had come to know as my uncle's. The letter was also free of the spelling errors that were characteristic of Hippolyte; yet, the voice of the letter was still very much his own. As to why a member of the military police wrote the letter for him, I have imagined a few scenarios-one of them being Hippolyte had somehow injured his hand. His next letter to Prosper raised even more suspicions and questions—questions to which I still have no answers.

Hippolyte was a foreign man in a foreign land in a tenuous time. In December of 1921, Egypt was roughly two months away from being granted "limited independence" by Great Britain, which had occupied Egypt since 1882. After nearly forty years of British colonial rule,

Egyptians were anxious to regain their freedom. In his letter to Prosper, Hippolyte wrote about "police disturbances." My interpretation of his phrasing is that these were not civil disturbances that required police intervention but rather British Colonial police causing problems. Hippolyte was alarmed enough to plan a hasty departure.

Tensions between Egyptians and British colonials had been building for decades—most likely beginning long before June 13th, 1906 when British military officers clashed with a group of locals in what became known as the Denshawai Incident. This would be a prime example of a "police disturbance" as Hippolyte phrased it. British officers were sport-shooting pigeons that were the property of some local residents. While the incensed villagers were protesting the loss of their livelihood, a British officer fired his gun and, among others, shot the wife of a Muslim prayer leader. Angered, the villagers attacked the British soldiers. One British officer fled the scene and headed back toward the British camp. Before reaching it, he collapsed from the heat. An uninvolved villager who was administering aid to the heat stricken man was shot and killed by British soldiers who believed he had slain their companion. The following day, more British soldiers were brought in and they arrested fifty-two local men.

A trial led by a British court soon followed. Several Egyptians were convicted in the soldier's death on the grounds that they had incited the soldier to run, thereby causing the heatstroke that killed him. The "guilty" men were flogged and sentenced to hard labor. One of the men was hanged in front of his own home. The British court dismissed an Egyptian police officer's eyewitness testimony and sentenced him to two years in prison and fifty lashes.

George Bernard Shaw—the author Hippolyte encouraged his sister to read for his ideas on birth control—wrote an article about the incident and was harshly criticized for his perspective, which favored the Egyptians.

> Instead of showing understanding for the peasants' self-defense against the officer's tactless blundering, the colonial administrators viewed the natives' actions as a dangerous popular insurgency that had to be dealt with harshly.

In the years following the Denshawai incident, the inflation and food shortages that caused starvation among Egyptians—but somehow not the British—led to a rise in anti-colonial sentiments. The subsequent exile of leader Saad Zaghul by the British in 1919 led to revolution. Egyptians from all walks of life, merchants, peasants, the elite, civil service and the clergy alike, began demonstrating against the British all across Egypt. Although this led Great Britain to recognize Egyptian independence, it would take another revolution in 1952 before the country was actually free from British occupation and control.

There was always something interesting happening wherever Hippolyte had been and Prosper even remarked so in a letter saying, "Polyte Dear Friend it seems that after you pass a country is some trouble started." In a different way, the same thing was happening to Doug and me. Twice after checking into a hotel after a long day of walking, we turned on the television. In between ubiquitous Jackie Chan and Japanese occupation war movies, we caught news stories about areas we had just left a hundred miles behind being devastated by torrential rains. We sat silenced and in awe as violent rivers of brown water carried away houses, cars and people leaving behind gutted, crumbling and muddy ravines. I'd always be anxious to turn the channel. I didn't want to dwell on those images for too long. One of my fears was that I would somehow get Doug killed on this trip.

One afternoon as we walked along the highway, the skies darkened and it began to pour so heavily that we were drenched in seconds. A truck pulled up beside us and the driver pushed the passenger door open and patted the empty seat. With water streaming down our faces, we declined his offer and told him that we wanted to walk. He shook his head sternly, pointed behind us and drew a zigzag shape in the air. I thought about the implications of what we were preparing to do—accepting a ride when the point of the trip was to walk. I listened as the lightning strikes got closer and closer and decided the integrity of the walk was not worth getting killed over. Less than a kilometer down the road there was a small village and we suspected there was a hotel there, too. I wanted out of that storm as quickly as Hippolyte wanted to pass through Egypt. The images of houses being carried away and corpses face down in muddy brown rivers ran through my mind. Dripping wet, we clambered in and the driver grinned through our apologies for soaking his seats. A minute later we slid out of his truck and onto the street as rushing water flooded over the tops of our shoes. We stepped onto the sidewalk just as a deafening bolt struck. The surprise of it nearly knocked me off my feet. The driver threw back his head and laughed as he motored away. Doug and I spent the next few minutes wading up and down the street, looking for what our GPS indicated were accommodations until we finally squished and sloshed into a hotel lobby, safe and sound. Our room was a hybrid hotel room/ "mahjong parlor." Two felt covered tables lined opposite walls. We spent the night in several such hotels.

Back in the blissful cool and dry winter of Alexandria, Hippolyte walked twenty miles to Kafr Ad Dawwar and then another twenty-eight miles to Tanta, where in a letter he told his family he'd had a nice rest. From Tanta he walked approximately fifty-one miles to Cairo. All totaled, he traveled roughly ninety-nine miles in four days, averaging just under 25 miles per day, considerably slower than the thirty mile per day pace he usually kept. I chalk this up to harried sightseeing excursions. Despite his desire to pass though quickly, my uncle was quite taken with Egypt.

It was in Cairo on December 17th that he was interviewed at the Egyptian Stock Exchange by a French newspaper. I have no idea what brought Hippolyte to the exchange in Egypt. Perhaps it was in a financial district where he was able to exchange currency or wire money home. Whatever the reason, I laugh to myself when I conjure the image of my road-worn, barefoot uncle once again in a building full of men wearing suits. The last time he was interviewed was because a woman had fainted in reaction to his very presence.

THE WORLD TOUR ON FOOT

> We have received this morning in our offices at our newspaper a visit by an original American, MSSR Hippolyte Martinet, who is making a tour of the world on foot. A face tanned and weathered by the sun and open air, lively blue eyes, beard and hair like Robinson Crusoe, this person who is circling the globe barefoot and without a hat and carrying on his broad shoulders all his camping materials.

Indifferent to the luxuries of hotels, he either sleeps under a sky full of stars or responds to the invitations made to him by his admirers. He carries with him post cards that show him with his faithful road companion, a black fox terrier. He offers these cards to anyone he meets and who becomes interested in his mission, in order to get a few coins, he uses to procure provisions for the road.

We passed a few questions to him, to which he answers amiably in a very pure French with just a hint of an accent. He speaks very well in English as well, and a bit of Italian.

Q: Have you been on the road very long?

A: I left Seattle (USA) in April 1920. After crossing the continent on foot and crossing the Rocky Mountains, I embarked in New York and reached Belgium. I've crossed France step-by-step and worked about four months in the war-devastated areas. I have to tell you that I made the Atlantic crossing on a Red Star line steamer on which I worked as a crewman. After having been to Nice, I re-crossed the French Alps to find myself in Genoa, Switzerland. Then I went back to Italy and to Brindisi and Albania and Greece. From Piree I then went to Alexandria, from where I left last Monday, December 12 at 11:00 am.

At Cairo I was offered the hospitality of the local Englishmen at Babo El Hadid. They even offered me a bed that I was obliged to refuse, not wishing to acquire any bad habits.

Q: How do you support yourself and take care of your needs during your road trip?

A: I work when I don't have any money. Then when I earn a bit, I economize. By only drinking water at the source (streams, rivers etc.) and eating frugally, my needs are minimal. I never ask anything of anyone, but there are those charitable friends, nice people, that will offer me some eggs or a cup of milk, which I accept with a good heart.

Q: Sleeping outside in various conditions, are you never sick?

MSSR Martinet sighs without responding and shows us his muscular arm just below his vest.

> Q: And do you wish always to see new faces without seeing your friends or relations?
>
> A: My needs in life are significantly different from other men such that I don't have the same needs. The study of man, each following diverse country is for me a giant attraction.
>
> Q: Will you continue for a long time your Globe-Trotter life?
> A: I will pursue my walking journey and I intend to call at the Sudan then to Tripolitania, Libya, and then Tunisia, Algeria and Morocco.
>
> Q: And then?
>
> A: I believe I will continue on to Seattle where I have brothers and sisters who are anxiously waiting for me to offer as a gift to me, a fiancé.
>
> The Globe-Trotter consented to pose for a photograph for our journal and then he left with his heavy equipment supported by his forty-three-year-old shoulders.

Doug and I noticed that our needs were becoming different too. A closet full of clothes awaited me back home, but in China, I wore the same tan pants and orange plaid shirt every day and the same forest green pants and purple shirt every evening. Doug also limited himself to two outfits. After a few weeks, the shirt I walked in every day was permanently soiled with road grime no matter how many times I washed it. Even when we were clean, we looked filthy. Back home, I would have never worn these clothes publicly, but in China, I didn't care who saw me. Although my arms weren't muscular like Hippolyte's, my body was changing. Both pairs of my pants were now falling off of me. I had literally walked my butt off.

CHAPTER THIRTY-SIX

The Accident

Chinese drivers have to be some of the best in the world. I say this because in large cities there is an impossible number of cars on the road at any given time, all honking and passing one another, all seeming to disregard any and every traffic law, and yet we never saw a car accident. Not... a... single... one. This defies all laws of both physics and probability. Traffic in China's larger cities was terrifying. I can't remember if there were lines painted on the streets or not. If there were, motorists drove as if they didn't exist. Granted, we have all rolled through a stop sign when there is nobody around. But driving into oncoming traffic to pass another car on the left? We saw it over and over again and it seemed perfectly acceptable. A family of five on a motorcycle? Back home, the parents would be arrested for reckless endangerment and the children put into foster care immediately. In China, they were simply another family trying to get by. There were other transportation *oddities* we witnessed.

Long distance passenger buses often passed us on the highway. Instead of seats, there were rows of bunk beds that stacked four high. Televisions were placed strategically throughout the bus to entertain the passengers. Doug and I saw one of these buses parked along the side of the road. We stuck our heads inside the open door to have a look around. Of all things, the television in the front was playing a compilation video of footage shot from inside buses during high speed crashes—bodies being thrown around like rag dolls. It was horrific.

We frequently saw semis broken down beside the road. Instead of using orange cones or flares to warn motorists, drivers hacked fairly large branches off trees and placed them every 100 feet or so apart, starting a good 150 yards behind their stopped rig. In this manner, other drivers were alerted to the semi that was partially blocking the single lane.

Along rural routes in the U.S., there are often rest areas where a motorist can pull off the highway and sleep if necessary. In China, you just stop your car in the middle of the lane, put it in park, and close your eyes. The first time we saw a sleeping motorist, we approached the vehicle like a crime scene. The motor was still running, and the driver was slumped over the steering wheel. We assumed he had a heart attack while driving. Worried, we discussed how we were going to report this emergency to China's 911 with our limited Mandarin. We decided it would be best to keep it simple and say, "Man sick. Highway 324" and then tell them the kilometer number. Maybe that would be enough information to summon an ambulance. Yet before either of us could reach for our phones, the man stirred, lifted his head, rubbed his eyes and gave us a big smile before driving away. He could have at least pulled his car part way onto the shoulder. He could have turned on his hazard lights, but apparently neither are necessary in China.

Once we witnessed an accident involving two motor scooters. One man went flying over the handlebars, his arms stretched out in front of him like he was Superman. He slid belly down through the gravel and got up, the front of his shirt torn to shreds. I cringed and nearly crumpled from pain synesthesia. Weeks later, I saw a man on a scooter crash as he went through a deep rut in a dirt road. By the time I reached him, he was sitting up and clutching his chest. I thought he might be having a heart attack, but he pointed to the rearview mirror and I understood that it had jabbed him in the chest when he crashed. I offered him my cell phone in case he wanted to call for assistance, but he waved me off, righted his scooter which was bleeding oil, and limped away using it like a crutch.

Doug and I veered off the highway one afternoon to buy some water and snacks and find a cool place to sit. Even though it was an overcast day, it was still hot as blazes. Rested and re-fueled, we headed back to the 324. Across the two-lane highway and a few yards behind us, a man in shorts paced back and forth in his flip flops, his cell phone to his ear. The skin on his legs was scraped and bleeding. He walked to the shoulder of the road and peered down into the wooded ravine. He had somehow crashed his scooter and it had slid off the road and landed below. I stopped and called to Doug, "This whole trip has been about people helping us. It's our turn now. Let's help that guy get his scooter back up to the highway." I knew Doug would be willing because seven months prior to this incident, we encountered a woman in a broken down golf cart on a residential street. I drove behind Doug as he pushed her a half mile back to her home. A HALF MILE! I knew he'd be up for helping this guy. It'd be a cinch.

As we crossed the highway, we noticed something fifty feet ahead of us. It was the guy's scooter, the one we assumed was in the ravine! We left it where it was and hurried back down the road to his side. I looked at his feet and shuddered with sympathy pain. He seemed oblivious to the fact that the nail of his big toe was bent straight up, torn from the bed. The man headed back to the edge of the ravine and Doug and I followed him. Down below, we saw the figure of a tiny man laying among the trees. The scooter driver climbed down and picked him up, cradled him in his arms as though he was a child, and carried him up to the street. From what Doug and I could deduce, the old man had been struck by the guy on the scooter. He must have been going quite fast considering how far the scooter had skidded down the highway and how far the man had been thrown into the ravine.

As they neared, I could see the man's leg had been broken badly. The bones of his tibia and fibula stuck through the skin and his foot dangled at a grotesque angle. He laid him beside the road. My stomach lurched. I'd never seen a compound fracture before. It wasn't bleeding but the bones were clearly visible and a delicate pink color. I looked away and took a few deep breaths before turning my attention to the injured man. He had to have been close to ninety years old, not much more than five feet tall, and couldn't have weighed eighty-five pounds. His eyelids fluttered but never opened and he whispered and muttered words I could not understand. He moved his broken leg, bent his knee and tried to put his foot flat on the ground. "No, no buddy," Doug said in a soothing voice as he straightened the man's leg and lowered it to the ground. I took the man's hand in mine and his fingers moved almost imperceptibly. We verified that an ambulance had been called and then we waited. The man wasn't bleeding, but it was clear he had suffered serious head trauma. Thirty minutes later, two men driving a white minivan showed up. The driver opened the back doors and pulled out what appeared to be an orange plastic snow sled from the otherwise completely empty interior and laid it beside the injured man. They seemed very preoccupied with his broken leg which, while certainly problematic, wasn't what Doug and I found most concerning. The man still hadn't regained consciousness. They lifted him onto the sled, loaded him into the back of the bed, closed the doors and drove away.

Later we realized we should have brought the shopkeeper to the scene of the accident to see if he could identify the injured man. Certainly, everyone knew each other in such a small, rural area. I have no idea what became of him, but I think of him from time to time. What happened to him was my biggest fear. I worried every day that one or both of us would be hit by a car, truck, or a bus. Now I worried we could be hit by a scooter.

CHAPTER THIRTY-SEVEN

Hippolyte In Baghdad

Everyone has a travel horror story. If you are lucky, yours merely involves lost luggage or a cancelled flight. Once early on in my travels and due to an overbooking at the youth hostel, I found myself without accommodations and was ready to spend the night in a graveyard in Edinburgh. A man saw me peering over the wrought iron fence I planned to climb over once it was dark; a conversation ensued and I learned he spent six months living in a city 100 miles to the north of my home town. He ran a hotel, had one vacancy and offered me a room for the night at hostel prices. One summer while traveling in an extremely rural area of Sumatra, a wasp stung me in the knuckle of my ring finger. As the hours dragged by, the agonizing throbbing pain moved up to my wrist, elbow, and then my shoulder. I vacillated between self-pity—thinking I might actually die because my neck and throat seemed like the obvious and logical progression—and pride, feeling like a full-fledged adult because for the first time in my life, I had purchased repatriation of remains insurance so my body could be shipped home. With tears streaming down my face, I staggered to the reception area of the hotel. The sympathetic manager offered to escort me to the village *pharmacy*, which turned out to be a wooden shack where I was able to procure three antihistamine tablets from a ten year old boy. Then there's that one Christmas Eve I was beset by a pack of street dogs in Laos. None of the people watching that spectacle unfold came to my aid, but I'm going to pretend it was because they knew I had street cred and could hold my own... and that fortified me. I won't necessarily call these three events *cherished* memories, but even twenty-nine years later, these misadventures are among my favorite stories to share. As Ibn Battuta, the 14th century Moroccan scholar and traveler of the medieval world said, "Traveling—It leaves you speechless, then turns you into a storyteller."

For as long as my uncle had been traveling and for as far as he walked, he had not been just lucky, he'd been blessed. No traveler is immune to bad fortune and good luck is not infinite; eventually, it's bound to run out. Hippolyte's did, and in a letter to his brother-in-law Prosper, my uncle alluded to the fact that there was enough to make a story. Whatever he planned to tell them, be it about his misfortunes or some other adventure, his family would just have to wait. Maybe in anticipation of writing a book about his travels, Hippolyte was beginning to hone his craft as a storyteller and developing the skill of the teasing hook that draws in a reader. Or, perhaps guardedly he shared the events in his letter, only after he was out of the territories where the stars first turned against him.

Hippolyte left Egypt in the last days of December, setting his sights on Jerusalem and then Damascus Syria, from where he penned a letter to his brother-in-law. Even though his letter is dated "3-10-1922," I think it was written on February 10th and he accidentally wrote the numeral "3" instead of "2." Geographically and chronologically, it seems more accurate. If I correctly interpret Hippolyte's route and timeline rather than follow the route as dictated by the dates of his letters, he would have walked a total of 715 miles from Giza to Damascus in roughly forty-four days. His pace was a leisurely sixteen miles a day, a speed that Doug and I could have easily matched. Below is the letter I believe was written on February 10th.

> Damascus Syria
> 3 10 1922
> Friend Prosper
>
> Was trying to make Basra & then let you have some news but some how greatly delayed. Therefore will hasten matter for have more to tell than I really can write, in fact enough for to make a story to begain with Cairo one must visite & see said city to have

an inspection of what like is life in this mad world, however was very welcome there but had the misfortune an auto run Gigi my faithful dog in. I didn't cry but that was all, now from Cairo to Jerusalem had a splendid hike also very welcome in fact nothing on earth just like the Holy City, but would you believe that I had to come to the Holy Land for my worse struggle, that's to say was attacked by 3 robbers. I sure was clean-out, however a man determination will take him over the world was taken in by a missionary & then was sent to see the Emir, that's to say he's like a King. However he look at me & said you're the 8 profit. Therefore I'll make good your entired lost & see you safe out of my territory. Now in Syria on to Damascus was again attack but no harm done. I come to realize it's very dangerous to travel among wild Arabs alone.

Therefore made up my mind to wait for a caravan across the Syrian desert, in fact I am putting up with the owner of same a Pasha that is also royalty whatever he may he's the most congenial man thus far, made me his guest in his own mansion. In fact I am welcome in Damascus not like a hobo rather like one of this royal being or a profit, believe me its very interesting to visit royalty, also nobility & have had plenty of in this city, also was given more generous gift for postcard than any other city save New York, therefore in case anything should happen to me inform yourself from the American Consulate in Baghdad Maspot, by the way I have met a number of American tourists here have taken a supper with them in the Damas Palace that's same a hobo in his bear feet.

My very best wishes to all also regards
Your friend as ever Hippolyte

When I read that Gigi had been run over by a car, my breath caught in my throat. Although he touches upon the incident only briefly, I can sense his loss through his sentimental choice of words. Gigi was his *faithful* dog. I read into his phrasing, *I didn't cry but that was all.* Perhaps wisely, he denied himself the catharsis of tears. After all, he was a stranger in a foreign land where the spectacle of a grown man crying in the street over the loss of an animal might be interpreted unfavorably. Chronologically,

Hippolyte standing in front of The Sphinx

the next photo I have of my uncle was taken not long after he lost his sole companion. Hippolyte is in Giza, walking alone in front of the Sphynx. He is midstride; I can see his running corks clutched in his hands. He looks caught off guard, deep in thought and lonely without his travel partner.

Gigi wasn't a big dog, but I'm sure she provided Hippolyte not only with companionship but protection as well because it was while traveling without her that Hippolyte met with more misfortune and was robbed. Twice. He told his family that he lost everything in the robbery that took place in Jerusalem, Palestine. I believe this is why I don't have a copy of the letter from Prosper that was waiting for my uncle in Egypt. In my imagination, I always picture Hippolyte holding letters from his family, reading them again and again until he knew them by heart. These letters would have been the only items in his backpack that were truly irreplaceable. While in the Holy Land, Hippolyte had new postcards made. This time, a sketch was used rather than a photograph.

After he was robbed the first time, Hippolyte had the good fortune to meet a missionary who gave him an introduction to the Emir, Prince Abdullah, who ruled Transjordan and its successor state, Jordan, from 1921-1951. Prince Abdullah claimed that he was the 38th generation direct descendant of Muhammad. Coming from such a distinguished lineage, I find it all the more remarkable that the Emir believed my uncle to be the 8th prophet.

The prophets are sent by Allah to share a message. They all preach the same message, but each preaches to a different group of people in language that is appropriate to them and their time. The 8th prophet was Ishmael; scripture says that he and his mother were cast out of their home and nearly died in the desert. Like Ishmael, Hippolyte was far from home and walking through the desert. If my uncle had shared his credo on the nature of his fellow man with the Emir, I can see how it led him to the conclusion that my uncle was an incarnation of Ishmael. To a spiritual person, the connection nearly begs to be discovered. Verses of the Quran could lead an earnest believer to that conclusion.

> *Give the relatives, the destitute and those who when on a journey have become needy, their dues.* 17:26
>
> *Worship Allah and associate nothing with Him, and to parents do good, and to relatives, orphans, the needy, the near neighbor, the neighbor farther away, the companion at our side, the traveler...*" 4:36

Hippolyte was his own self-fulfilling prophecy, surviving on the kindness and generosity of his fellow man, giving every person he met the opportunity to fulfill this religious obligation. In its own way, it made perfect sense.

I don't know what conversations transpired between Emir Abdullah and Hippolyte, but the Emir replaced all his stolen possessions. He also promised Hippolyte safe passage throughout his territory. I have no idea how my uncle's safety was ensured or achieved, but he made it out of the region without further incident only to be robbed again thirty-seven miles after crossing the border into Damascus, Syria.

The fact that Hippolyte reported that he received no harm in the second robbery implies that he had been injured during the first robbery. It must have been frightening. I wonder if he entertained the idea of packing it in and heading home, or was he as steadfast as ever in his commitment to his beliefs? After the robberies, was he still comfortable sleeping outdoors or did he fall asleep only out of sheer exhaustion?

Because it would have been impossible for Hippolyte to travel the vast expanse of desert alone and on foot, he joined a caravan to Baghdad. In Egypt, in a newspaper interview, Hippolyte reported that when he was in Cairo, he had been offered a bed but turned it down, "not wishing to acquire any bad habits." I think that after being robbed twice, my uncle set his principles aside, and in the interest of safety accepted an invitation to stay at the mansion of a Pasha rather than sleep unprotected in the outdoors. Maybe Hippolyte had been spooked by the two robberies. But then again, who wouldn't be at least a little intrigued by the offer to sleep in the mansion of a high-ranking officer. It certainly made me feel less guilty about how Doug and I were living while on the road. A handful of times we stayed in commercial hotels, but the majority of the time we were staying in rooms that had been built above the family home or business. Maybe it was at the Pasha's mansion where he met the American tourists with whom he dined at Damas Palace. I believe these are the American men with whom Hippolyte took supper.

In 1922, the Pasha of Syria was Ahmed Djemal. I believe this is the Pasha with whom my uncle met. He and three other Pashas were responsible for the Armenian, Greek and Assyrian genocides that in combination killed between 2.1-3.5 million people. If Ahmed Djemal was indeed the Pasha, I'd like to believe that Hippolyte was unaware of his host's history when he accepted the invitation.

My uncle's next letter was not just written by another hand but was typed by another hand, and whoever transcribed it took some liberties with his verbiage. The first time I read it, it gave rise to dark suspicions that weren't completely assuaged even after I saw his signature at the bottom of the page... proof that he was alive. I remembered in his last letter he had instructed Prosper, "In case anything should happen to me, inform yourself from the American Consulate in Baghdad." Of course, I know nothing nefarious happened to him, but what must his family have thought? Had I received this letter, I would have assumed the worst, that Hippolyte had met with a foul end and someone was trying to hide that fact. In the end, I found the letter amusing. To begin with, it was typed and had at least eight spaces between each sentence and there was no trace of Hippolyte's colorful Creole. The register was exceedingly formal, as evidenced by the highbrow greeting, "My Dear Davis," rather than Hippolyte's Quaker-ish form of address, "Friend Prosper." Whereas the closings of his previous letters ran anywhere between five and eighteen words, the longest being "I'm enjoying the best wish you all the same also regards to all very truly yours friend Hippolyte Martinet," the terse and formal closing of this letter read, "With kindest regards."

Basrah, Mesopotamia

21st February 1922

My dear Davis,

I've received your letter of the 23rd January which was handed to me on my arrival in Basrah, and I'm glad to get your news. It is interesting to read of the fact that you have had a bad time with rain and frost especially since I have not seen either frost or rain for some time back. I hope I shall be able to fulfill your expectations that I shall be home for Christmas, but I very much doubt it, and think the farthest I will manage by that time will perhaps be Hong Kong. I had the most interesting journey across the desert from Damascus to Baghdad and again from Baghdad to Basrah, and although I encountered a certain amount of difficulty on the way from time to time I managed to get through. The leader of the caravan with which I crossed was a most excellent type of Arab and did me well.

I am leaving Mesopotamia in a day or two for Persian and thence to India and I will probably be in Karachi in about a month or six weeks time. My next address should be in care of the American Consul in Calcutta, India. I am glad to say that I am keeping excellent health and the desert country is as healthy as any in the world. You might tell Marie that I should have liked to have been home in time to act as godfather to the stranger.

With kindest regards,
Hippolyte

The caravan trip took twenty-one days and Hippolyte reported that it was enjoyable. In conducting research, I read two books about desert caravans. My impression is this, at the time Hippolyte would have been crossing, the desert and its people were in a way, timeless. There was little to no technology to make his trip any different from a caravan that crossed 500 years ago. The only thing that would have changed in that time would be the gentle curve of the dunes that were endlessly shaped and reshaped by the scorching desert wind.

In February, the temperatures would have been in the cool fifties. This is where the wisdom of Hippolyte's decision to winter in France factors in. Had he crossed that desert in the summer, daytime temperatures could have been as high as 120 degrees. Sand temperatures can be thirty to forty degrees warmer than air, meaning 120-degree heat will raise sand temperatures to a blistering 160 degrees, too hot even for Hippolyte's thick-soled feet. I don't know if my uncle walked across the desert sands or if he rode on camel. It's possible that he did walk, and this is why sandals were also listed among his final possessions.

Finally in Baghdad, Hippolyte once again made the news. This article was published in at least twenty-six different U.S. papers. The text of the article never varied, but the headlines did: "A Bum Before Calif," "Yankee Vagrant Reaches Bagdad," "American 'Vag' Wins Over Calif," "A Bonafide Globe-Trotter Who Hails From Seattle, Travels in Bare Feet and is Generally Penniless" and "Feisul's Audience To World Tramp." The *Oakland Tribune* ran the article on August 30th, 1922.

SEATTLE HIKER IS RECEIVED BY BAGDAD'S RULER

Bagdad, Mesopotamia, July 12 Hippolyte Martinet, an American, who hails from Seattle Wash. And who claims to have tramped barefooted over half the globe, arrived in Baghdad today, shoeless as well as penniless.

With long hair hanging over his neck to protect it from heat and cold, a beard that had not seen the sheers for two long years, a kit weighing about 20 lbs flung across his back and a sign pinned across his breast to proclaim to the world that he is a globe trotter, Martinet presented himself to King Faisel and told the following story.

Tired of my profession as a cabinet-maker and feeling that a tramp around the world would benefit my health, I set out from my home on April 19th, 1920. I reached New York 4 months later and managed to get passage across the Atlantic, reaching Southhampton in September. After a tramp to London, I embarked for Antwerp.

From Antwerp, I worked my way through the devastated regions. Quitting Paris, I tramped to Havre and thence to Nice. From Nice I crossed to Switzerland and gradually worked my way down to Brindisi. I crossed to Albania and then to Greece. Taking a boat I crossed to Egypt reaching Cairo in December last year.

After roaming about Egypt, I struck towards Palestine and then to Damascus where I joined a caravan, crossing the desert to Baghdad in 21 days.

Martinet plans next to go to Bazra, then Bombay, Japan, China and San Francisco.

Emir Faisel, who displayed great interest in Martinet presented him with a check for $200.

Emir Faisal was the brother of Prince Abdullah, the Emir of Jordan who replaced Hippolyte's meager stolen belongings. In 1920, Faisal became the King of Greater Syria and eventually King of Iraq, ruling from August of 1921 until 1933. During World War I, Faisal worked with Captain Thomas Edward Lawrence, a British intelligence officer who was involved in the Arab Revolt. Lawrence's written accounts of his experiences brought him fame. The 1962 movie, *Lawrence of Arabia*, was based on his life.

CHAPTER THIRTY-EIGHT

Getting What You Ask For

Weeks into our walk, the blisters on the bottoms of my feet had healed into tough callouses and I had found my groove. We were absolutely loving our journey through China. Few people have the time and opportunity to see a country this way, and Doug and I were extremely grateful that our jobs provided us the flexibility. We both agreed wholeheartedly that if one has the time, the best way to truly experience a country is by walking it. A country is not solely its monuments and buildings; it is also its people. Almost anywhere else in the world, two backpacking Westerners wouldn't turn a single head, but people stopped on the highway to meet us every day in China. To be honest, I enjoyed the little breaks. Had people been disinterested in us, it would have been a completely different trip and certainly not as enchanting, memorable and cherished. I felt so embraced by the enthusiasm of everyone we met. It engendered a feeling of warmth and positivity inside me. It was exactly like Peace Pilgrim said, "The world is like a mirror. If you smile at it, it smiles back at you." I think I must have projected that sentiment out into the universe. I just can't remember who smiled first.

The flora was as interesting as the fauna. Although we walked through regions that farmed potatoes, the most magnificent mushrooms we had ever seen or eaten, grapes, bananas, barrel cactus, mangos and lychee, the one constant was rice. From beginning to end, the cultivation of rice has to be the most labor intensive, stooped over, back-breaking work imaginable. When we began our walk, the shoots were a vibrant pale green, emerging just a few inches from the surface of the shallow and still waters that reflected the nearby mountains. As the shoots grew taller, more water was added to the paddies, and when the stalks eventually began to bend and bow under the weight of the concealed grains, the water was drained. Gradually, the green stalks faded into a golden-yellow and were eventually cut down and harvested. Trucks hauled the cut stalks away and then later, we would see them laid out on driveways and sidewalks, where the kernels were left drying in the sun, winnowing baskets at the ready. Later the rice stalks would be burned in the fields. Finally, the paddies would be flooded again and new rice planted. We witnessed the entire life cycle of the grain that provides nineteen percent of the world's consumed calories and uses roughly one third of the world's fresh water supply.

We were eating our fair share of rice while we were there. We had it with every meal in one form or another. The change in diet and level of exercise were having an effect on both of us. More and more often when we gave our postcards to people, the recipients would look at the photo of Doug and me, point to him in recognition, but then look at me, mild confusion registering on their faces. In the photo, my face was round and full, my hair dark and styled. The current version of me... not so much. My face was considerably slimmer and tanned, and my hair was sun bleached and wrecked from the heat and humidity. To prove that was indeed me in the photo, I'd mirror my postcard self by puffing out my cheeks and holding both hands out in front of me to slightly round my belly. Then I'd pantomime walking and, still using my hands, gradually show myself getting slimmer. In my rudimentary Mandarin, I'd tell them approximately how many hundred kilometers we had walked.

Before traveling to China, neither Doug nor I had ever heard of Nanning, a city of nearly seven million in Guangxi Province near the border with Vietnam. When we arrived there, we headed straight to an international package delivery company, expecting a shipment of postcards and supplies we had sent ourselves. As we waited for our box in the loading dock, I spied an enormous scale. I took off my backpack and stepped on. The numbers were displayed digitally and in kilograms. I stepped off and used my phone to do the calculations. I had lost approximately thirty pounds over the course of six weeks, walking seventeen miles a day and subsisting on rice, or rice noodles, eggs and vegetables. A few minutes later, we had our package and went to look for a hotel.

The sole of Doug's hiking sandal was cracked and was threatening to break in half, so that evening he went in search of new footwear while I stayed at the hotel to update our website. As he walked out the door, I asked him to look for a pair of pants for me. I typically have resolute faith in Doug, but it waivered for a second when I recalled a story a friend told me about asking her husband of twenty-five years to buy a box of panty liners for her. He came back with bladder control pads that resembled the old school maxi-pads that were held up with what amounted to suspenders worn around the waist. When Doug returned from his shopping expedition, he handed me a brand new pair of pants that fit me perfectly. He really is my hero.

With our sartorial problems solved, only one predicament needed to be addressed. Although I had cinched the hip belt on my backpack as tight as possible, it still hung loosely on my frame. This meant the weight of it hung on my shoulders. I needed to figure out a solution because it was becoming painful and would likely worsen. I needed to somehow increase the thickness of the belt pads so my hips could once again support the weight of my pack.

Unfortunately, that was not the only problem I was having. My hip bones were beginning to project and without the protective padding of fatty flesh, my femoral nerve was getting irritated. I had developed something called meralgia paresthetica. When the area wasn't feeling numb, shooting burning pains ran up and down my legs even when I wasn't wearing my backpack.

The next time we stopped at a roadside store, I scanned the shelves for something suitable and walked out with a terry cloth hand towel. I folded it in thirds and put it between my lower back and the pack. The towel was a less than perfect solution, slipped frequently and soaked through with sweat in less than an hour. I bought a second towel and put them between my body and the hip pads. That worked better, but they too slipped and shifted and needed frequent readjustment, which was too time consuming.

I decided what I needed was some sort of tape to secure the towels to the hip pads. Duct tape, I mused, wasn't suitable because it would leave a gummy residue on the towels and was *too* durable. If I was going to wash the towels every night, I would need a different kind of tape. As we were walking along the highway, it came to me… electrical tape. It wouldn't get too sticky, and would be easy to remove. As I walked, I thought about how I might ask for or pantomime electrical tape if I was in one of the rare areas where I had no phone service and couldn't find an internet image. Minutes later, something on the ground ahead of me came into view. It was an unopened, clear plastic package with the letter M written in black marker upon it. I picked it up and ran to catch up with Doug so I could show it to him. It was exactly what I had asked for, a roll of electrical tape. In the end, it didn't provide the solution I had hoped for, but it was still astonishing that of all of the things we had seen on the side of the road in China—discarded piles of shrink wrapped fermented duck eggs, cartons of milk bulging in the hot sun, 50,000 empty plastic water bottles—it was exactly what I had been wanting. And why, in the middle of rural China, had someone inscribed the packaging with my initial (I chose to see the letter as an M rather than as a W) … I will never know.

I tried the electrical tape method for a few days but was unsatisfied because the towels wadded up and twisted from the constant movement. Still in search of a fix, I went online and posted my predicament on a hiking forum. The next morning, I was surprised to see a number of responses. The only suggestion that was even remotely viable given my current location was to place pieces of foam rubber between my body and the hip pads.

I tried to imagine where I could procure such an item. This would be even more difficult than trying to find electrical tape. As I continued walking, there it was on the shoulder of the road… my piece of foam rubber. I picked it up, dusted it off and put it in the outside pouch of my backpack. In the end, it wound up being too stiff and unyielding so I discarded it, all the while thinking of what I could engineer to solve my problem.

I needed something softer, not *overly* yielding, that would slide like a sleeve around the hip pads. It would need to be something I could adjust in case I continued to lose weight. Then the solution came to me. Water wings! Two hours later… there they were, hanging from a rickety display outside a store. I still choose to believe this was the universe answering my calls—especially in light of the fact we weren't anywhere near a body of water and people in this part of China didn't have swimming pools. I bought them on the spot. Unfortunately, they too proved an inadequate solution because when I put my backpack on, the air squeezed to the outer side of the water wing and provided no padding at all. In the end, I went back to the folded towel method. Even so, I couldn't believe how everything I had asked for was put in my path. I still have my roll of electrical tape and the towels, too. I don't think I'll ever get rid of them.

CHAPTER THIRTY-NINE

Firecrackers

Of all China's many contributions to world civilization—silk, the abacus, the compass, the umbrella, paper making, even noodles—fireworks have to be my favorite. They are such an important part of our yearly Independence celebration that I think we forget we didn't invent them. Where I'm from, Southern California, fireworks and firecrackers are illegal and aren't sold in stores or roadside stands like they are in other states. However, if you live near the border, one can cross over into Mexico, buy some and smuggle them back. Under normal circumstances, I'm a law-abiding citizen, but my weakness is things that light up, spin, shoot into the air and explode in a glorious shower of colorful sparks. And that heady sulfur smell that I find so addicting… it is the cherry on the top of that delicious Class A misdemeanor sundae, which is punishable by up to one year in county jail and/or a fine up to $1000.

Back in our early thirties, a group of friends and I went down to Mexico to have lunch and search out said contraband for an upcoming Fourth of July party. We made our purchases and headed for home in the mid-afternoon when lines at the border would be shortest. As we idled, slowly inching closer and closer to the checkpoint, my conscience began to get the better of me. By the time I pulled my car up to the U.S. Border Patrol Agent's kiosk, my heart was racing and my palms were sweating. The border agent said something I didn't quite hear but was probably the single word, "Citizenship?" to which I replied, "What?

Fireworks? Fireworks? I don't have any fireworks!" The border agent rolled his eyes, shook his head and waved us through. Yes, I freaked out and this is exactly why I don't usually break the law. I'm a bad liar. I get *Reefer Madness* level paranoid and I will unintentionally throw myself and everybody with me under the bus. Even worse, I'll back that bus up and drag everyone with me into Secondary Inspection. Thirty minutes later, I was still buzzing off a mix of shameful embarrassment and self-induced fear endorphins. We went back to Mexico for fireworks the next year, but I acted way cooler. Somebody else drove and I sat in the back. Little did I know that someday I'd visit the country that invented them.

Meanwhile, back in China, when we were having our first noodle breakfast just before beginning our walk, two huge rolls of firecrackers blew up on the sidewalk right in front of us. It seemed such a random time and odd location to light them off. At that time, we didn't yet understand their significance. Over the next few days, we noticed a wide array of firecrackers for sale in the roadside stores where we stopped for water and snacks. Most were in bricks or rolls and some had scary and foreboding names written in English. Several times Doug and I saw men with missing fingers and disfigured, burn-scarred hands. We'd look at each other, nod knowingly and whisper, *Widow Maker*, invoking the name of the most dangerous looking firecracker we had ever seen in our whole entire lives—the one that looked like a single stick of dynamite. Doug was fond of the rolls of firecrackers. He'd buy the biggest ones he could find and I'd strap them to the back of his pack. Some measured at least eighteen inches across. The skinniest firecrackers were on the outside and they got progressively fatter towards the center. A similar roll would probably cost $30 in the United States, but in China they were the equivalent of a mere few dollars.

Doug started buying them whenever they were available, which was almost every day. At those prices, he couldn't resist. He'd wait until a reasonable hour and when we were well out of town, he'd light them off. It became part of our daily routine—wake up, walk, light off firecrackers, eat some noodles, walk, look for firecrackers to light off the next day, walk... It was always a disappointment when we couldn't find any. I enjoyed our little ritual, even though it caused a few arguments.

Trailing behind Doug as usual, I'd look ahead and see him standing well off the shoulder of the road, looking into a ravine and then walking away. My curiosity piqued, I'd wonder what could be there and hurry to the same spot. But instead of seeing an exotic specimen of delicate flower or a hen with a brood of adorable, fuzzy chicks scratching around for their breakfast, a roll of firecrackers with a delayed fuse would explode ten feet in front of me. As previously mentioned, I love firecrackers... when I have some warning, but these unwelcomed surprises were fraying my nerves. As soon as the ringing in my ears stopped and my ability to hear returned, I'd chastise him for not giving me any warning. He'd tell me he had mimed lighting them off; I'd counter that I hadn't seen or understood any such gesturing and he'd call me a killjoy. A few days later, it would happen all over again. It was the only time we bickered during the entire trip.

One afternoon we stopped at a store for water and Doug pointed to a roll of firecrackers he wanted to buy. The shop owner looked at us sternly and said, "mùdì", which we knew meant "grave," as in burial plot. He refused to sell any to us and so we left not really understanding what the problem was. At another shop further down the road, we were able to buy some and so our morning ritual continued uninterrupted. A few weeks later, a large bus rumbled past us and from the back window a woman tossed lit firecrackers followed by handfuls of small, rectangular papers which fluttered to the ground. Our curiosity piqued, we trotted after the bus to see what she had thrown. Some of the papers were very small bills of Chinese currency valued at a few U.S. cents. The other papers, which also appeared to be currency, were larger and brightly colored. A few Chinese characters were printed on one side below a drawing of a bearded and mustached man wearing an orange robe and headdress. The other side bore a landscape in blue ink. Across the top, a banner read in English, *HELL BANK NOTE*. The denomination of the bill was $50,000,000. The shopkeeper's single utterance, "mùdì," in combination with his admonishing look, then began to make sense. The money and firecrackers the woman threw out the window were funerary items. Doug and I laughed and speculated as to why the currency was in US dollars. Does the devil do more business with Americans? Does he prefer the relatively stable US dollar to the Chinese Renminbi? We gathered a few of the Hell Notes and the smaller Chinese currency and I put them in my backpack. That evening I took photos of the "money" we had picked up and posted the story on our website. Then I ironed the bills flat with my hands and tucked them in between the pages of my journal to keep as souvenirs.

As for the two rolls of firecrackers that blew up the morning we set out to finish Hippolyte's walk… I accepted them as a blessing and a good omen. And all those firecrackers we had been lighting off every morning… I decided that without even knowing it, we had, in the Chinese tradition, been honoring Hippolyte the entire time. Our morning ritual took on new meaning. Now Doug waited until I was standing beside him before lighting the fuse while I said my uncle's name quietly to myself.

CHAPTER FORTY

Alone With the Police

Doug and I stood at the edge of a small town, staring down the highway that disappeared into the distance. Although we logged eighteen miles that day, neither of us felt tired. According to our GPS, the next town was over fifteen miles away. However, neither of us had that kind of energy in our reserves. Because suitable camping spots were still difficult to find, we decided to turn around and look for a hotel. Almost immediately, we found one that looked inviting. Its glass doors were fogged with condensation and upon entering, we were met with a blissful blast of air-conditioning. Doug asked if there was a room available and the clerk smiled, which we understood to mean yes. We produced our passports, she looked at them briefly and then gestured for me to follow her outside. Doug had already eased into the sofa and was looking awfully comfortable, so I told him to relax and that I'd take care of everything. In the past, clerks had made photocopies of our passports, so I assumed the woman was taking me to a neighboring business with a copy machine.

She pushed the door open and we stepped back out into the sweltering heat. I followed her across the road, down the street and into a large empty parking lot. I looked at the signage above the building and recognized it immediately. My stomach dropped and my heart skipped a beat. I was being taken into another police station. Despite how our last encounter with the police had ended, my fears were not allayed.

She pushed open an enormous, heavy door that closed with an

ominous thud behind us. We entered a large room that was empty and still. Our footsteps echoed off the walls and high ceilings. The hotel clerk walked to a door on the right and knocked. A voice on the other side responded and the clerk pushed the door open. Inside, a shirtless man was seated backwards on a wooden chair while a woman in a police uniform massaged his back. There was a modest-sized desk up against the wall, but by far the biggest piece of furniture in the room was a giant bed frame. There was no mattress on it, just a flat wooden surface where a mattress should be. Since beginning our journey through China, Doug and I had slept on a few beds like this, albeit they were always twin sized. The man straddling the chair, clearly annoyed that his massage had been interrupted, stood up, put on his shirt and led us to a room across from his. He unlocked the door and pointed to a sofa. He left and locked the door behind him.

For the second time since our arrival in China, I found myself gazing wistfully out a window secured by sturdy bars. Only this time Doug wasn't with me. I took a seat on the sofa and did my best to settle in. The woman sat across from me. We smiled at one another briefly and then fell into awkward silence. As I scanned my surroundings, my eyes stopped on a picture placard that told me everything in the room was being audio and video recorded. I considered looking for cameras but thought better of it, not wanting to do anything that would appear suspicious. If there were indeed cameras in the room, there would be no way for me to post a status update on my social media account like I had done the time Doug and I had been brought in by the police. I watched as the woman from the hotel relaxed and eventually nodded off into her armchair, unconcerned about whatever fate might await me. What did she care if I got arrested and did time in a Chinese prison? Twenty long minutes later, I heard a car pull up in the parking lot and then voices as someone entered the building. Next I heard the sound of keys. The door opened a mere few inches—perhaps in anticipation of me trying to make my escape—and a different female officer entered the room. The officer who had been giving the chief a massage peeked her head in before abruptly closing and locking the door behind her.

Once again, an off-duty police officer with English skills was brought in to figure out what exactly we were doing in China. Her English skills were minimal and no better than my Mandarin. However, she had a translation app on her phone, which we passed back and forth for the next hour and a half. There is a limit to what you can do with a translation app, and the horror of the "nice fresh rape" mistranslation, the catalyst for our Mandarin lessons, was still in the forefront of my mind. I opted to use gestures and mime to reply to her questions, peppered with the few applicable Mandarin words I knew.

Her first question was, "Why are you in China?" I told her in my very limited Mandarin that my boyfriend and I were walking 1,200 miles from Dali to Shenzhen. Her expression was skeptical, so I reluctantly pulled out my phone and showed her pictures we had taken along the way. I never let her hold my phone; I was too nervous about the VPN app I had hidden away in my game folder. She asked if we were working in China, if we were traveling with a group, or if we were with an organization. I replied *no* to all of her questions. As nerve-wracking as our first police interrogation had been, at least every question was asked with a smile and our answers received in kind. The woman who was grilling me now seemed disappointed by all my responses.

Next she asked, "You walk?" I told her in Mandarin, "We walk from Dali to Shenzhen—1,200 miles." "You go by car?" she queried. "No. We walk," I replied. "You go by bus?" she asked with raised eyebrows. "No. We walk," I reiterated, trying to hide my frustration. I contemplated taking off my shoes and socks and showing her my hideously calloused feet as proof but thought better of it. Instead, I mimed getting up in the morning, which I achieved by closing my eyes, letting my head loll to the side, opening my eyes again, stretching my arms over my head, blinking several times and doing my best to look like as innocent as newborn Bambi. Then I marched in place and said "Èr shí wǔ gōng lǐ"—*twenty-five kilometers,*" after which I pantomimed exhaustion, wiped actual sweat from my forehead (because unlike the hotel where Doug was waiting for me, this room had no air conditioning) and then feigned going to sleep, folding my hands alongside my cheek, closing my eyes and doing my best to look angelic. Then I pantomimed getting up at the crack of dawn, pointed at my watch and told her, "4:00 in the morning." "But tomorrow you go by car?" she asked. I buried my hands in my face and took a deep breath. I looked up at the police officer and then at the hotel clerk, who was examining her cuticles. Would I ever be released from this room, and if I got locked up, what would the clerk tell Doug when she returned to the hotel without me? An hour before as we stood on the highway at the edge of town, I felt energetic. Now I was bone-tired and weary. Suddenly exhausted from completing eighteen miles that day in ninety-five-degree heat and humidity, I replied, in Mandarin—*We walk. We walk. We walk. We waaaaaaaalk.*

I sat down on the couch and waited for her next round of questions. I repeated my performance again and again as she queried, "Yesterday? Day before yesterday? Tomorrow? Day after tomorrow? Two days after tomorrow? Last week?" She asked what town we were headed to next and the best I could offer was somewhere twenty-five kilometers down the highway. She also wanted to know how old I was, how old Doug was, what we did for a living, if we had visited other countries on this trip, and a few questions that I simply didn't understand. By this time, even that mattress-less bed in the police chief's office/massage room started looking good. I began to wonder if there was something wrong with me. Some people, I thought to myself, take their vacations at island resorts. If I were one of those people, I could at this very moment be relaxing on a beautiful tropical beach, face down on a massage table, sucking a fish-bowl-sized frozen cocktail through a three-foot-long straw as I listened to waves crashing on a sandy, white shore while steel drum music played in the background. Instead, I was trapped inside a police station playing charades with a police officer who was no doubt annoyed that she was called in on her day off. Just then, my phone buzzed with a text message from Doug, who asked what the heck was going on. I told him I was at the police station again and to stay put. I figured one of us needed to be on the outside just in case things went south. After everything Doug has done for me, I figured it was my turn to take one for the team.

Eventually, the barrage of questions ended, our passports returned, and I was free to go. The whole process had taken nearly two hours. By the time I got back to the hotel, Doug had just uncapped and taken a drink of his second beer. He held it out to me and, gratefully, I accepted the bottle and drained it with one unladylike chug. It felt and tasted better than any cocktail with an umbrella ever could have. I sighed heavily as I felt the stress leaving my neck and shoulders. I swung my backpack over my shoulder and followed the clerk up three flights of stairs to our room with three twin-sized beds with glorious, plastic-covered Hello Kitty mattresses.

CHAPTER FORTY-ONE

Ouch!

Throughout our walk, we kept track of the miles. One hundred miles, two hundred miles, three hundred and fifty miles. In the beginning, there were so many miles ahead of us that it was disheartening. The imbalance felt defeating. Then we started measuring in a different way: one eighth of the way finished, one quarter, one third and then one day we broke the halfway point and I finally quit doubting myself. I went from, *I don't think I can do this* to *I'M DOING IT!* After that, the miles seemed to fly past and my perspective changed. Every mile we walked meant less time in this amazing place. The days and miles were being stolen away from us.

Then one early morning in July, Doug calculated we had less than three hundred miles left, and it sounded so easy—almost *leisurely*. It was still dark outside, and we were getting ready to leave our hotel. I stood up like I have stood up hundreds of thousands of times before, took a few steps forward to grab my sandals... and kicked a bed leg... **hard**. I heard a loud *CRACK*. Doug heard it too. Instantly, I was in excruciating, unbearable pain and I crumpled into a heap on the foot of the bed. It was agony. It was of all things... my right pinky toe. I gave myself a minute to catch my breath before I stood and tried to put weight on it. Searing pain shot through my entire foot and I collapsed back onto the bed. I knew it then. The walk was over.

Actually, I was surprised that it hadn't happened sooner. I've always been terribly, if not comically uncoordinated. Long ago I resigned myself to the fact that I'd never be the elegant woman turning heads as she glided into the room. I'd be the woman who tripped upon entering the room, and I would probably have toilet paper stuck to the bottom of my shoe, but that's ok. It's who I am. I had never really been bothered by my clumsiness before. However, this time I was devastated and broke down into big, ugly, heaving, snotty tears.

For the next several hours I lie on the bed, rigid with pain. I sent Doug out to look for ice, and one protracted and tortuous hour later he came back with a green pea-flavored popsicle. That was the closest thing to ice he could find. If I'm completely honest, in that exact moment, I probably cried again. A few hours later and still in pain, I decided I needed something prescription strength. Doug went downstairs to the reception desk to inquire about a doctor. Minutes later he was helping me to the lobby. By the time we made it downstairs, a taxi was waiting for us.

After a short ride, the car pulled up in front of a hospital. I protested vehemently as the driver got out of the car to open my door while he called out to someone at the top of the drive. I tried explaining that I only wanted a doctor, but things spiraled out of control from there. The next thing I knew I was in a wheelchair being pushed into the building. We went down a corridor, out another door, and into a hallway where people in various stages of distress waited in line. A woman with an infant perched on her hip stood at the head of the line. She held up a length of bamboo from which hung a clear, glass bottle with an IV line that ran to a needle inserted into the back of the babe's hand. Whoever was pushing my chair left me at the head of the queue. "Bu, mei yào. Mei yào!" I repeated, "No, I don't want" was the closest I could come to expressing my mortification with the situation. "Wo yào!—*I want!*" and I pointed to the end of the line, but next thing I knew I was being helped onto a table to have my foot x-rayed. A few minutes later I was in another room, this one with beds and benches filled with people who all turned to look at Doug and me.

A woman in her 70's, staff in her hand, came and stood beside me. A strip of torn cloth was wrapped around her shin, covering a wound that had bled through the makeshift bandage. More of the walking wounded stood up and gathered around. "Please, no. Please, no," I whimpered as I buried my face in my hands, believing that I certainly deserved to be at the end of the triage list. I felt a hand on my shoulder and looked up to the woman with the bandaged and bleeding leg, who was looking at me sympathetically.

Then three doctors entered the room and stood in front of me. One of them showed me my x-ray, and I saw the problem immediately. The two bones that were supposed to be on top of one another were slightly askew. The second doctor conferred with his smart phone, looked at me, and with a friendly smile said, "Dislocated. Must pull." I nodded my head as one doctor held my leg out straight, another grabbed me around the ankle, and the third doctor grabbed my pinky toe and pulled for what felt like an eternity. I screamed the entire time, alternating between, *Ow! Stop!* and, *Please, no*! All were peppered with a few choice R-rated modifiers, none of which they understood but nevertheless found amusing. I knew of no other way to end this torture. The doctor finally stopped when I leaned forward in my wheelchair and tried to punch him in the shoulder. He dodged my weak blow even though my reach would have missed him by two feet. Everyone was laughing at me... including myself. It was the most simultaneously comical and painful experience of my life.

I've never dislocated anything before, but I knew the pain should have subsided immediately once those two little bones were realigned. But it hadn't subsided. It was worse. Unbeknownst to any of us, the actual problem was that I had also torn the tendon and/or ligament in my little toe, which was now an angry shade of red. Thinking they hadn't successfully realigned the two bones, they resumed the collective pulling. My shrieks carried to the far wings of the hospital and to the ears of the chief of orthopedic surgery, who recognized some choice English words... and that's how we met Dr. Vincent.

CHAPTER FORTY-TWO

A Year In Limbo

I prayed that somehow Doug and I would be able to finish the walk. If we took one week off, we'd have to walk twenty-one miles per day to complete the last 300 miles. I explained to Dr. Vincent why we were in China and what we were doing and asked if he thought it would be possible for us to continue if I rested my foot for a week. He told me that it would not. Any hope I held onto was gone. I was crestfallen. The fact that the injury that ended our walk had zero "wow" factor only added insult to actual injury. Why couldn't I have been bitten by a venomous snake or mauled by a panda? He sent for another cab, gave me an envelope of pills for the pain, and exchanged phone numbers with Doug.

The next morning Dr. Vincent called Doug and asked if I would be interested in trying Eastern medicine. By that time, I had consulted with a friend, the wife of a chiropractor, and she suggested that since I was in China, I should ask for acupuncture—something I was already familiar with—and a treatment I had never heard of before—cold laser therapy. Doug asked Dr. Vincent if the hospital offered either, and it did. He offered to pick us up at our hotel on his way to work but said he would not be able to bring us back to our hotel afterwards because he had a surgery to perform.

When we arrived at the hospital, a wheelchair was waiting for me and Dr. Vincent escorted us back to the room where I had previously received what I now refer to as the "Toe Yanking." Dr. Vincent said a few words to a clinician and left for the operating room. The clinician briefly paused the wheelchair in front of a woman with a baby sitting on her lap. The infant, about nine months old, had five needles sticking out from the top of his head. "Nǐ hǎo shào hā ěr—*Hello sweetheart,*" I said with a smile. He smiled right back, reached up, and pulled out three needles. A nurse rushed over, took the needles out of his chubby and dimpled little hand and deftly reinserted three new needles while he stared at me with unblinking eyes. I thought of all the other babies we had met on our trip thus far. He was one of the few who didn't burst into tears at the sight of us.

She helped me onto a table where I lie on my back with my head on a pillow. A cart bearing a machine with cords and clamps was rolled to my bedside. Another female patient came and stood at my side. She sympathetically patted my hand and murmured comforting words as the clinician stuck needles into my foot and little toe. Then she attached the clamps and rotated the dials until my fourth toe began to twitch. By the time my therapy session was over, Dr. Vincent had returned. He told us that his surgery was cancelled and he could take us back to our hotel.

Our private and narrated tour of Beiliu began the moment we left the parking lot of the hospital. Dr. Vincent pointed out places of interest while taking the most scenic route through the city. As we neared our hotel, he mentioned that since we planned to stay in Beiliu until I was able to walk at least a little, we might want to upgrade to a nicer hotel. I waited in the car while he and Doug went to look at the first place, which although of similar caliber, appeared to be a bit nicer than our current accommodations. When they returned, Doug declared that the hotel was a big improvement and that we'd be happier there, but Dr. Vincent still had one more hotel to show us. We rolled up a steep driveway, where water from a stone fountain cascaded down marble steps and into a tiled pool. As we pulled into the porte cochere, a uniformed man emerged from the shiny chrome and glass entrance and opened the passenger door for Doug. This place had all the hallmarks of the lavish hotels I never stay in because somehow, even though I was born in the 60s, my inner-child grew up during the Great Depression. After Dr. Vincent got out of the car, Doug whispered to me, "I'll go look to be polite, but we'll stay at the other hotel." Doug went inside while Dr. Vincent stood out front in the shade and waited. When Doug returned, Dr. Vincent asked him what he thought. Doug replied that it was lovely; however, we didn't want to spend that much money. Dr. Vincent asked us to wait a moment while he went inside. He returned a few minutes later and told us he'd been able to negotiate a better price. It was much better and we couldn't pass it up. It was a resort with a bar, a restaurant, a swimming pool and best of all... an ice machine!

Our new accommodations were splendid. The carpet was thick and soft, so when I had to crawl to the bathroom, it felt like my knees were on little pillows. I spent the next few days in bed with bags of ice beside my elevated foot as it was still too painful to have anything touching it. For over a week, I slept every night with my foot sticking out from under the bedding, as even the weight of a sheet touching me was insufferable.

One evening Doug helped me downstairs to the hotel lobby where there was a restaurant that looked out onto the hotel pool. I was still racking my brain to find an explanation—aside from kicking a bed leg—for hurting my foot. I needed a reason. It seemed so unfair and the only way I would be able to accept that we weren't finishing the walk this year was to find that reason. All through dinner, I scanned the pool, keeping track of every child in the water until it was too dark to see and our empty plates had been cleared. It was crazy and morbid, but I thought that if I could point out a drowning child and be responsible for that child being rescued, then it would all be worth it. The reason for hurting my foot would be saving the child's life and I could go home happy. But nobody drowned and no life was saved, so I went to bed. The only thing that gave me any amount of comfort was the fact that the protagonists of all good stories have challenges and setbacks. Would anybody read The Odyssey if Odysseus sailed straight home after the Trojan War? Of course not. Dear Reader, with a healthy dose of embellishment and artistic license, I could have made this part of the story absolutely riveting. I could have had you all on the edge of your seats. Alas, I cannot. I tell my story with honesty and integrity. Thus, our odyssey contains no kidnappings, monsters, sirens nor cyclops—only a mangled pinky toe that sometimes aches when the weather turns cold.

Every day that week, Doug and I went back to the hospital for my acupuncture and cold laser therapy treatments. After six days of treatment I was well enough to hobble short distances, and we were ready to make our way back to Hong Kong. We went to the cashier to settle my bill for six days of acupuncture, cold laser therapy, the initial x-rays, toe yanking and pain pills. It came to roughly fifty dollars.

That evening, Dr. Vincent had us to his home for dinner. We met his son, who had taken the Western name Steve, and his wife, Hong, who even complimented me on my chopstick skills. It was a delicious dinner and a lovely evening. We took photos around the table, said our goodbyes and then Dr. Vincent drove us back to our hotel.

The next morning, we took a cab to the bus station and began our slow journey back to Shenzhen. For a while we drove along the 324, the same highway we were supposed to be walking down. I eventually quit looking out the window. Every mile marker we passed made me feel like a failure. I wasn't supposed to be passing them from a bus window.

Two weeks and several bus rides later, Doug and I stopped at a nature preserve called Dinghu Mountain Resort. It was filled with beautiful streams, waterfalls and trees. A damp cave, water dripping from its walls and ceilings, housed 100 Buddha statues. I held out my open palm, caught a few drops, and let them drizzle onto my pinky toe. Later we saw a sign outside that said something about the special purity of the ions in the water. We met a young man named Ting Feng in the parking lot and gave him one of our postcards. That evening I logged into our website and wrote about our visit to the park. I commented about how far I was able to walk over the course of several hours by taking lots of little breaks. The next day I found a message from Dr. Vincent in the comments section.

"I am glad to know that you have been able to walk a long distance. Your rehabilitation is my desire! Your behavior touched me, let me to rethink the true essence of life, bless you!" We had gained a friend in Dr. Vincent, and I knew that in less than a year we would be back in Beiliu to resume our walk.

I also found a message from Ting Feng. "Hello my friend, I am glad to meet you. Your tenacity and optimism have affected me. I hope you gain more love and know more good friends. I wish you happy every day." That wasn't the only message he left for us. He saw my post about finding the funerary money and left a message in the comments section below the photo. "There's a human being in the middle of the note like Mao in RMB. He is the King of Hell, he is not only the ruler but also the judge of the underworld and passes judgement on all the dead. He always appears in a male form, and his minions include a judge who holds in his hands a brush and a book listing every soul and the allotted death date for every life. In our ritual, we avoid picking the hell money up by throwing out from a funeral family, it brings you very bad luck, burn it if you still have it." I'm not usually superstitious, but when I read his message, I immediately thought about my toe and Doug and I burned the bills in our hotel trashcan.

We flew home a few days later, and for the next ten months... I waited and watched the calendar. My mind was always on China. I was still so disappointed that the trip hadn't ended how I wanted it to and berated myself frequently for kicking that bed leg. If only my foot had landed an inch to the left, even a half inch... To this day, I still give every piece of furniture a wide berth. I vacillated between thinking it had happened for a reason and being upset that we weren't able to just walk the last three hundred miles and return triumphant. I wanted my denouement! This was not how it was supposed to end and this wasn't what I wanted. However, if I hadn't kicked that bed leg, we never would have met Dr. Vincent. I also thought about potential disasters that were averted when my toe met that bed leg. Maybe something much worse was supposed to happen to us down the road and my clumsiness had saved us.

We settled back into our lives, went back to our jobs, slept in the same bed every night, and I counted off the days just as I had counted down the miles. As the holidays came and went and we welcomed in a new year, the numbers got smaller, the waiting more manageable, and then it was time to go back to China and finish Hippolyte's walk.

CHAPTER FORTY-THREE

Back to China

When I was in my twenties, I met a woman who told me a phenomenal travel story. It bordered on supernatural. During the 70's, she was just out of college and vacationing in San Francisco. She went to a park and there met two men from Australia. They did touristy things together for a few days and had a wonderful time, in her opinion. When it came time to part ways, she suggested they exchange phone numbers and addresses. One of the men told her that it wouldn't be necessary. "Travelers always meet again," he assured her, and so they bid farewell with no way of ever reaching one another. Mind you, this all happened back in the days before email made communication convenient and social media made finding someone, even someone from another country, relatively easy. Their casual farewell left her feeling bewildered and rebuffed. Two years later while vacationing in Greece, she walked into a bar and there they were... the two men she had met at the park in San Francisco. I have no idea what forces brought them back together again, but what the Aussie said had proven true. When people travel, they meet again. They left it up to the fates and had been reunited. We, on the other hand, did not want to leave meeting Dr. Vincent again up to the cosmos. Our last night in Beiliu, Dr. Vincent invited us to his home for dinner. Before we said our goodbyes, we all connected on the app WeChat. Over the next ten months, we sent holiday greetings and checked in with one another periodically.

Several weeks before our anticipated return to China, we sent Dr. Vincent our itinerary. We planned to fly to Hong Kong and from there to Nanning where we would take a bus to Beiliu. We also invited Dr. Vincent and his family to dinner at our hotel. Despite our willingness to take the bus, he insisted on picking us up at the airport in Nanning, a five-and-a-half-hour round trip drive from Beiliu. The previous year when Doug and I flew into Kunming, we disembarked not knowing a soul in this country of 1.3 billion. This year, we had a friend waiting for us at the airport.

As Doug and I were being driven through Nanning, memories flooded back to us. We had been in this city of nearly seven million people roughly a year ago, only we had been walking in the dark morning hours. At that early hour, the normally bustling metropolis that boasts twenty-one of China's tallest buildings was nearly silent. Even the air was still. Somewhere along the street that we were being driven down was the corner on which we found a 150 lb. dead pig lying next to a broken end table. I couldn't begin to imagine where the pig was living before it wound up curbside. As we continued on our chauffeured drive, we looked out the window and excitedly pointed out sites we recognized. I was overjoyed and relieved to be back. We were finally going to finish Hippolyte's walk.

Exhausted from travel and the time difference, we fell asleep in the back of the car after an hour or so of driving and woke up just before we arrived in Beiliu. What took us nearly ten days to walk flew by in two hours and forty-five minutes. Lychee season was at its peak and vendors holding bags of the delicious, red fruit stood on every corner. We drove through a maze of streets until Dr. Vincent found the man who sold the best lychees, and then he bought a bag for us. We had one full day to get Chinese SIM cards for our cell phones and an evening to spend with Dr. Vincent and his family. Our second and last night in Beiliu, we met at the restaurant of our hotel for dinner. It was obvious Dr. Vincent's son, Steve, had been practicing his English because we were able to speak with him so easily this time. He even interpreted for his mother, who asked if I would give her a Western name. Her first name, Hong, means *red* in Mandarin. Doug and I pulled out our cell phones and showed her pictures of both a rose and a ruby and asked her to pick the one she preferred. She picked the one I would have selected for her, the ruby. Having no children, I've never had the privilege of naming someone. It was an honor. We exchanged small gifts and Dr. Vincent presented us each with wooden bead necklaces. Mine was made from fragrant sandalwood. We wore them every day. Now they hang from our bedside lamps.

The next morning, we were up at 3:30 and on the road by 4:15. We officially resumed our walk from the driveway of the very hotel where our journey ended the previous year. I couldn't wait to take that first step. I wiggled my toes in my sandals, remembering both the physical and emotional pain that I experienced nearly a year ago when I kicked that bed leg. Then we took our first steps towards Shenzhen, eating lychee for breakfast and enjoying our first sunrise as we walked along the shoulder of the highway.

They say you can't go home again, that you can't step in the same river twice, but it felt like everything was just as we had left it. It was as though everything had simply stopped and waited for us while we went home. People still smiled and waved to us as we walked along the highway. Our favorite snack treats were all still there, even the ones I didn't venture to try, like sweet pea and corn-flavored ice cream pops. Oreo cookies still came in odd flavors like red bean cake and pork. I had never been so happy to see giant chicken feet and fermented duck eggs in shrink wrap packages. They all told me that we were finally back. The one thing that wasn't the same that summer was the heat. It was worse than I could have imagined. We wouldn't find out until after we went home, but it was one of the hottest summers on record in China. I had experienced this kind of heat and humidity before, in India, but I was considerably younger then.

When I was planning my trip to India, I knew I was going to be traveling during monsoon season and I knew it would be hot. I was, however, completely unprepared for how hot it would actually get. If you ask Google about monsoon season in India, a cute little graphic pops up, and under that it says:

> "Monsoon or rainy season, lasting from June to September. The season is dominated by humid southwest summer monsoon, which slowly sweeps across the country beginning in late May

or early June. Monsoon rains begin to recede from North India at the beginning of October. South India typically receives more rainfall."

This description makes no mention at all of the extreme heat. My trip pre-dated Google by a good six years; even so, Google's description would have in no way prepared me for such a vexatious and punishing weather phenomenon. "Summer monsoon, which slowly *sweeeeps* across the country." Ha! It sounds feminine, graceful and almost...gentle. Not even close, Google! Monsoon is a sadistic dominatrix. She is cruel and merciless. She hears your safe word and laughs in your sweaty face. And then she cranks the heat up higher. She chokes you with humidity levels that hover at 99%. She teases you with the possibility of rain that could lower temperatures into a bearable range, easing your suffering, but she never delivers.

Monsoon temperatures range between 95 and 105 degrees, but it's not the heat that makes it uncomfortable or dangerous. The humidity is so high that even the locals find it difficult to breathe, especially those with asthma. Every year during monsoon season in India, the department of transportation schedules additional trains to Hyderabad, where asthma sufferers line up by the thousands to ingest a traditional remedy that supposedly cures asthma forever. They swallow a live, guppy sized fish called a *murrel*, which is stuffed with a paste made from a secret family recipe.

In late May of 1992, my flight into Bombay arrived eight hours late and landed at 2:00 am. The British man who sat next to me on the airplane offered me a ride to my hotel. When we stepped outside the airport, it felt like I was wading through the hot and muggy air. It was so thick, it was a wonder I couldn't see it. I chalked my discomfort up to the fact that I was exhausted from travelling nearly thirty-five hours straight. As we drove through the dark streets, I saw men sleeping sprawled across the hoods of their taxies or slumped in the backseats of their auto-rickshaws, waiting for their next fare to wake them.

I had reserved a room at an upscale hotel and planned to look for more modest accommodations the following day. I checked into a beautiful air-conditioned hotel, went to my room and slept until 9:00 am. I dressed, stuffed my travel guidebook in my purse, went downstairs and ate a quick breakfast. Excited to see what Bombay looked like in the daylight, I headed across the lobby for the revolving glass door. I pushed the panel and walked into the cylindrical enclosure. The second I stepped outside, I was hit with a choking blast of heat and humidity far worse than what I had experienced the night before. It was like being in a steam sauna and made me feel as though I was suffocating. I took a hard left and followed the revolving door right back inside. Once indoors, I perched nervously on the edge of an overstuffed chair outside the hotel salon where women were having their eyebrows threaded. I felt immediate panic and a solid dose of regret. "Maybe you're over reacting. Maybe it's all in your head. Maybe the heat feels worse coming from an air-conditioned room," I attempted to gaslight myself. I tried again. Boldly, I walked through the revolving door again only to be met with the same wall of heat and humidity. I followed the door back inside so quickly that I felt dizzy.

Eventually, I did venture out. I was forced to. I had only booked one night at that hotel and needed to find more reasonable accommodations; I had budgeted $10 a night. That day, I walked along the shore of Juhu beach. I took an uncomfortable and lurching ride on the back of a camel and I watched a snake charmer blow a hypnotic melody on his punji as he tried to draw an unwilling and uncooperative cobra from its reed basket. Eventually, the charmer used the punji as a stick to poke at the cobra until it rose lethargically, flared its hood and swayed for a few seconds before languidly retreating to the relative cool of its woven cage. The heat was too much, even for a cold-blooded reptile. Monsoon season isn't restricted to India. It spreads across Bangladesh, Myanmar and into China. Hippolyte walked through all these countries during monsoon season.

The summer Doug and I returned to finish Hippolyte's walk, the weather was even hotter and more humid than the previous summer. It broke records. It was so extreme, I feared it might break me. And as a person prone to heat exhaustion, I feared it could kill me, too. One morning, a group of men approached us while we sat on the front steps of a store, enjoying the sliver of shade provided by the eaves of the roof. Our backpacks and trekking poles leaned against the side of the building. Exiting the store with cigarettes, they stopped to survey us, sweaty and disheveled, finishing our waters that less than a minute ago had been blissfully cold but were now tepid. The cut-up of the group grabbed my trekking poles, one in each hand, and bent deep at his knees as he acted out skiing down a steep and snowy mountain. Imaginary tree branches whipped and battered him in the face as he bombed down the non-existent slope and crashed into a heap. He was a gifted and talented mimic who had us all laughing. The best part was that for that brief moment, I was on a frozen mountain with him and I forgot about how hot it was. I stood to leave, grabbed my props and felt no embarrassment over the giant wet spot my thighs had left upon the pavement.

I have no idea how Hippolyte survived in that heat. Maybe, like Doug and I, he walked in the early mornings and sought out shade during mid-day and afternoon. I wonder what my uncle Hippolyte would have thought about the modern-day advantages Doug and I had as we walked through China. We wore moisture-wicking clothing, had a lightweight tent, air mattresses and a water purifier in our backpacks. What would Hippolyte have thought about Doug and I staying in hotels with fans and sometimes air conditioners? Neither of us had the willpower to shun the use of these comforts when they were available.

I was appreciative of these amenities but felt guilty and spoiled for using them knowing that Hippolyte lived exclusively outdoors without any reprieve from the elements. But, it wasn't just an issue of willpower. There was a day the previous summer when I'm certain air-conditioning saved me from heat stroke. I would have been a fool to deny myself this life saving measure on some sort of mis-guided principle, which leads me to this realization. Had Hippolyte understood the risk and had it been available at the time, he probably would have taken anti-malarial medication.

Because of the intense heat, we began waking at 2:00 am and were on the road by 2:30. Still so hot at this hour, our clothes were drenched with sweat in ten minutes. The roads were deserted but we were far from alone. Thousands of cicadas screeched so loudly that it was like being at the hardware store while someone is cutting keys. We had to raise our voices to be heard over them. Frogs croaked from rice paddies and roadside canals, and bats dipped and flitted in the light of the occasional street lamp, eating all the bugs they could before the rising sun sent them back into hiding. There was so much beauty we missed while walking in those dark hours before sunrise, but the heat only got worse as we traveled further south and east. As we walked in those dark morning hours, the towering emerald green mountains that by daylight reflected their images in the still waters of rice paddies now appeared to us as hulking dark sentries. By 9 a.m., those same mountains wavered in the heat. By 10:00 am, if I was lucky, we had checked into a hotel. Doug would occasionally explore and I would sometimes join him but more often than not, I stayed indoors regardless how lovely our surroundings may have been.

But it wasn't just the landscape and scenery we missed by walking so early in the morning. We also missed engaging with the people who greeted us as we traveled along the highway. I felt a bit like a Golden Retriever because there wasn't a person we encountered whom I didn't immediately and enthusiastically adore. Admittedly, our experiences off the highway weren't always as idyllic. We had been chased out of a few hotels, twice interrogated by the police and there were a couple times when Doug and I paid "the tourist tax" and were charged far more for a meal than we would have been charged back home. If these establishments had Yelp reviews, there would have been a $$$$ out of $$$$ below the establishment's name and a five star rating despite the fact that we were seated on eight-inch-high wooden stools at plastic tables while chickens weaved between our feet, hoping for a dropped morsel. Once, Doug was charged $30 for a two course breakfast. Back home, if I spend $30 for breakfast there's a decent chance I'm leaving with a mimosa buzz. But really, we were only grossly overcharged twice, and both times we tallied how many meals, bottles of water and bags of fruit we had been gifted and called it even, opting to believe that perhaps the person really needed the money.

The previous summer, we often stopped at town squares to sit on benches and watch large groups of people doing something akin to tai chi that was choreographed to music. Or, when presented with the opportunity, we would sit and listen to an ensemble of octogenarian musicians performing in small, shady parks. I missed watching these gatherings that to me were as culturally valuable and relevant as a visit to a museum.

Specifically so I could entertain children that first summer, I packed my disappearing scarf trick. The following summer, I brought everything I needed to make balloon animals. But, because of the hours we kept, I only had a dozen or so opportunities. One morning, I created a balloon sword and hilt for a four-year-old boy. Within seconds, he partially dismantled it, put it over his head, squeezed it over his shoulders and shimmied it down to his waist. He then proceeded to parade around the lobby, hands on his hips proudly donning his anatomically correct accoutrement. This story serves as an example that, despite how hard we try, sometimes things don't materialize as we plan. There is a Chinese proverb that states, "Man's schemes are inferior to those made by heaven." I prayed that we'd be safe and injury free on this trip. Another Chinese proverb felt fitting. "A bit of fragrance clings to the hand that gives flowers." I decided to keep making balloon animals... but no more swords.

CHAPTER FORTY-FOUR

Hippolyte In India

A newspaper article published after my uncle's death stated that Hippolyte intended to walk along the east coast of the "Gulf of Persia" but was denied entry by "the British representative in Persia on account of the many dangers" and therefore took a boat from Basra to Karachi which then was still part of British India. The partition of Pakistan which would include East Pakistan, now known as Bangladesh, wouldn't take place for another twenty-five years. What exactly these *dangers* were, I don't know. The Soviet Socialist Republic had invaded towards the end of 1920 but had withdrawn by 1921. There was a British coup d'état the same year in an effort to stop the Bolsheviks from penetrating Iran, as this was a threat to Britain's colonial possession of India. Either of these events might have caused-the representative to bar Hippolyte's entry. This is where things get confusing, because a different newspaper article, also printed after his death, says that Hippolyte *did* go through Persia and from there to Afghanistan, through the Khyber Pass and then to Calcutta, India. I didn't know which article to believe, so I did the math. My calculations indicate that he ignored the directions of the British representative and walked straight through Persia, otherwise there are sixty-four extra days.

Whatever his route, Hippolyte definitely passed through India because he had more postcards made there. My cousin Artie thinks Hippolyte walked to Bombay because the name of the company, Bombay Art Printing Works, is printed at the bottom of the card. I couldn't understand why

POST CARD.

I am an American, walking around the globe with my dog as companion. I started on April 19, 1920 at Seattlewash without a penny in my pocket.

We both earn our livelihood by the sale of our picture post cards.

H. MARTINET.

Bombay Art Printing Works.

Address

my uncle would walk so far south only to walk north again to Calcutta. I considered the possibility that Hippolyte laid over somewhere in the north while he sent an order to the printing company in Bombay and waited for new cards to be printed and delivered to him. Artie adamantly insisted it would have been impossible for Hippolyte to get cards made without actually going to the printer himself. Still, I just couldn't imagine why my uncle would go on such a long errand. This nagged at me for years until I eventually searched the internet for Bombay Art Printing Works and immediately found a company by that exact name in Udhna, an area of Surat in the state of Gujarat. It's been there for generations and from there, it's a straight shot due east to Calcutta.

My uncle's presence in India was noted there and at home. At least four different articles were written about him. This first one was the least embellished. While it made no mention of my uncle meeting the College Square Swim Club, a photo of him and the club ran with the article. It was the first time I saw Hippolyte with bare upper arms and legs.

THE MODERN REVIEW V. 32 (1922)

A Globe-Trotter

An American globe-trotter named H. Martinet, who is doing the world mostly on foot, walking bare-footed, has been creating a mild sensation wherever he appears. He is not encumbered with either purse or with superfluous luggage. His exploit certainly indicates the possession of pluck and resource. His experience will also be more varied and intimate than those of travelers who tour round the world in the ordinary way.

This next article was published in 1936, in of all places, Australia. Sadly, the author buried the lede and the name of the man the article was written about was never mentioned. In a little over thirteen years, Hippolyte's passage through India had become the stuff of legend.

THE PORT MACQUARIE NEWS AND HASTINGS RIVER ADVOCATE

Saturday 2 May 1936 page 7
Walking Round The World

Recently an old, whiskered negro, aged seventy-five, set out to tramp from Los Angeles to New York, a distance of 3000 miles, to see his sons. He has based his life on John the Baptist, and decided that he would not accept a lift on the way. He carries a long pole, which serves the dual purpose of a walking-stick and a fishing-rod. The oddest of all unusual walkers was Hippolyte Martinet, who, starting from Seattle, tried to walk round the world. Penniless, he walked across the continent, then to France by boat, and from there through Europe and the greater part of Asia.

Walking through India, he was mistaken for a great new prophet, his tangled locks and blue eyes giving him a wild, imperious look, and mile-long queues of pilgrims, rich and poor, came from hundreds of miles, bearing gifts of gold, silver, jewels and fruit.

My cousin, Brian, found the following article in an unlikely publication called, The Gillette Blade, which I believe was a trade book.

AMERICAN GLOBE TROTTER ARRIVES IN INDIA

Will celebrate his return to U.S. A. by using a Gillette

Reprinted from the "Statesman" Calcutta, India

Our special representative resumed his search for Mr. Martinet, the American globe-trotter walking round the world, yesterday in the morning. News was received of passengers by 33 Down train having seen the globe-trotter marching along the railway line towards Howrah.

Our representative took a train which was returning empty from Howrah to Santragachi. He found the railway staff at Howrah and all along the line agog with excitement waiting for Mr. Hippolyte Martinet.

At Santragachi, conflicting versions of the traveler's journey were current. Some said that he was seen at Andul, others that he was near Bourea and still others that he was midway between Bourea and Anul.

He arrived in Calcutta to time, as he had declared his intention of arriving here on Independence Day.

Mr. Martinet went to Spence's Hotel for dinner, as he said he had been told by someone he met that it was the best place in India for a hearty meal. People left their tables and crowded round the globe-trotter at Spence's Hotel. He told then that it was the best meal he had had for many a day.

After dinner, some Americans asked him to go to Pelit's as the Americans in Calcutta who were celebrating Independence Day with a dinner were expecting him there. Mr. Martinet is so bronzed that Mr. Reid, of the United States Steel Products Co., who first saw him did not know that he was talking to an American. Mr. Martinet was heartily cheered by the gathering when he appeared in its midst—a picturesque figure with his uncommon costume and free bearing.

The representatives of Messrs. Muller and Phipps (India) Ltd. Agents for the Gillette razor gave Mr. Martinet a handsome gold (new improved model) Gillette razor, but Mr. Martinet smilingly declined the offer to have a shave there and then, but promised that when he accomplished his feat of walking, round the world he would celebrate his return to his country by using the Gillette which he had received as a gift.

This article was picked up by the *Seattle Star* the week of August 14th, 1922.

SEATTLE HIKER IS WORSHIPPED OVER IN INDIA

Barefooted Martinet Keeps on Walking Tho Interviewed

Hippolyte Martinet, bare-footed, bare-headed "globe trotter" who set out from Seattle October 1920, to walk his way around this world, is reported by the Calcutta "Englishman" to be arousing much interest and excitement among the people of India.

"The Englishman" is a daily newspaper of Calcutta which in a recent issue tells of sending its "representative" to interview "this man in khaki" who was setting the people all "agog."

According to the account, the paper's representative had trouble in keeping up with Martinet during the interview. Martinet did not stop walking, keeping his pace at what was estimated at 40 miles an hour, and traveling meanwhile thru the little settlement of Andul, Bengali and Santragachi.

When Martinet, a man 5 feet, 8 inches in height, with dark brown hair, left Seattle in 1920, he declared his intention of hiking around the

> world. He made his way across the United States in four months. He sailed to England, then left for the continent to walk thru France, Italy, Albania, Egypt, Arabia and finally into India, where it is said the Hindus now are bowing down and worshiping him as an "avatar", an incarnation of the deity, when he passes thru their villages. They have heard of his achievements and are said to be astounded. Martinet, it is reported, however, does not stop anywhere longer than for food and drink, which the people gladly give him. He continues on around the word, wearing no hat, no shoes and declaring himself to be "just globe-trotting".

Either the comment about my uncle walking forty miles per hour was tongue in cheek, or the author of this article intended to say Hippolyte walked forty miles *per day*. That feat no longer seemed remarkable to me even though Doug and I, because of my slow pace, never managed to walk more than twenty-four miles in a day. I was amused to see that once again my uncle was mistaken for an ascetic; in this case he was identified as a sadhu. To an outsider, a sadhu might be mistaken as a homeless person. Some sadhus are nomadic, wandering roads with staffs and begging pots which people fill with food in exchange for blessings and prayers. While Hippolyte didn't carry a staff or a begging pot, I can understand why someone would mistake him for an ascetic. It must have been refreshing for him. After all, he was in India, where a wandering person might be revered. In the United States, a wanderer could be arrested, as Hippolyte knew from experience.

Sadhus are regarded as holy men and representatives of God. They make up one half of one percent of the population in India. Some begin the path as children, offered up by their parents as thanks for good fortune or because they recognize that their child demonstrates an affinity for spiritual life. Others are orphans who have been adopted by sadhus. Becoming a sadhu is also a means of respectfully escaping marital obligations. By becoming a sadhu, one can transcend a lower caste, which thereby allows them freedoms that would be unattainable within their caste. Self-knowledge and a pressing desire to share the way to liberation guide others to this path. The ultimate aspiration is to achieve enlightenment wherein it is impossible to differentiate between opposites.

Therefore, there is no good or bad. Dirty is clean. Death is life.

A vow of poverty and chastity is taken when one becomes a sadhu. Often their only possessions are ritual objects. They wear loincloths or crude clothing constructed from grain sacks. Some wear no clothes at all and cover their bodies in ashes from fires or human cremations. They grow their hair into long, matted locks that they cut only after the guru who initiated them dies. Others wear wooden chastity belts or, in a demonstration to prove they have transcended their sexuality, lift blocks of stone that are hung from their genitals by strips of cloth. Other acts of mortification are practiced. They remain forever standing until their feet develop sores that require bandaging. Sadhus will stand upon only one foot or raise an arm straight up in the air without ever lowering it...for years on end. They only eat food that is offered them and, because they have transcended and it is impossible to differentiate between opposites, there is no good or bad food; as a result, some eat garbage or even excrement—human or animal.

I spent nearly a month traveling in India in 1992. I lost count of how many temples I visited where I bowed and was blessed by men in gauzy, flowing robes. Some of them might have been sadhus although, at that time, I had never heard the word. Because I would never presume to tell a holy person how to bless me, I accepted whatever benedictions they bestowed upon me. Across the board, they all prayed that I would find a husband. Soon. I was twenty-six and had no idea that my "best before" date had long since expired.

One of the most vivid memories I have of India is the morning following my late-night arrival in Agra. I woke up and left my hotel room to explore my immediate surroundings. I wandered only a few blocks away when I heard the chiming of cymbals, music, chanting and singing as a group of twenty or so people turned a corner and walked towards me. As they neared, I looked up and into the face of the person leading this procession and saw a man wearing a brightly colored sari and garish make up. *She* was bedecked with gold jewelry in her nose and ears and golden bangles jangled as they slid up and down her arms. When she saw me, her face broke out into the most beatific and adoring smile, as though I were a long and nearly-lost-forever friend. She stretched her arms out towards me as if to pull me into an embrace.

I'm embarrassed to say that I responded by nearly breaking into a run as I headed back to my hotel. Unfazed, they continued on their way. As the sounds of their revelry and music faded, I thought... "phew!", having no idea I had been invited into the arms of one of the more obscure sadhu, the sakhi. While ten percent of sadhu are women, most of whom are widows, only men can be a member of this sect. They forever adopt the dress of women as well as aggrandized feminine mannerisms. They are not as widely and readily worshiped as the other sadhu and are often disparaged, treated with suspicion, mocked and jeered. I've always felt like a bit of an outsider myself and regret my reaction. In my defense, I was alone and even though I was excited to be in India, I was completely overwhelmed by my environment. I was afraid I would be swallowed up among them and disappear forever. I regret my judgmental reaction when instead I could have walked into those welcoming arms and received her blessing.

When someone blesses another person, he or she is asking God to bestow divine favor and protection upon that individual. I am reminded of a story my friend Holt told me about a trip he took to Cuba in 1970. When he was twenty-two, he joined The Venceremos Brigade, a coalition of students from the United States. In a show of solidarity for the Cuban Revolution, they labored side-by-side with Cuban workers cutting cane in the fields. One night there was a party and Holt wandered off to sleep on a table away from the noise. When he woke the next morning, he found two freshly-eaten and picked-clean chicken bones deliberately arranged in a cross beside him. He interpreted them as a protection charm, picked them up and put them in the breast pocket of his shirt. As a young man traveling and occasionally in need of the acceptance and favors of strangers, he often carried chicken bones in his breast pocket. In the event he met people who had a cat, their pet would be drawn to the scent in his pocket and nuzzle him. His rationale was that if people saw their cat trusted and liked him, they would like and trust him as well.

I was moved that someone had laid those chicken bones down beside my friend. Maybe someone intending to do him harm saw those bones and backed away. Maybe those bones arranged in a cross saved his life. I thought about how easily they could have escaped his notice. It made me think about my Uncle Hippolyte, a stranger in foreign lands, sleeping outdoors every night. Maybe he received help all along his way, even if only in the form of chicken bones. After all, any blessing is worth receiving.

Another one of Hippolyte's postcards from India

CHAPTER FORTY-FIVE

Last Letters

The intolerable heat of monsoon is alleviated, albeit only momentarily, by the torrential rains. I was walking to the train station in Bombay when, without warning, it began to pour. My clothes were soaked in seconds. The rain came down in sheets so heavy that I struggled to see as I made my way up the sidewalk. Water streamed down my face and I made no effort to wipe it off. It would have been pointless. Two minutes later, the sidewalk was breached by water that was rushing down the street. Minutes after that, the water was at mid-calf level. My overstuffed backpack was getting drenched. I could feel it getting heavier. I worried that if I lost my balance and fell backwards, I wouldn't be able to get up and I'd drown in the murky water that I imagined might eventually make its way to the Ganges. Ten minutes later it stopped as abruptly as it had started. The river of water abated into a stream and then a gentle trickle in the gutter before stopping altogether. In flat areas, where the ground was saturated, the water stood in ankle deep pools, perfect breeding grounds for mosquitos.

Given one inch of standing water, a female mosquito can lay 300 eggs at a single time. Within a few days, the eggs will hatch into pupae, and in two to three days the pupae will become flying mosquitos. Within twenty-eight hours, females can breed. Worldwide, there are roughly 198 million cases and 584,000 deaths due to malaria every year. The statistics are heartbreaking. Malaria is caused by a one-celled parasite that is transmitted through the bite of the female mosquito. Once the parasites are in your body, they travel to your liver where they mature. They then enter the bloodstream and infect red blood cells. In 48 -72 hours, the parasites multiply, causing the red blood cells to burst.

I met a man who told me he had contracted malaria while traveling in Laos. He was staying in a backpacker hostel and went to bed after a day of sightseeing. He woke up three days later in a hospital with no recollection of even feeling ill beforehand. Fortunately, he was discovered by hostel staff who took his unconscious and fevered body to a hospital. They saved his life. He spent several more days in the hospital before being released. Even then, it was another week before he was well enough to travel.

Symptoms of malaria include chills that cause moderate to severe shaking, high fever, pain in the abdominal muscles, headache, confusion, and gastrointestinal problems including nausea, vomiting, and diarrhea. Within ten days to four weeks of contracting the infection, symptoms will present. This means Hippolyte could have become infected while walking through India, Bangladesh, Myanmar or China.

He missed mail in all of these places. I'm sure this was a huge disappointment to my uncle. The only thing that might have softened the blow was knowing that after over two years traveling, home was in his sights. All of Prosper's letters to Hippolyte found their way back to Los Angeles unopened.

Los Angeles Calif
June, 22, 1922

Dear Friend Martinet

Your letter was received which we was all glad to have of your news and at that was good news as you was enjoying good health and still on a go glad your trip across the desert was a good one. Dear friend, we are all well here, well from what you say you will be her in time for the next stranger as for this one, she arrive on the 6th of June. She was Christian last Sunday her name is Marie Theresa. Mother and baby is fine and doing well. Have no news from the old home last news anyway high water had the folks that is left out there.

The baby Prosper referenced in this letter was Marie Teresa, born to Blanche and Hippolyte's sister, Marie Louise.

Los Angeles Calif
Sept. 28, 1922

Dear Friend Hippolyte

Your letter was received and also your picture glad to hear that you is well and still hiking. From your picture you surely are in good order for us we are all well. We had an increase in the family on the 13th of a baby girl. Blanche and the family is fine doing nicely and also the rest of us, Marie Louise and baby is fine she just left a few minutes ago she is neighbor to us and me I just came from Honora him and family is well also at Edwards.

Polyte Dear Friend it seems after you pass a country is some trouble started how is the situation where you are now from the newspaper there is about to have war over there take care of you self its quite a while since I have heard from Uncle Nonone. Uncle Lazar is still in here but always talking about going back to Chicago but I don't think he is going to go all his children is here. Friend Polyte, I don't know what kind of weather you are encountering in (illegible) we are having hot weather at lease have had its beginning to be better now. Well Friend Polyte as it's the same thing over and over again. I haven't to say to you hoping to hear from you soon again. I will close with love to you from us all

Your friend
P. Davis

The increase in the family that Prosper referenced in this letter was their daughter, Blanche Cecilia. I spoke to her in 2015. She recalled, as a child, hearing her mother and father talk about her Uncle Polyte. Blanche Cecilia told me that at the age of ninety-three, she still lived independently, drove and wore high heels.

Burma, Akyal
August 3, 1922

> Dear Friend, I was I receipt of your letter. I had hardly time to answer. From Cairo I have come down to Akyal district of Burma and am now making plans to go to Hong Kong, a Chinese town. It gives me pleasure to hear of my neighbor. I am mistaken to be a Shadhu by the India folk. I was in the desert when your kind letter missed my hand. I am in a hurry. Hoping this will find you hale and healthy with best respect I depart.
>
> My letters may be posted C/Co American Consul, Hong Kong.
>
> Friend... Martinet
>
> Regard to all

This is the last known letter written by my uncle. It was so short. I can only imagine that he was feeling well when penned this letter. I'm sure he would have written more if he even suspected it would be his last. I'm not sure where Akyal is. I searched for it on maps. I contacted newspapers, universities and heritage preservation organizations in Myanmar but received no response. I wanted to know what this place was like.

I traveled to Myanmar in 2006 during a relatively quiet political period. It was nine years before the mass exodus of Rohingyas fleeing sectarian violence and murder. In order to stay in touch with family and friends, I had to open a new email account because mine, which was linked to an online news site, was forbidden and blocked. Aung San Suu Kyi was still under house arrest. It was dangerous to even speak about her. When she was mentioned, it was only as "The Lady." Overall, the people were kind and friendly. They were also wary of foreigners, who they suspected might be acting as agents of the government. In larger cities, streets are monitored by secret police. Even so, I met a couple men who were brave enough to talk to me and ask me what life was like outside of their hermit kingdom.

I was enchanted with Myanmar, especially Bagan, which is now the largest archaeological zone in the world and recently became a UNESCO World Heritage Site. Hippolyte would have most likely passed through this town. It is one of the most picturesque and tranquil places I have ever visited. The city of Bagan covers 40.15 square miles and is dotted with more than 2,500 temples and stupas. One can walk into or climb a temple, but stupas are smaller, usually solid and have no entrance. The first stupas erected are said to contain portions of the Buddha's ashes that charge the structure with the energy of the Buddha himself. Many people in Myanmar feel it is their sacred obligation to build one, regardless of size, at some point in their lifetime. No matter where one stands in Bagan, one is within view of a stupa or temple. It is nearly impossible to be anywhere in Bagan without feeling the overwhelming devotion.

CHAPTER FORTY-SIX

Earache

Our first morning walking, the temperature had reached 89 degrees by 9:00 but the weather app on my phone told me the "real feel" was 109. From that point on, I avoided looking at that app as much as possible. Seeing that the temperature *felt* like 114 degrees—as it did one day—even though it was only 103 was not helpful.

By the third day, we had found our groove and settled into a routine. We'd wake at 2:00 or 2:30 and begin walking. By sunrise, we had typically walked nine miles, the last three with rumbling stomachs because we hadn't eaten anything since our late-afternoon dinner the previous day. We'd stop for breakfast if we found a restaurant and then walk a few more hours. With any luck, we'd check into a hotel by ten a.m. By seven p.m., we were asleep. This was the schedule we had been forced to adopt. We were at the mercy of monsoon.

Culinary diversity is lacking in China, and by the end of the previous summer we swore we never wanted to eat another noodle again. We had eaten them for breakfast every morning for close to seventy days. Four months after our return home, we suddenly had an insatiable craving for them. We called local traditional Chinese restaurants, but none of them served this breakfast menu item. I tried recreating them at home, but there was always something missing. Back in China and now sixty miles into our walk, we still looked forward to them every morning.

After three hours on the road, our growling stomachs and the sky lightening faintly from black to deep blue told us it was time for breakfast. In the distance, we saw several tall towers huddled together like they were sharing a secret. Surely, we thought, there would be a restaurant there. We quickened our pace in anticipation of those delicious noodles. A few minutes later, the secret was revealed. We had been fooled again by another one of China's brand-spanking-new ghost towns. Sometimes as many as twenty towers in groups of four occupied an eight-acre plot of land beside the highway... with nothing else around for miles... floor after floor of empty residential space and not a trace of a single human being. The previous summer, I read there was enough unoccupied residential floor space in China's ghost towns to completely blanket the city of Madrid. Madrid covers 233.3 square miles. For the sake of comparison, Chicago is 234 square miles and New York is 302. Like the others we had encountered, it appeared this town had nothing to offer us, not even shade at this dim, early hour. We walked through this town of empty promises, dead leaves scuttling about our feet. The quiet was eerie. Like walking into an empty cathedral, it commanded our silence. It dared us to speak in anything above a whisper and quelled our juvenile temptations to throw back our heads, shout, and listen to our voices echo off those hollow towers.

Often, living villages are razed to make way for new construction. We were delighted to see that at least one had been spared and sat behind the stand of unoccupied towers. It was barely six a.m., but several businesses had their lights on and doors opened. Out on the street, a man holding a thermos and disposable plastic cups poured hot tea and handed it to Doug and me. His restaurant wasn't opened yet, so he directed us to the one next door, where we each ate a bowl of noodles. As we were leaving, we saw a woman out front preparing to cook something. A steam tray and a glass pitcher of milky white liquid sat on a folding table. Intrigued by her ingredients and implements, Doug and I stopped to watch. She poured the liquid onto the tray and within seconds it began to congeal into a solid. Doug and I looked at each other with excitement. We knew what this was! It was one of our new, favorite dishes. She added minced, pickled vegetables and green onion, rolled up the crepe-thin rice noodle she had just made, and drizzled soy sauce on it. Our enthusiasm was not lost on the street side chef, and she gave us each one for the road. Carb loaded and absolutely unable to eat another bite, we waddled towards the highway.

Less than an hour later, we found ourselves in an industrial part of the province. Mile after mile of nothing but one warehouse after another on both sides of the highway lay ahead of us. The roll top garage doors of each building were open and revealed massive sheets of marble that lay one against the other in metal racks. Delivery trucks rumbled past us, adding the sound of their screeching brakes and horns to the shrill screech of saws cutting stone. All of this was made worse by the fact that I had been suffering the last two days from a painful earache and my blisters were back in full force. This section of road was nearly as bad as the granite quarry from the year before, but at least this was flat. Four hours later, it was all behind us. By the time the ringing in our ears had ceased, we found ourselves in a blissfully quiet town. We had walked eighteen miles and decided to stop for the day.

We checked into a hotel, left our backpacks in our room and went back out into the heat to have lunch at the street side restaurant downstairs. A man and his year-and-a-half-old grandson were at a table across from us. When Doug finished eating, the man sent his grandson to our table with an unlit cigarette in his tiny hand. When Doug reached for it, the tot retracted his hand momentarily and then deftly stuck the cigarette between Doug's lips. He returned seconds later and handed Doug a lighter.

With my ear throbbing, I limped across the dusty street and into the medical clinic. The doctor pointed to my feet. I shook my head and pointed to my ear, pantomiming my head bursting when I bent down to tie my shoes. Using my translation app, I told the doctor it felt as though I had a snail in my ear, that I was having difficulty hearing and that I was in considerable pain. He led me to a chair and then retrieved a plastic, rectangular drugstore flashlight similar to the one my grandmother had in her nightstand in 1972. Granny's smelled like Ben-Gay. This one did not. I realized the flashlight ear canal inspection was nothing more than an exercise in medical protocol when the beam hit me directly in the eye and didn't even make me reflexively squint. He looked in my ear, assured me there was no snail, wrote out a script and pointed to the pharmacy window across the room. I handed the prescription to the pharmacist, who went to various drawers and cabinets and counted out shiny, brightly-colored pills of various shapes and sizes. She sorted them and then wrapped them individually in packets made from folded pieces of paper torn from a magazine. The doctor instructed me to take one packet of the multi-colored pills in the morning and the other at night. They gave me a shot of what I assumed was an antibiotic and a bottle of drops for my ear. Anxious to take my first dose, I emptied a pack of pills into my hand, took a sip of water and put the pills in my mouth. Instantly, my mouth was flooded with the taste of sugar. I paid the cashier $4.30, and then he, the nurses, pharmacist and I posed for pictures in the street in front of the clinic. I asked one final question before walking back across the street to our hotel room, "When ear better?" The doctor said it would be better in two days. It wasn't.

Back in our hotel room, we looked at our GPS and realized there were options for the next forty-five miles of our walk. We could stay on highway 324 as it went up and over some mountains, or we could get off the highway and take a slightly longer but less arduous route that skirted those mountains and eventually rejoined the 324. The faster, more direct and steep uphill route had its appeal, but everything about a day or two of walking on level ground placated my fiery blisters. We decided to hire a taxi to take us along each route and make an informed decision thereafter. We showed our GPS to the taxi driver and directed him to first drive us along the route that bypassed the mountains. We loved everything about this detour. The gently winding road was flat and tree-lined with tons of shade. There weren't any hotels, but under a bridge at the seventeen-mile mark as if just for us, lay sheets of brand-new cardboard... thick, long and wide enough for us to sleep comfortably. I was ready for this adventure-within-our-adventure in China.

We asked the taxi driver to take us through the mountain route on our return. Within minutes of entering the mountains, we had completely changed our minds. All thoughts of walking the country road and sleeping under a bridge were abandoned. What we were witnessing was the most visually stunning landscape we had seen throughout our entire walking journey in China. Out of nowhere, beautiful grey limestone towers rose up thousands of feet into the air. They were covered almost completely with lush green vegetation; Doug and I spotted two caves way high up the almost completely vertical sides. The place felt ethereal, magical... primeval. *This*, I thought, is where dragons live. On our way back to our hotel, we asked the driver to stop at a roadside convenience store/restaurant hybrid for our early dinner.

While we were eating and lamenting that we didn't have time to walk both routes, a man on a motorcycle stopped to buy cigarettes. It was clear he was either very close friends or related to the woman who was single-handedly running the establishment. She unwrapped the cloth that held her eight-month-old daughter to her back and sat the child in her lap while they chatted. The man got our attention. He wanted us to watch something. He took his wallet from his pocket, retrieved a one kuai note, and handed it to the baby. She waved her hand back and forth in front of it dismissively. He handed her two kuai notes and she waved the money away again. Then, he handed her a crisp, bright red 100 kuai note. Her face lit up, and with a huge grin she snatched it out of his hand and squealed.

The remainder of the drive back to our hotel was less impressive. This would comprise the bulk of the following day's walk, but we knew we would be rewarded the second day with those mystical mountains as well as a visit with that cheeky little tot. Back at our hotel, we got ready for bed. I put the drops the clinic doctor gave me into my ear, took a handful of sugary pills, brushed my teeth, and looked forward to what we would be seeing in two days.

CHAPTER FORTY-SEVEN

On the Lam

Our alarm went off at 2:00 and we were out the door and on the highway by 2:30. This day's walk would only be ordinary Chinese beautiful. The spectacular mountains that left us in awe when we scouted out the two routes were still over twenty miles away. We kept a steady pace throughout the first dark hours of morning, stopped for a quick breakfast and by 6:30 were back on the road.

Contrary to our expectations, the part of China we were walking through did not become less rural as we ventured south. The vast majority of the time we were in the countryside, which was what we preferred. In a small field, a billboard advertised, of all things, a Buddhist temple. Even though it would take us a few miles out of our way, we decided to explore this detour. We followed the sign that led us onto a narrow, paved path that meandered through banana, lychee groves and pig farms. We stopped to stare in awe at a huge sow and counted twenty pink piglets nuzzled up to her belly, sleeping through the cacophony of dogs that barked in our wake. Ahead of us, a woman walked with two water buffalo traipsing behind her.

After thirty minutes, the temple came into view. It sat on a hillside and overlooked a landscape dotted with ponds. We crossed a small, stone bridge and headed up the drive to the temple. Men and women in plain clothes greeted us, handed us bottles of cold water and offered food. A monk donned his yellow robes and led us inside the temple. He gave us each four sticks of incense and we lit a stick and said a prayer at each of the four altars. I was reminded of the temple Doug and I visited the first day of our walk the year before. As I did then, I asked for protection on our journey. We had left that temple with an Asian pear, tamarind pods and candies. When we left this temple, we were given a small Buddha figurine. I tucked it into Doug's backpack, we said our thanks and were back on the road.

Hours later, just as the sun reached its blistering peak, we exited the highway and headed for what our GPS told us was the town's sole hotel. It was easy enough to find, and I walked in feeling like I did every time we checked into a hotel in China—triumphant... because we were that much closer to Shenzhen despite blisters and an earache, but most of all because I had done it without succumbing to heat stroke. Through a door behind the front desk, I could see a two-story building and doors with numbers on them. What a relief, I thought. Normally we were taken to a room on the third floor. My blisters were so painful that knowing a cool shower and a place to lie down were only a flight of stairs away was enough to make me giddy.

Seconds after our arrival, a man emerged from a door behind the reception desk and we requested a room for the night. The discourse that transpired left us with the impression that we were mistaken and that we were in fact not at a hotel. We apologized, stepped back outside into the wavering heat and wandered up the street. While we were consulting with our GPS, a group of friendly and enthusiastic, young men approached us. We told them we were looking for a hotel, and they pointed down the street to the establishment we had just left. Perplexed, we crossed to the other side of the street where we encountered another helpful man. We asked him where we might find a hotel and he escorted us back into the very same building from which we had been turned away.

At the sound of voices, the proprietor emerged to find us standing in the reception area of what he had previously tried to convince us was not a hotel. Clearly exasperated, he pointed to the street again. Doug pulled out his cell phone and made a call to Luxi, our contact in Dali; after a brief explanation, he handed the phone to the proprietor. He talked to

Luxi for at least a minute and returned the phone to Doug. Luxi was as confused as we were. It was indeed a hotel that was licensed to rent to Western tourists, except *we* were not welcome there.

By this time, a young man whom we assumed was the proprietor's son got involved. Sensing he was sympathetic to our plight, I handed him one of our cards. He read both sides and tried showing it to his father, who brushed him aside. We watched hopefully as he tried to convince his father to rent us a room. We even showed him that we had money to pay for the room, but he uncrossed his arms only long enough to point to the door. The young man and the stranger from across the street continued to plead our case, but still the proprietor refused us.

The disappointment of walking into a fully operational hotel with vacancies and being denied a room was worse than walking into a ghost town. All I wanted was a shower and place to prop up my feet and cool my blisters. Simple comfort was being withheld because some stranger, for no explainable reason, didn't like us. I was indignant and lost all interest in ingratiating myself to this man who had a beef against backpackers. I pulled out my phone, opened my translation app and typed in the simple phrases, "You not nice. You very mean man!" and showed it to the angry proprietor. He read the text and stomped off, retrieved a key ring from behind the front desk, walked out the door and climbed on a scooter. He was spitting mad, and I was only able to understand one word he said before he took off down the road... "*police.*" I had taken things too far. Doug was still trying to talk to the son when I interrupted. "We have to leave now! He's gone for the police!" Grabbing our backpacks, we walked hurriedly out the door just in time to see a bus inching away from the curb a block up the street. My blisters felt like they were tearing with each footfall as we chased after it, but I disregarded the pain. I was too afraid of what would happen if the police caught up with us. Fortunately, the bus stopped, the doors opened, and like fugitives we ducked in.

The moment we stepped in, almost every face that had been looking down at a cell phone turned up and greeted us with cheers and smiles. No longer seedy transients, we gratefully rejoined the ranks of D-list celebrities. It felt so good to be loved again! The bus attendant followed us as we walked to the only empty seats in the back. He answered my only pressing question, and I was dispirited to hear that the nearest hotel was twenty-five kilometers away. I pulled some crumpled bills from my pocket, but the attendant waved it away before returning to his station. As the bus veered onto the narrow and winding highway, Doug and I distributed our postcards to our neighboring passengers. Although we couldn't recall seeing any hotels or businesses on this stretch of the highway during our reconnaissance drive, we discussed disembarking a few kilometers up the road. However, our fear that angry hotel guy would have the police looking for us kept us in our seats. We were worried about what would happen if the police found us. If we had twice been brought into the police station for merely walking, what would happen in this situation? Then, just as those beautiful mountains came into view, the skies darkened and rain poured down so hard that the windshield wipers, even at full speed, were effectively useless. We peered out the window through a veil of rain for a glimpse of those beautiful mountains. Visibility was so poor that we couldn't even take photos. Instead, I counted the crumples in the guard rail that ran along this stretch of narrow highway. I was disgusted with myself and felt so guilty about this bus ride until I remembered Hippolyte's caravan ride across the desert. The rain stopped just minutes before the bus pulled over to let us out. The attendant pointed to a building directly in front of us. We turned around and said goodbye to everyone on the bus and stepped off, hoping our luck had improved.

When we entered the building that we were assured was a hotel, we drew the attention of four men who were gathered around the front desk. Our luck had indeed changed. They broke into huge smiles, and again we were greeted with cheers as well as a chorus of resounding hellos. One man took our backpacks and set them in a chair while another led us to a world map on the wall. He handed me a pushpin and invited me to mark our hometown. We distributed our postcards and California state flag stickers. It was one of the easiest check-ins ever and we were led to a room on the third floor.

After we showered and washed our sweaty, grimy walking clothes, we went downstairs to inquire about a restaurant. One of the men walked with us to the door and pointed to a building just down the road. Doug walked and I hobbled a hundred yards or so, and like the people on the bus and the men at the hotel, the room erupted into cheers when we entered. We were ***loving*** this town! A woman cooked for and served five men sitting around a long, rectangular table. They moved down and made room in the center seats for Doug and me. We asked for two vegetarian dishes and two beers. Hearing the word *beer*, the room erupted into cheers again. Two deliciously cold bottles were delivered and uncapped. Then seven plastic cups appeared, and beer was poured for everyone. Between cups of beer and bites of food, a man read our palms. I have no idea what he saw, but judging by the look on his face and how our day was shaping up, it was all good. Noticing we had emptied our plates, the waitress walked across the room to where a five-gallon stockpot simmered over a propane tank. She removed the lid and pulled out a metal hook with a meaty carcass hanging off it and offered some to Doug, who paused briefly. Reading his mind, I intervened with my best dog imitation, "Ruff-ruff?" She nodded and smiled. Doug politely declined and the room erupted into laughter again.

By midafternoon we were back at the hotel. "Delicious food and cold beer!" we told our hosts and explained that we would be leaving at 2:30 in the morning. "Tài rè le. *It's too hot,*" we said, pointing outdoors. With that, we said good night and headed upstairs. An ancient-looking thermos of hot water had been placed beside our door. I brought it inside and when we woke up at two a.m., the water was still hot enough to make tea.

CHAPTER FORTY-EIGHT

Hippolyte Reaches China

DEPARTMENT OF STATE
WASHINGTON

October 14, 1922

Mr. Jules Martinet
St. Martinville,
St. Martinville Parish,
Louisiana

Sir:

The Department regrets very much to have to inform you of the receipt of a telegram dated October 4, 1922, from the American Consul at Yunanfu, China, reporting that your nephew, Hippolyte Martinet, died at Siakwa, Yunan, China, on September 30, 1922.

Upon the receipt of further information in regard to the death of Mr. Martinet you will be promptly advised.

It is respectfully requested that if practicable you furnish the Department with any information you may have in regard to the names and addresses of the next of kin of Mr. Martinet.

I am, Sir,

Your obedient servant,

For the Secretary of State:

Director of the Consular Service.

I believe the first family members to be notified of Hippolyte's death were his Uncle Jules in St. Martinville, Louisiana and his brother Honorat in Los Angeles. I don't know how Blanche and Prosper received this devastating news.

China Inland Mission,
Talifu, Yunnan,
October 11, 1922

The American Consulate
Yunnanfu, Yun.

Dear Mr. Myers:

I am returning herewith the form of your report of death with all that I know filled in. I am afraid I should not have filled in this form as I see from a second reading of your letter that you were only sending it so I should know what information was desired. I am sorry I made this mistake. I think you have practically all this information in my previous letters.

The report from the Chinese was that Mr. Martinet was a Foreign Beggar. He had very little money and would not use it, but asked the people to give him food. For example, he would stand by a meat-seller's stall and hold out his hand as the beggars do until some one would cut off a piece and give it to him. He would take it and swallow it raw, and then beg for more. One of our Christian boys saw this. Some of the Chinese have asked me why our government issues passports to such men. My answer has been that no doubt they did not know what he intended to do. I expect Mr. Martinet was driven to do such things through no fault of his own, thinking perhaps his money would not hold out till he reached Canton. He was also handicapped by a lack of knowledge of Chinese. I should say he was nearly starved.

Herewith is a statement of his funeral expenses. The first few items were paid by the Chinese in Hsia-kuan before Mr. Fergusson went after him and I am enclosing the receipts from the Chinese. The other items I paid myself.

Paid at Hsiakuan

Sep. 30,	1 Pinewood Coffin	$15.00
	1 Telegram Hsiakuan to Tali	.99
Oct. 1,	200 sheets Tough Paper (to put in coffin)	.20
	1 pair Trousers (clean)	1.20
	Watchman's wages (2 days)	.50
	Sanitary Charges (by landlord)	2.00
	Cotton Coverlet (wadded)	3.00
Oct. 2,	9 coolies to carry coffin to Tali	9.00
Oct. 3,	6 coolies to go to cemetery and lower coffin into grave	1.00
	Grave diggers	3.60
Sep. 30,	1 Telegram to Yunnanfu	1.08
Oct. 2,	1 Telegram to Yunnanfu	.45
		$38.02

There were also a number of small items paid by Mr. Yang at Hsiakuan, Mr. Fergusson, Mr. Liu, and myself, but they would not amount to much. As far as Mr. Fergusson and I are concerned we want no thanks but were glad to do what we could and wish we could have done more, but the Chinese gentlemen will no doubt think it strange if there is no word of appreciation from his friends and others.

You spoke of enclosing confirmation of telegram. There was no such enclosure so I am wondering if it was forgotten.

Yours sincerely
(Signed) Allyn B. Cooke.

Only one item in the list of funeral expenses was not immediately clear to me, "200 sheets Tough Paper." I did some research and learned that ashes or lime are placed in the bottom of the coffin and sheets of paper are laid over it.

By the time Hippolyte crossed into China, it had been nearly two and half years since he had left Seattle and he had walked approximately 15,000 miles. There was nothing that indicated he was ill or ailing. Quite to the contrary, the American Consulate reported that he was "well clad and… appeared to be in good health and must have been so as he had walked from Bhamo (Burma) in four and a half days, over thirty miles a day."

As he was conserving money, instead of staying at a "Chinese Inn," they made accommodations for him and he was allowed to stay at the consulate for three days while he waited for a "passport". I assume the word passport meant a visitor visa. They insisted he accept a felt blanket and other supplies. "He was especially warned that the road was arduous and mountainous but that had no effect on his resolution. Though he had money of his own, he refused to take more than $15 and $36 was remitted to the American Consul general at Hongkong."

I think Hippolyte sent the $36 to Hong Kong because he was wary of being robbed again. My best guess is that he was earmarking that money—equal to $522 in 2020—for his return passage and did not want to lose it in the event of another robbery. Walking thirty miles a day, it would have taken him roughly forty days to get to a port near Hong Kong. The $15 he kept –valued at $217 in 2020 would have allowed him the equivalent of $5.40 a day for food. Doug and I were spending roughly $1.50 per meal per person in China. We agree that neither of us could eat $5.40 of food in a day. Because Hippolyte slept outdoors and had no lodging expenses, $32 would have been plenty of money to see him to Hong Kong.

As for the conflicting report of his appearance and perceived health—one document reported that he was well clad and in good health while another claimed he looked nearly starved. I attribute this discrepancy to malaria. When he wasn't sick with malaria, my lean uncle looked healthy and well dressed. When he was sick with malaria and perhaps delirious, he was the "starved…foreign beggar" who was imploring for and eating scraps of raw meat.

Reports of his death were published in multiple newspapers around the world. The article below, while a lovely tribute to my uncle, makes several errors. The conversation between Hippolyte and Honorat referenced below would have taken place in 1919 at the latest. I'm not sure how this next error escaped the editor's attention. The headline reads that Hippolyte died in India but the fourth paragraph states correctly that he died in Yunnanfu, China. It also states that he died from Yellow Fever. I have several documents reporting that Hippolyte died of malaria. Additionally, I emailed an epidemiologist at Johns Hopkins University, an expert in the history of epidemics, disease, and public health in China and provided information about my uncle. She shared my letter with colleagues at Tufts University, Duke University, Barnes University and Yale, all of whom specialize in the history of disease in that region. They concurred that there was no Yellow Fever in China and that Hippolyte most likely died from malaria.

I have a photocopy of this newspaper clipping but have not been able to find its source.

REVEAL DEATH IN CHINA OF L.A. MAN WALKING ROUND GLOBE BAREFOOT

The last official record of Hippolyte Martinet's heroic attempt to walk around the world barefoot was written in Judge Paul McCormick's court Friday, when administrators of Martinet's estate were appointed.

Martinet succumbed to exposure and privations in the province of Yunnanfu, China, where consular reports said his death was due to fever.

He had walked from Los Angeles to New York, and with the exception of sea voyages across the Atlantic, the English channel and the Hellesopont, he'd walked every foot of the way to China. His route led him across France, Switzerland, the Balkans, Greece, Turkey, Persia, Afghanistan and through the Khyber Pass into India. Skirting the southern foothills of the Himalayas, he had swung through Indo-China up into the Chinese republic where he met his death September 30, 1922.

Martinet according to his brother, Honorat Martinet 218 Richard Street, who was appointed his administrator had money forwarded to him in care of American consuls on his route. Most of his estate consisted of money in banks where he had stopped. It aggregated $4000, it was said.

Martinet left Los Angeles in 1920, expecting to make the circuit in three years and then settle down in his business.

He resolved to wear neither hat nor shoe during his trip and to distribute money as charity wherever he went. He refused to accept money, however, although his letters told of many efforts to "endow" him by wealthy men who heard his story on four continents.

NEARLY REACHED

By Junier B Wood.

Special Cable to *The Star* and *Chicago Daily News*

Hongkong, Nov. 7—With his goal almost in sight, death in a lonesome village in Yunnan province, ended the courageous attempt of Hippolyte Martinet an American, to walk around the world.

Like many better sung and better known explorers, Martinet overcame all obstacles except the last.

A letter from M.S. Myers, American consul at Yunnan Fu, to Consul General H, Gale at Hongkong, Tuesday reported that Martinet died at Hsaikwan, Yunnan province, on Sept 30 and was buried there by an American missionary.

Death, the letter says was due to exhaustion and lack of proper nourishment.

Had Premonitions of Death—When Martinet passed thru Tongyouh, in the western part of Yunnan province, eleven days preceding his death, it is believed that he had a premonition of his coming end for he called on the British consul at Tengyouh and after arranging for forwarding a small sum of money, requested that Consul General Gale at Hongkong be asked in case of accident to him to notify Miss Blanche Davis Los Angeles. Consul Gale, after inquiring of Miss Davis whether she wanted the money forwarded on her instructions, used the sum to place a marker over Martinet's grave.

Martinet's sporting attempt to circle the globe on foot had aroused interest throughout the entire near east and the Orient. Britishers especially appreciating the physical endurance necessary in the attempt, assisted him with small contributions wherever he stopped.

(By Junius B. Wood) (Special Cable to The Denver Post and the Chicago Daily News.) (Copyright, 1922.)

This first time I read this article, I cried. It still brings tears to my eyes. It was published in the *Los Angeles Times* January 26, 1924

MAN'S INHUMANITY TO MAN?

A man of the name Hippolyte Martinet died the other day in China of yellow fever. These facts are unimportant. Nobody knew him yesterday; tomorrow nobody will remember him.

But his death gave him a brief moment of publicity in Judge McCormick's court when his brother applied for letters to administer his estate. Hippolyte left an estate that was worth a trip to court and the consumption of a judge's valuable attention. That is something worth pondering.

For in the due course of the dry court procedure necessary in settling the deceased's affairs a story came to light in reference to the man who died of yellow fever in China that was supposed to be so unusual it was given a paragraph in the news items of the day.

It seems that to prove the abundant humanity prevailing in mankind Hippolyte set out penniless, hatless and shoeless to beat his way around the world, dependent entirely on the goodwill of strangers. The venture was a complete success. He circled the globe on charity. And left behind an estate worth administering.

The strange thing is not that Hippolyte was able to circle the globe on charity. The strange thing is that anyone should see anything strange in the feat. So that he went about the experiment with resolution and confidence it would have been very surprising had he not succeeded.

Bobby Burns was barking up the wrong tree when he said, "Man's inhumanity to man makes countless thousands mourn." On the contrary, it is man's incredibly foolish generosity that keeps three-quarters of the human race so near the border line of want. Nine-tenths of the normal folk in the world get ten times the kick out of giving that they get out or receiving.

In fact, it is the only hope of getting a chance to give that keeps alive the incentive for receiving. Countless thousands have had reason to mourn a bad balance between these two human operations because they are allowed their generous instincts to predominate. And have died happy in their memories.

But he who has the ability to circle the globe on charity will leave an estate that is worth administering. Professional receivers fortunately are a negligible minority in the scheme of humanity.

As the author of this article said of my uncle, "nobody knew him yesterday, tomorrow, nobody will remember him." I politely disagree. My great-great Uncle Hippolyte met countless people throughout his journey around the globe and I'm certain he was remembered by many of them. And now that they are gone and he is gone, I am writing this book in hopes that he will be remembered by anyone who reads or hears about his story.

CHAPTER FORTY-NINE

Our Last Miles

Before Doug and I left for our return trip to China, we had talked ourselves into believing that certain aspects of travel would be easier the second time around. They weren't. We were facing all the same old challenges as well as some new ones. For example, in urban areas, internet service, normally stellar even when we were in the middle of nowhere was now weaker and sometimes non-existent.

Finding a hotel was as difficult as ever. Dripping with sweat and exhausted, Doug and I stood on a street corner and asked a group of shop owners where we could find a hotel. One man indicated that the nearest was several kilometers back the way we had come from, another insisted there was no hotel in that location and that the closest one was several kilometers further up the road. While they stood there arguing, a woman on a motor scooter rolled to a stop to see what the ado with the Western folks was all about. Once she was up to speed, she began yelling at the men, gesticulating wildly and pointed out that in fact, the nearest hotel was thirty feet away, directly across the street from where we all stood. In ten strides, we had walked into the empty reception. Even so, as happened in cities, it still took us thirty minutes to check in as the clerks pored over our passports. Only eighty-six miles lay between us and Shenzhen. Doug and I estimated that over the course of our journey, we had walked at least an additional twenty miles looking for overnight accommodations.

By 3:00 am the next morning we were out of the city, walking along the highway that bisected a field that spanned for miles towards the dark horizon. Rain began to fall, lightly at first but within minutes, it came pouring down. We counted the seconds between the lightning flashes and thunder of the nearing storm. Up ahead, we found a building with a cement pad under the awning. Dripping water, we shed our backpacks, spread out our ground tarp and lay down. Our respite from the rain beside this 100 square foot building became one of my favorite memories of the entire trip. Quite by accident, we discovered that we could make farting noises by pressing our lower backs into the ground. We lay there for the next two hours laughing until we were breathless as we improved our technique. When it finally stopped raining, we stood up to put on our backpacks. Curiosity got the better of me and I peeked behind a tarp that was covering something propped against the wall. It was a motorcycle and two helmets. Only then did it occur to us that we had been on the porch of someone's home.

Five days later, our alarm woke us at 2:30 a.m. It was an exciting and somber sound. This would be the last day of our 1,200 mile walk. Outside it was thundering and raining so heavily, we were surprised we had been able to sleep through the din. We lay in bed for the next hour drifting in and out of sleep until the rain finally stopped.

The ferry terminal was only twelve miles away. The rain came and went as we walked. The first part of that morning I walked so fast that for once, Doug was behind me. We were still in the countryside and I was so grateful for our beautiful surroundings. This was how I wanted to remember China—fields, green mountains and random little vegetable garden plots everywhere. Even so, I was looking forward to being in the metropolis of Hong Kong, allowing my blistered feet to heal and seeing a doctor about my earache which had worsened. The pain from the blisters would subside into something bearable after fifteen minutes of walking but the pain from the earache dominated my attention. I had taken to sitting or walking to the right of Doug because it had become difficult to hear him.

With roughly five miles to the ferry terminal, we realized we should have exited onto an access road two miles behind us. Our GPS indicated that the access road was on the other side of the expansive field we stood beside. Doug began detailing our two options, "We can backtrack two miles to the access road and add four miles to our walk or... ". I chose option "or" and marched into the field of knee high weeds. Doug followed as we passed towering banana plants.

After a few minutes, the access road came into view but we soon discovered that an irrigation ditch separated us from it. Our options were to retrace our steps through the field we had just crossed, backtrack another two miles to the access road and walk another two miles to be two hundred feet from where we were standing or... I wanted no part of that backtracking nonsense. Not knowing how deep the water was, I unclipped the waist belt of my backpack, balanced it on my head and stepped into the murky, brown water that came up mid-thigh. Doug climbed in after me and a few seconds later, we scrambled up the bank on the opposite side.

We followed the access road to where it re-joined with the highway. Typical of China, we went from rural, quiet bucolic countryside to the pandemonium of the city. This time, we were in the port city of Shenzhen. A two-lane bridge with no shoulder lay ahead of us. We surveyed our surroundings looking for an alternate route that was safer and didn't require that we invade the lane space of eighteen wheelers, but there was none. Doug took the lead as we stepped onto the bridge. We hugged the railing as closely as possible as a stream of semis with empty trailers rumbled past us. My heart raced and I craned my neck to look over my shoulder endeavoring to make eye contact with every driver. I wanted to know that we were being seen. It was the longest, most harrowing, adrenaline-pumping twenty-five yards of our journey.

Thankful to be off the bridge, we followed a shaded sidewalk for the next two miles. My pace by this time had slowed to a near crawl, each step was agonizing. I tried not to think about what bacteria might have been living in that murky brown canal water as my feet squished in my socks. It took us five and a half hours to walk twelve and a half miles but at last, we stepped into the parking lot of the ferry terminal. We had done it. Ninety-six years after he had begun his walk around the world, we finished Hippolyte's journey.

I had enjoyed the sense of purpose and resolve I had felt and now that the walk was over, it was gone. I was going to miss that sensation, that feeling of having a mission, that I was doing something meaningful. Yet, there was still a book to write and that journey still lay ahead of me—every bit as overwhelming as those 1,200 miles had at first seemed. But instead of feeling doubt, I decided to approach it like I had approached our journey through China but instead of mile by mile and on some days step by step, I reminded myself to take it page by page knowing that some days, I would have to take it word by word.

EPILOGUE

Though we have hopes and aspirations, what happens to our story is not always in our control. I'm sure Hippolyte never thought his story would end with him dying in China. That first night I read about Hippolyte, the night I discovered the truth about my family, I excitedly scrolled through his itinerary. Line by line, I followed him as he circumnavigated the planet until everything came to a crashing halt. In disbelief, my eyes took in the sentence again—this time as a whole. "Dali, Yunnan, China Died September 30, 1922." I read it over and over again until the sentence that put a period at the end of Hippolyte's story instead of an ellipse finally sunk in. I had no idea that sentence would eventually send me to China, to walk 1,200 miles across a country I would grow to love so much. And so that night, a chapter of my life story began where Hippolyte's ended.

His story wasn't supposed to end in China. He was supposed to sail from Hong Kong across the ocean to an awaiting family. As his ship pulled into the port of Los Angeles, he was supposed to think that even though he had never lived in Los Angeles, it felt good to be home. He was supposed to search the crowd for the faces of Blanche and Prosper as he disembarked. He was meant to have a long hug with his baby sister and an unashamed embrace with Prosper. He was supposed to sit in a chair in his sister and brother-in-law's home as his nieces and nephews took turns picking up his dusty backpack that smelled not just of rough sack fabric but of far-away places. They'd take turns trying it on; the younger, smaller ones would buckle under its weight and they'd all laugh.

After the kids had reluctantly gone to bed, he, Blanche and Prosper would sit at the kitchen table. As a clock chimed away the hours, they'd pick over cold, leftover supper and talk about everything that had happened in his absence. When it was late and they were all yawning and too tired to stay up talking but not yet ready to go to bed either, they'd finally stand up and when Hippolyte grabbed his pack and shuffled off to sleep on the porch rather than on a sofa or in a child's empty bed, Blanche and Prosper would chuckle and smile. Blanche would fall asleep, for the first time in over two years, knowing where her brother was and that he was safe.

Hippolyte was supposed to wake up the next morning and walk into the kitchen and sit down at the table for a cup of coffee, and after the first sip close his eyes and smile because he hadn't tasted his sister's coffee in so long. At the stove, Blanche stepped away from sizzling and spattering bacon only long enough to present her brother with a gift—a stack of blank paper, a fountain pen and a bottle of ink and maybe, that day, he'd begin writing his own book. He was supposed to go see his boys—who had spent the last two years of their lives living with their uncle—and be a part of their lives. Eventually, he'd find that earth-loving woman and spend the rest of his life with her.

That's the ending I want, not the one where I finish the walk for him over the course of two summers. I want the ending where all of these years later, somewhere I know that his book is sitting on someone's shelf. Maybe it's even on my shelf. I would prefer that my uncle lived even though it means that I never got to go to China TWICE and have amazing life-changing experiences. One of the most tragic things about his death is that he had this absolutely amazing journey and he never got to share it with anyone. But Doug and I did, and it was more beautiful than I ever could have imagined.

I feel truly blessed because I found my earth-loving man and I love him so much for helping me honor my uncle. I am so grateful to Doug, my cousin Clare and Hippolyte for making that journey happen. I don't know how my life will end. I try not to think about it. Regardless, I hope the life I lead will inspire someone to do something that changes their life for the better and that it sends them on an adventure that is as fantastic as the one Doug and I experienced, an adventure that renews their faith in humankind and reminds people that like that article said, this world needs more professional receivers for in the act of receiving, we are also the gift givers.